Sexual Deceit

Sexual Deceit

The Ethics of Passing

Kelby Harrison

LEXINGTON BOOKS
Lanham • Boulder • New York • Toronto • Plymouth, UK

Published by Lexington Books
A wholly owned subsidiary of The Rowman & Littlefield Publishing Group, Inc.
4501 Forbes Boulevard, Suite 200, Lanham, Maryland 20706
www.rowman.com

10 Thornbury Road, Plymouth PL6 7PP, United Kingdom

Copyright © 2013 by Lexington Books

All rights reserved. No part of this book may be reproduced in any form or by any electronic or mechanical means, including information storage and retrieval systems, without written permission from the publisher, except by a reviewer who may quote passages in a review.

British Library Cataloguing in Publication Information Available

Library of Congress Cataloging-in-Publication Data Available

ISBN 978-0-7391-7705-1 (cloth : alk. paper)

™ The paper used in this publication meets the minimum requirements of American National Standard for Information Sciences—Permanence of Paper for Printed Library Materials, ANSI/NISO Z39.48-1992.

Printed in the United States of America

For MJM

Contents

Introduction: Many Have Passed; Some Have Failed ... 1

1. Passing in Abstraction: *The Theoretical Organization of Passing* ... 33

2. The Good, the Bad, and the Oppressed: *Ethical Considerations* ... 61

3. Thoughtfully Produced Sexuality: *Sexology and The Queer Academy* ... 93

4. Those Shoes Look Pretty Gay, Or at Least Bi-Curious: *Style and Sexual Identity Passing* ... 113

5. Political Perversity: *Queer Sexuality and the Moral Majority* ... 141

6. Practicing to Preach: *Gayness as a Practical Identity* ... 163

Conclusion: Social and Legal Implications of Sexual Deceit ... 179

Bibliography ... 203

Index ... 213

About the Author ... 221

Introduction
Many Have Passed; Some Have Failed

How should we treat each other in light of our sexual identities? What do we owe each other based on shared sexual identities? How are we to support lesbian, gay, bisexual, transgender and queer (LGBT/Q[1]) people in our personal spheres, in public spaces, in our professional roles? These types of questions about other types of oppressed identities have been of central concern to moral philosophers; these questions in the context of sexual identity are of central concern in this book. My basic guiding intuition is that when we are deciding how to frame and disclose our identities, especially when those identities are not necessarily favorably received, we must make decisions guided by our ethics.

In particular, this book is about sexual identity passing. Passing is something that we do with identity. "Passing" designates a successful self-presentation in line with a socially favored identity at the expense of an "authentic" one—e.g., passing for white when black, heterosexual when LGB/Q, cisgender[2] when transgender, etc.—this basic definition will be complicated and problematized throughout the pages that follow. It is an option for those who lie in a liminal space between a favored identity and a minoritized identity. At times it is the only option to make other life decisions work: careers, familial relationships, physical safety in certain regions. To decide to pass involves a complicated mix of social and psychological pressures as well as ethical commitments and values that elevate social goods and gains above personal authentic expression. Those who choose to pass nearly always choose to do so under a complex system of pressures, often to escape corrupt and unjust restraints on personal freedom, or to access greater levels of opportunity or power in a social system that privileges certain sexual identities, gender expressions, religious or ethnic identities, or racial self-presentations.

All forms of passing have similar elements: motifs, themes, psychological patterns, social restrictions. At times I will talk about racial, religious, ethnic, gender passing, or just passing in general. When the focus of this book is sexual identity passing, the focus is about sociality, not sexuality. More accurately, it is about the sociality of sexuality, including the politics of sexuality, and the politics of sexual identity. But, more foundationally it is about the ethical import of sexual identity.

Which brings me to the matter of the title. "Sexual Deceit" suggests infidelity—sexually cheating on a committed lover, or sexually straying from a spouse. At times, passing does entail a betrayal of loved ones—a denial of a relationship or presence within a community. In this sense the subtle connotation of infidelity is apt. However, more concretely, "sexual deceit" in this instance firmly suggests an infidelity to oneself and one's identity. To commit to a social identity is a complicated endeavor that we could readily understand as requiring fidelity. This process will be discussed at length in the latter half of this book, where I will present a theory of ethics, one that can build a collective or community and serve as a basis for a LGBT/Q social ethic. In so far as this process requires fidelity to identity, passing involves infidelity.

In order to build up to the constructive chapters—where I present a theoretical and ethical description of sexual identity which I call "gayness as a practical identity," I first set the stage through a myriad of theoretical and ethical problems that passing presents. Questions about the ethics of identity require, first, that we understand what is at stake in our theories of identity. I employ a number of approaches including narrative philosophy, phenomenology, postmodernism, queer theory, and elements of analytic philosophy. The next major task is to explore the framework of identity through an ethical lens. I am not committed to any particular theory of ethics, but instead first reflect on the ethical issues and then use particular theories where they are helpful and point out where they are not useful. In order to create a constructive ethic for LGB/Q people, I review the historical construction of contemporary sexual identities, and explore the tense contemporary relationship between ethics and queer theory.

The constructive chapters begin by first offering a new theoretical model of identity. The theoretical model I propose—style—is constructed such that it can capture and support the theoretical complexities inherent in the lived experience and conceptual parameters of passing. Style, I argue, also lends itself to an ethical understanding of identity that has both resonances with virtue theory and contemporary Kantian ethics. Having re-established a theoretical foundation, I take a particular look at some of the moral complexities of LGB/Q lives, namely shame and coercive lying. I establish the paradox of "the liar vs. the pervert" at the center of contemporary LGB/Q moral lives. Finally, I employ Christine Korsgaard's model of practical identity as a framework for an LGBT/Q social ethic. I spend the conclusion talking about some of the social, political, and legal implications of this ethic—which I call "gayness."

In this book I will proceed through arguments concerning the philosophical analysis of the concept of passing, the ethics of identity, the intellectual history of sexual identity, and contemporary theoretical issues in academic studies of gender and sexuality; I will then offer a theory of identity and a constructive ethic for LGBT/Q communities. First, however, in this introduction I will enumerate and explore some of the lived complexities of passing.

Integral to an ethical analysis of sexual identity is the social-cultural ethical framework known as heteronormativity. "Heteronormativity" is a complex matrix of social rewards and punishments that favor a binary gender system with opposite-sex couplings. Heteronormativity is the backdrop of sexual identity passing.

Through its subtle and overt ubiquity that is thoroughly infused into culture, heteronormativity structures sexuality. Some persons are rewarded for authenticity: monogamy driven heterosexuals. Others are rewarded for passing: everyone else.[3]

Passing is not the closet. The political lives of LGBT/Q people and the rhetoric of visibility and invisibility in the LGBT/Q communities often center around the socio-cultural trope of the closet. At the end of this introductory chapter I will say a number of things about what the closet is, and how passing is not those things. But, before I say what passing is not, I will take you through a summary of what a number of people have had to say about passing as a phenomenon in its particular contexts of race and gender.

It should be noted: passing is almost never a thoroughly pleasant subjective experience. There are certainly some who have reveled in the success of their identity performance, or relished their social gains to such an extent that passing seemed worthwhile, or even experienced such significant spiritual or psychological gains that passing was the only relevant option. But one of my basic guiding premises is that passing is not a desirable end in a utopic world that would allow all authentic expressions of identity, equal opportunity, and all individuals maximum freedom in pursuing a life that would allow them to flourish.

Racial Passing

The term "passing" originated in the American context of light-skinned black people who could pass for white in the United States. Judith Berzon argues in *Neither White Nor Black: The Mulatto Character in American Fiction* that the term "passing" possibly refers to a time when American slaves were required to have passes in order to travel. Some light skinned slaves were able to "just pass through" without the required documentation.

Racial passing is the primary context out of which the ethical and philosophical definitions of passing arose. The classic description of racial passing can be found in Gunnar Myrdal's 1944 analysis of race relationship in the United States: *An American Dilemma*. Myrdal describes passing as "crossing the caste line." He defines passing as someone light enough to look white, who can do both of the following: 1) deceive the white people around him/her, and 2) create a "conspiracy of silence" among the black people who know the truth.[4] He writes that if a white person would choose to pass as black it would be a "comparatively easy matter" because an American Negro does not need to "have any Negro features at all." He is referring to the one-drop definition of race, where visibility of skin color is significantly less important than the measurable heritage of African blood. He also notes that the person would remain "fairly unsuspected" because it is assumed that "nobody would want to descend in caste status."[5] So, already he offers us the basic definitions of classic racial passing: upward mobility and deception of the receiving class. Both of these elements of racial passing are shared with sexual identity passing. Myrdal, however, offers us a third element: "the conspiracy of silence," that is not necessarily shared. Only if someone who is passing for straight has previously been visibly LGB/Q or "out of the closet" or has had non-anonymous sexual encounters with individuals in LGB/Q communities could his/her passing also necessitate the silence and participatory secrecy of others.

However, Myrdal cites the requirement of anonymity for individuals who choose to racially pass. This leads him to claim that racial passing is "restricted to the larger cities where everyone does not know everyone else."[6] He does go on to specify that someone could pass within a small community, but that it would require movement into that small community. This requirement for large community/anonymity for racial passing is not the case for sexual identity. And the relationship between small community/large community is often inverse. Many LGB/Q individuals choose to pass in smaller communities because those communities tend to be more conservative in their evaluation of behavior. It is the larger urban environments that allow individuals to be honest and forthcoming about deviant sexual identities.

Myrdal also draws attention to the separate spheres of life that allow for selective and sometimes temporally-bound forms of passing. He argues favorably for the kind of passing for white to "attend theaters, lectures, concerts, and receptions." He argues that "such passing breaks the cultural and spiritual isolation of the Negro community and favors the dissemination of broader ideas and patterns into the Negro community."[7] He also cites what he calls the "relatively common" form of passing in the Northern and Border states where black individuals choose to pass professionally, but maintain a black social life.[8] He mentions that at times black youth would pass for white in educational institutions where they would be better received as white. Most of these elements are shared with sexual identity passing. It is certainly the case that many LGB/Q people pass professionally. It is also true that queer youth will choose to pass to minimize their exposure to homophobia in educational environments. The choice to pass for cultural events is not quite as common; however, choosing to pass for certain types of social events (weddings are a prime example) is common.

The role of gender politics and sexual relations plays a counter role in racial passing that is akin to the kinds of passing in sexual identity. Myrdal argues that in situations of professional passing, choosing to marry and settle down often creates a life dilemma where one must chose to stop passing. The decision to enter into a serious relationship, or the circumstantial instance in which that occurs, often creates a situation for the sexual identity passer to come clean. Myrdal points out that sometimes professional passing fails after a particular amount of time, and the passer must either voluntarily retreat from their social role, or find that they have fallen from the prestigious position that the passing afforded him/her. This can also be very true of the LGB/Q passer. He argues that Negro men have an easier time passing than do Negro women because of the constraints marriage-ability puts on women. He argues that a woman will have a hard time finding a husband if it appears that she does not have a kinship network which would be the social ties that must be severed if she were to pass.[9] So, Myrdal writes, "their chance on the white marriage market as lonely women without a known or presentable family must be slight." He goes on to write, "quite often marriage will put a stop to all dreams of passing, since it is less likely that the mate is also capable of passing."[10]

Myrdal spends some time exploring the question of why people who could pass would choose not to pass. He states that given the clear financial benefits of passing, it is easy to explain why light-skinned people would pass in the 1940's but significantly harder to explain why people would choose not to pass. He articulates a few reasons: 1) race pride or "missionary spirit" of wanting to fight for the cause, 2) social strain or nervousness caused by passing, 3) comparative social status (higher in the black community than white community), and 4) social life was better within ranks of Negro community.[11] All of these arguments have analogous positions within LGB/Q communities and assessment of passing.

Myrdal argues that for whites, "passing is an insult and a social and racial danger."[12] In the case of sexual identity it is quite contrarily true. The military mandate of "don't ask, don't tell" strongly evidenced that the heterosexual majority is made to feel *less* anxious when LGB/Q individuals pass. There is also the common cultural rhetoric that suggests that as long as LGB/Q people act straight in public, they are to be tolerated. The idea of sexual identity passing is heralded as a way to maintain social order, as opposed to the issue of anxiety that white people experience from the invisible transgression into their communities. Myrdal adds that the anxiety that racial passing provokes for whites is particularly due to the social strength evidenced by someone who can choose to break all the "personal and social anchorings" to enter into the white world.[13]

From the perspective of the African-American community, the decision to pass involves a kind of betrayal of one's origins.[14] For LGB/Q communities, deciding *not* to pass often entails betraying the values of one's origin. But in both cases it is the spirit of solidarity and a protective community that shields the individual in his/her attempt to pass. Myrdal argues that this is the case within the African American community.[15] It is generally understood in LGB/Q communities that you do not out lovers, friends, co-workers, or other social kin to non-LGB/Q people.

The most notable difference between racial passing and sexual identity passing is seen in the different ways in which each "community" is created and provides meaning for its members. We come to understand our identities, indeed we develop our identities within a social context. Kwame Anthony Appiah made this clear in his discussion of social identity in his thorough analysis of the intersection of ethics and identity in his 2005 book, *Ethics of Identity*. We build caring and supportive relationships with the people that surround us. This social network—one might argue—is a "primary good."[16] Given that a supportive social network, or a "family," is something each and every one of us should want no matter what else we also want should be considered at the very center of our discussion of community.

The idea of community in relation to racial identity builds on and from the care structure already in place in a kin network. Racial identity revolves around ancestral connection. Indeed, the very foundation of racial identity is passed from generation to generation. Families of origin will almost always be a part of one's autonomous adult racial identity.

The idea of community in relation to the LGBT/Q identity rarely if ever builds on or from the care structures available in a kin network. In fact, kin connections are often severed at the time of "coming out." The force of such a traumatic expulsion from one's family of origin, religious community, or support network cannot be overestimated. The recreation of "family" and "support network" within LGBT/Q communities emphasizes and addresses this radical reformulation of autonomous adult community.

Gender Passing, Intersex, and Modern Transgender Politics

Before I begin to talk about gender passing and the modern transgender community, it is important to acknowledge that the role of gender identity can play a significant role in sexual identity passing, or in an individual's ability to pass. Butch lesbian women and effeminate gay men have a harder time passing than feminine lesbian women and masculine gay men. The associations between gender identity and sexuality are politically problematic and based unfairly in stereotypes. However, the stereotypes and distinctions are readily employed inside the LGB/Q communities as well. Take, for example, the notion of "straight-acting," which is viewed as a type of legitimate and desirable social presentation of LGB/Q identities.

The phrase "straight-acting" usually refers to a gay man or lesbian that acts in accordance with the gender prescriptions of masculinity and femininity. Clearly the phrase "straight-acting" cannot refer to the type of sexual behavior the individual is employing. The practice of determining and identifying sexuality in accordance with gender self-presentation produces what R.W. Connell argues as "gendered sexuality."[17] For Connell, gendered sexuality refers to the broader structure that defines masculinity in opposition to both women and homosexuality. (Although Connell assumes masculinity as the subject of inquiry, one could understand femininity, here, under the same model as defined in opposition to masculinity and homosexuality.) Masculinity is meant to define both personality and object choice, and entwined in this subject formation is a historical hatred of effeminate men with same-sex object choice.[18] "Straight-acting" refers to the ability of the gay/bisexual/queer man or lesbian/bisexual/queer woman to act in accordance with the personality of heterosexuality, without engaging in the practice of it. Not surprisingly, this can sometimes lead the straight-acting gay/lesbian to a social-cultural position that discredits and shames non-straight-acting gays/lesbians. In the final chapter I will argue against the use of gender identity in the formation of a queer sexual identity.

Gender Passing

Throughout the first chapter of this book, I will talk about gender passing as an historical example of passing that is similar to sexual identity passing. Historically (at least before 1850, and more ambiguously through the 1970's), I think these examples work nicely as clear representations of boundary transgressions. The modern era, however, of gender identity politics and the rise of the transgender/transsexual community as a class of persons fighting for recognition and rights significantly complicates the notion of gender passing. What I'd like to do, before explaining these new difficulties and passing logics, is to present a case of gender passing in the modern era that unambiguously demonstrates the aspects of passing through gender identity that much of this book is exploring.

Norah Vincent's memoir *Self-Made Man* is a narrative re-telling of her year living as a man: Ned. She traverses a number of "male" spaces, including a blue-collar bowling league, heterosexual dating (Norah is a lesbian, but this is her first experience of dating heterosexual women as a man), a monastery, and a "masculinity in the wilderness" retreat. Her journalistic writing style and her subtle attention to human interaction make the memoir a pleasurable read, but more importantly the self-designed experiment in passing, combined with her subtle attention to social dynamics makes for a nice first person account of the psychological pressures of passing.

By the end of her year-long experiment Norah has a nervous breakdown from her year as Ned; she is briefly hospitalized. What is it that she thinks drove her to this state? She blames it primarily on the psychological pressure of her "imposture"—particularly the associated and necessary deception of others that took place at the same time she was attempting to craft relationships of trust. She found this to be a miscalculation on her part. Norah explains:

> I began my journey with a fairly naïve idea about what to expect. I thought that passing was going to be the hardest part. But it wasn't at all. I did that far more

easily than I thought I would. The difficulty lay in the consequences of passing, and that I had not even considered. As I lived snippets of a male life, one part of my brain was duly taking notes and making observations, intellectualizing the raw material of Ned's experience, but another part of my brain, the subconscious part, was taking blows to the head, and eventually those injuries caught up with me.[19]

Vincent never considered this psychological toll in terms of an ethical dilemma. In fact, the exact word she uses elsewhere is "method." She considered her experiment to be a performance, with the world her (his) stage, and the ethical dimensions did not impact the framing of her experience. Is it fair simply to resolve her experiment in terms of "method"? Her "audience" did not willfully submit to a suspension of disbelief to her performance, and while her ordinary interactions may not be cause for concern, her relationships of intimacy (including ones of a sexual nature) should give even the morally callous reason to pause. Vincent does engage the rhetoric of sin and penitence, arguing in the end that she paid a high emotional price for her "meddlings," and that fact provides her with a certain degree of absolution.

There are two other elements of her journalistic narrative that I wish to extrapolate for the purposes of this academic evaluation of passing: her description of the moments of residual uptake to her performed gender identity as "freezing" and the energetic demand of a life performance. Both of these elements help to illustrate the phenomenological quality of passing.

Her observation that people interact with strangers in a gender coded way is hardly a new observation. But her opportunity to see the rupture in the fabric of society when her gender identity was not cleanly able to be categorized is insightful. She describes it metaphorically as a kind of freezing:

> It was the freezing that always struck me most. People will literally stand paralyzed for a moment, sometimes when they don't know what sex you are. You can see the confusion registering, or with polite people, being suppressed, and then you can see the adjustment being made either for an extremely uncomfortable and robotic neutral ground between the two.[20]

Witnessing the registering and discomfort of her (his) casual interlocuters began to take its toll on the psychological ease of Norah's ordinary life. And the energy needed to maintain some semblance of balance in her internal world was something she needed to put in writing.

> Ned was an imposter and imposters who aren't sociopaths eventually implode. Assuming another identity is no simple affair, even when it doesn't involve a sex change. It takes constant effort, vigilance and energy. A lot of energy. It's exhausting at the best of times. You are always afraid that someone knows you are not who you say you are, or will know immediately if you make even the slightest false step. You are outside yourself in two senses. First because you are always watching your self from beside or above, trying to get the performance right and see the pitfalls coming, but also because you are always trying to

inhabit the persona of someone who doesn't exist, even on paper. You don't have the benefit of a script or character treatment that can tell you how this person thinks, or what his childhood was like, or what he likes to do. He has no history and no substance, and being him is like being an adult thrown back into the worst of someone else's awkward adolescence.[21]

Needing to falsify the entirety of one's history, or at least large chunks of one's family origins, childhood, adolescence, and some portion of one's adult life is necessary for some types of passing (racial, gender, class) and not for others (sexual identity).[22]

But the exhaustive cost and cognitive dissonance between "one's true life" and "one's life narrative for consumption" also has its own phenomenology, and the psychological stress of this dissonance was something she chose to emphasize time and again.[23]

Cross-Dressing, etc.

The context for gender passing has significantly changed over the last one hundred and sixty years or so. In the colonial period, for example, there were ordinances that forbade people from "disguising themselves in public or wearing clothes associated with a particular social rank or profession."[24] Beginning in 1848, there were laws about gender regulation (prohibiting dress of opposite sex clothing) around the country that lasted up through 1974.[25] Of course in the modern day it is much more acceptable for women to wear men's clothing (suits, ties, dress-pants) than it is for men to wear women's clothing (dresses, skirts), and much of this has to do with the dress reform that was begun by feminists in the mid to and late 19th century. Before the mid 20th century, it is important to consider the gender context that granted economic benefit to women who passed as male, giving them much greater freedom to travel and find work.[26]

Many of the anti-feminists in the late 19th century equated gender reform with cross-dressing. Cross-dressing remains a viable gender identity option for those who are not transgendered, nor wish to gender pass. Along the broad spectrum between gender passing and transgender identity are many types of gender identities and expressions—of which cross-dressing is only one, but also historically the most easily recognizable. Also included along this spectrum are those who identify or are identified as transvestite, genderqueer, bigendered, genderfluid, third-gendered, drag performer (queen and king) and gender deviant. All of these individuals can be misrecognized and misidentified through our gender binary of male/female to produce the effects of passing. "Gender deviant" is perhaps the best over-arching term for all of these classes of gender identity and makes considerable room for mis-readings, multiple readings, and complicated gender self-understanding. "Gender deviant" simply refers to an individual who falls outside of our ordinary everyday understanding of male/masculine and female/feminine. Very closely related is "genderqueer" which refers to anyone who resists gender norms without wishing to change his/her biological sex.[27] "Bigendered" is someone who has both masculine and feminine qualities. "Gender-fluid" is someone who moves freely between genders.[28] Third-gendered people have a history within the Native Americans as Berdaches, as Hirja in India, and Kathoeys of Thailand. These are historically and socially approved classes of persons that are considered to be both male and female (they are gendered as female and sexed as males). Drag queens and kings are typically individuals who dress in cross-gender clothing for the purposes of entertainment or theatrics. "Transvestite" is a word coined in 1910 by a German sexologist to refer to what he called an "erotic urge for disguise." The base of the word was drawn from the same Latin base as "vestment" and literally referred to a cross-dressing.[29] "Cross-dressing" was originally coined as a non-judgmental replacement for transvestite and is "usually considered to be neutrally descriptive of the practice of wearing gender-atypical clothing rather than associating that practice with an erotic impulse."[30] Cross-dressing has a tendency to designate males more often than females, as women who cross-dress have greater freedom to live their daily lives as masculine or butch women. Julia Serano, transsexual activist, has argued that there is a cultural obsession and anxiety that surrounds male cross-dressing that is simply not shared for female cross-dressing. She has coined the word "effemimania" to describe this cultural obsession with male cross-dressers.[31]

Intersex

"Intersex" is another gender category and identity that also complicates the story of gender passing. Once known as "hermaphroditism," intersex designates "a variety of congenital conditions in which a person has neither the standard male nor female anatomy," endocrinology, or chromosomes.[32] Currently, intersex is considered a medically treatable condition by the general medical profession. If a child is born with abnormal genitals (typically, too large of a clitoris—over one centimeter, or too short of a penis—under two centimeters) surgery will be conducted on the infant, usually turning the child into an anatomically "correct" female, with the parents encouraged to raise the child as a natural member of the female sex. The assumed success of these surgeries is based on a belief that children are psychosexually neutral until around the age of two.[33] Many of these children grow up to have serious sexual dysfunction, experience significant gender dysphoria, and sometimes experience a confusing shame stemming from childhood and the numerous unexplained medical inspections of his/her genitals.

Many intersex individuals describe the medical procedures done in their infancy as a kind of medicalized and (en)forced involuntary gender passing. The surgeries are often performed without full disclosure to the parents of the social and sexual difficulties of some adults after the surgeries, and the parents keep the knowledge of the surgeries away from the patients (their children). Given the lack of full disclosure, the parents cannot give truly informed consent, nor can the patient give consent given his/her age. Many adult intersex patients confirm that their childhood surgeries and the encouraged silence around their differences and "surgical alterations only served to enforce feelings of isolation, stigma, and shame—the very feelings that such procedures are attempting to alleviate."[34] The ethical questions around intersex identity are created and enforced by a medical system that recognizes only two genders. The lack of respect for the autonomy and self-governance of gender identity and sex can create life-long problems.

Recognizing intersex as a valid location along the continuum of gender identity means that our understanding of sexed bodies needs to be more complicated than male and female.[35] It is also important to remember that, while a small percentage of the overall human population, the total number of intersex people is significant.[36]

Modern Transgender Politics

The "T" in LGBT captures the breadth of a community that is based much more in questions of sex and gender identity than in questions of sexuality. "Transgender" is a term that has gained significant popularity since the 1990's, and refers to people who live across the boundary of gender away from the gender they were born into. One can be transgender without any changes to their sex organs or hormonal levels. One can also identify as transgender and take opposite gender hormones. The most important aspect of the definition of "transgender" is what Susan Stryker emphasizes as "the movement across a socially imposed boundary away from an unchosen starting place."[37] Please note that the very definition of transgender emphasizes a movement across the gender line that we might also think of as passing. The most popular way of referring to individuals who are transgender is through the shorthand of MTF (male-to-female) or FTM (female-to-male). Even these short-handed ways of capturing identity emphasize the transitional and boundary crossing aspects of transgender identity.

Typically if one has had surgery, the term utilized to describe his/her identity is "transsexual." This term can be traced back to sexology in the late 19th century and refers to "people who feel a strong desire to change their sexual morphology in order to live entirely as permanent, full-time members of the gender other than the one they were assigned to at birth."[38] Surgical interventions became popular during the mid-20th century, and hit the broader public consciousness through media exposure in 1952.[39] In the current medical climate, in order to qualify for transsexual surgery, one must be diagnosed with Gender Identity Disorder (GID) by a trained psychiatric professional. Stryker writes that "GID is very controversial within the transgender communities. Some people resent having their sense of gender labeled as a sickness, while others take great comfort from believing they have a condition that can be cured with proper treatment."[40] The diagnosis of GID in combination with a period of time lived as the desired gender with the help of hormones before going through with surgery allows for the individual to make a legal change in gender on all relevant government documents, including a birth certificate.[41]

It is key to remember that transgender and transsexual people can be of any sexual identity.

The campaign for transgender rights began in 1975, with towns and cities nationwide beginning to adopt trans protective ordinances.[42] Discrimination of transgendered people is still very common, even by large LGBT/Q rights organizations. "Transphobia" is the term for "an irrational fear of, aversion to, or discrimination against people whose gendered identities, appearances, or behaviors deviate from societal norms."[43] Julia Serano argues that transphobia (as well as homophobia) is rooted in oppositional sexism, which is "the belief that female and male are rigid, mutually exclusive categories, each possessing a unique and non-overlapping set of attributes, aptitudes, abilities, and desires."[44] She argues that it is the attitude of oppositional sexism that creates the anxiety around lesbian, gay, bisexual, and transgender identities. Oppositional sexism would also explain the anxiety and fears that can surround people who pass especially in relation to gender and/or sexuality. In addition, Serano strongly notes that there is a particular cultural hostility towards trans women that centers on a mockery of both their femininity and their transition away from masculinity. She recognizes this as trans-misogyny and convincingly argues that it cannot be overlooked when we consider the contours of the fight for trans rights. She also argues that this should unite transgender rights activists and feminist activists. [45]

Modern Transgender Politics—Cissexual Privilege

Key to understanding both the cultural background of transphobia and transmisogyny, as well as the framework of identity that makes the logic of transgender passing work, is the concept of *cissexual privilege*. The prefix *cis* means "on the same side as" and when added to the suffix sexual or gendered it is meant to highlight the unstated assumption in words like "man," "woman," "male," or "female" which is that the individual is non-transgendered.[46] Using the prefix *cis* draws attention to the asymmetry in gender identity that sets transgender outside the natural framework of human gender. Cissexual privilege refers to the rights and social abilities of people whose gender identity matches their birth gender, many of which go unseen and unexamined. Two key aspects to culture that allow cissexual privilege to flourish, Serano argues, are gendering and cissexual assumption.[47]

Gendering is the process of classifying and identifying the gender of other people, quickly and usually unconsciously, based on just a few visual and/or audio clues.[48] This process of gendering privileges cisgendered people as few cisgendered people have had the experience of being misgendered. The experience of being misgendered is common for all transgendered people before they transition and for many transgendered people after they transition. Gendering is usually considered to be a natural observation by cissexuals, but trans activists demonstrate that gendering is speculation.[49] The corollary to gendering is ungendering, which commonly occurs when a transgendered person discloses his/her trans identity. Ungendering is the process by which cissexual people start to look for details or evidence that the trans person is no longer living in his/her birth gender.[50] The process of ungendering is socially and politically problematic for trans people. The process of ungendering someone who it turns out was passing would have significantly different political undertones given the passing individual's existential commitments to his/her birth gender.

Cissexual assumption is the day-to-day presumption by cissexuals that everyone they meet is also cissexual.[51] In alignment with that presumption is the projection that everyone else feels as comfortable in their physical and subconscious sex as they do. This cissexual assumption is particularly burdensome for transgender individuals who have not yet begun to transition. This assumption that s/he feels natural in his/her assigned gender makes it difficult to articulate gender dissonance and dis-ease. This creates a burden on transgender individuals to come out as trans, where cisgender people have the comfort of assumed recognition.[52]

Another form of gender discrimination occurs when people distinguish cisgendered people as biologically or genetically male or female. Julia Serano argues that the use of the words "biological" or "genetic" most often stand in for the use of the word "natural" in the pejorative way that is employed in homophobia. She writes, "most cissexuals want to believe that their maleness or femaleness is "natural" in the same way that most heterosexuals want to believe that their sexual identity is "natural.""[53] This can also be evidenced when transgender identity is described with words like "'emulate,' 'imitate,' and 'impersonate.'"[54] The cissexual privilege at play here is a gender entitlement based in the assumption that being birthed into a gender gives someone a greater legitimacy within its contours.[55] Julia Serano argues that this is one of the last places where Western culture practices a social class system based on birth. She writes,

> Cissexuals view their gender entitlement as a birthright. This is often a deceitful act, as many (if not most) cissexuals in our society tend to look disparagingly upon societies and cultures that still rely on class or caste systems— where one's occupation, social status, economic disposition, political power, etc., is predetermined based on an accident of birth. So while most Western cissexuals frown upon birth privilege as a means to determining these other forms of social class, they hypocritically embrace it when it comes to gender.[56]

This gender entitlement is maintained by a social order and culture that does not encourage recognizing gendering and cissexual assumption, nor do most cissexuals experience the negative side effects and inconveniences of others' gender entitlement.[57]

Cissexism is the natural extension of cissexual privilege and refers to "the belief that transsexuals' identified genders are inferior to, or less authentic than, those of cissexuals."[58] Serano cites two common examples: the purposeful misuse of pronouns and the insistence that trans people use a different public restroom.[59]

Modern Transgender Politics—Passing Logics

It should be clear by this point that we can't understand transgender passing in the same way that we would understand gender passing. The movement across the gender line is a definitional part of trans identity. When trans individuals "pass" for their identified gender, they are "passing" as cisgender, not "gender passing." So the logic of passing within trans communities includes both a transition across the gender line as well as a movement from the trans identity into a cisgender identity.[60] The failure to pass as one's identified gender is a different social experience than failure to pass as cisgender. For example, when a transman fails to "pass" as a man, the experience can feel like a failed gender identity, specifically in this case it is failed masculinity.[61] If an individual who is not trans is trying to pass as the opposite gender and fails to do so, the reaction may be one of anxiety, fear, embarrassment, or social rejection. If a trans person fails to pass as his/her identified gender, this experience will occur against the backdrop of a life of gender dissonance, and repeated misrecognition as the wrong gender.[62] The gender passer is likely to feel exposed and judged based on his or her behavior that transgresses social expectations of gender. The transgender passer, however, is likely to feel it as a larger affront to his/her identity: a failure of grander existential proportions. The failure to pass will be experienced as both transphobia and the employment of cissexual privilege.

Julia Serano argues that the experience of passing for a trans person can feel simply like "conditional cissexual privilege." This means that for a period of time the privilege of being recognized with all the benefits of a natural born gender are extended, with the recognition that those benefits can be revoked at any time and often are revoked when it is disclosed that the person is trans. An additional asymmetry exists for transsexuals after they transition. After transition the trans person cannot "pass" for his/her assigned or birth gender; this is not the way the social logic works.

Serano strongly argues that the logic of passing is embedded in the perspective of the majority, and in the case of transsexual/transgender passing, it is embedded in cissexual/cisgender privilege. She writes,

> Sometimes people work hard to "pass," and other times they don't try at all. Either way, the one thing that remains consistent is that the word "pass" is used to shift the blame away from the majority group's prejudice and toward the minority person's presumed motives and actions (which explains why people who "pass" are often accused of "deception" or "infiltration" if they are ever found out).[63]

She doesn't mention that the accusation of passing can be virulently placed upon someone by co-members of the same minority community, but her observation remains keen that the logic and rhetoric of passing focuses on the stigmatized individual rather than the stigmatizing majority. She also wants to shift the locus of action in passing. She writes,

> The crux of the problem is that the words "pass" and "passing" are active verbs. So when we say that a transsexual is "passing" it gives the false impression that they are the only active participant in this scenario (i.e., the transsexual is working hard to achieve a certain gendered appearance and everyone else is passively being duped or not duped by the transsexual's "performance"). However, I would argue that the reverse is true: The public is the primary active participant by virtue of their incessant need to gender every person they see as either female or male.[64]

Much like I will do in the later chapters, Serano recognizes the importance of the gaze upon the person who is passing. However, she locates the active element of passing in the gendering aspect of that gaze. And she writes that by employing the word "passing," the active element of that gaze is unfairly displaced.

It seems to me that both an analysis of the prejudiced majority and a look at the behaviors and logics of the individuals affected by that prejudice are separately and collectively important. One does not lose their moral agency or capacity to make decisions about identity under hostility, but certainly those decisions must be evaluated within the context that they occur.

The context of transgender passing is cissexual privilege, and Serano has a number of things to say about how the concept of passing furthers the agenda of cissexual privilege. First, she states that "most cissexuals are absolutely obsessed about whether transsexuals 'pass' or not."[65] Note the difference here between race and sexuality. Cissexuals find it to be a matter of intense curiosity as to whether or not a transgender person can pass. Historically there has been a significant amount of anxiety surrounding the passing of light-skinned African Americans. And there are laws and other forms of social encouragement and sanction for gays and lesbians who can pass. Serano explains that the only reason a cissexual should be concerned with the passing status of a trans individual is so that s/he can "exercise cissexual privilege over them."[66] And focusing on this ability to pass allows cissexuals to ignore their own privilege; the focus is on the transgression of social boundaries not on the content of the social categories on either side of the boundary.[67] Passing, of course, involves a double standard. Cissexuals don't try or need to worry about passing for transsexual. But all transsexuals know that "being accepted as members of our identified sex makes it infinitely easier for us to gain employment and housing, to be taken seriously in our personal, social, and political endeavors, and to be able to walk down the street without being harassed or assaulted."[68] Clearly cissexual privilege is a real, tangible, and desirable thing to acquire. Serano doesn't take a hard political line on whether or not one should be open about his/her trans status. But, it is clear that she thinks the rhetoric and logic of passing unduly and unfairly benefits the cissexual perspective.

There have been transsexual activists who have argued against passing, in the more classic way that this book understands the term, and under the rhetoric of trans to cis passing. Sandy Stone writes,

> For a transsexual, as a transsexual, to generate a true, effective, and representational counter-discourse is to speak from outside the boundaries of gender, beyond the constructed oppositional nodes, which have been predefined as the only positions from which discourse is possible.[69]

Obviously many transgender and transsexual rights and ordinances are dependent upon trans people standing proud in their trans identities and asking for rights and respect in terms of that identity. But Stone argues that there is also a cultural need for trans people to stand outside the gender binary and speak authentically from an outside location. She also thinks this is necessary for trans people to be honest about themselves in order to have authentic relationships; she takes her political argument and translates it into ethical terms. If trans people begin their interpersonal relationships (social, professional, or otherwise) from a platform of passing, they inevitably see significant damage and inauthenticity in those relationships because they "begin as lies."[70] Instead she encourages all trans people to take the "political action begun by reappropriating difference and reclaiming the power of the refigured and reinscribed body."[71] This is a strong identity politic that does continue to place the moral and political burden on the subjugated one who could pass. It is clearly in opposition to the kind of political/cultural analysis that Serano would have us undertake.

C. Riley Snorton, however, takes a different position in regards to trans passing. He argues that there is significant psychic value to passing. He argues that passing is the way that trans people make identity. He presents a unique argument that is not mirrored by anyone else who discusses trans passing or any other kind of passing.[72]

Snorton claims first that the "psychic art of passing"[73] is an essential means of self-knowledge. By this description of the psychic act he is referring both to how one narrates oneself to others, but also how one narrates identity to self. He writes that there is

> a form of psychic legibility evidenced by the experience of cognitive dissonance on the part of the one who passes. *Misrecognition*, therefore, is as important as recognition in the production of self, as the quality of feeling misrecognized/unseen/wrongly viewed serves as a context for the emergence of selfhood.[74]

The experience of passing, or misrecognition, has a psychic quality that creates a kind of jolt that requires a follow up of self-recognition. It enhances the sense of self by creating moments in which the internal self-inscription of identity must be more thorough. He also points out that passing not only allows many trans people to physically navigate the world safely, but it also allows for the avoidance of psychological harm.[75] One can experience social connection, approval, and all the social benefits of fitting in while passing, and not run the risk of damage by exposing a trans identity that would not be well received.

Snorton describes passing as a hopeful experience. He writes that passing has a restorative psychological value in the way that hope does, by helping to transcend beyond the material particulars of the current situation into a possible or fictional future/other location. It allows him to transform the scripts of gendered embodiment, and to create an identity beyond the constraints of his assigned sex. As a transman who is pre-op, no hormones, Snorton writes, "passing, like hope, keeps me sane, or at least helps me to cope in an environment that does not produce the identity I psychically inhabit."[76] This hopeful interpretation of passing is currently well framed by the social identity logics of the trans community, and I argue should be held in abeyance when considering other kinds of identity passing.

Narrowing the Focus: Sexual Identity Passing and the Closet

One of the most important distinctions to make up front, particularly in terms of the texts available in queer or LGBT studies, is the difference between "passing" and the "closet." The trope of the closet traditionally refers to a kind of identity falsification in LGBT/Q communities, referencing an ambiguously sociopolitical and psychological space that has developed in the 20th century. Throughout this book I will forgo what would undoubtedly be a fruitful investigation into the phenomenon of the closet. But it will serve us well to distinguish the closet conceptually from passing before we begin a more in depth investigation into sexual identity passing.

"Passing" and "the closet" each invoke different metaphorical associations. The closet functions as a spatial metaphor. It denotes a space where identity and knowledge about identity are hidden from view. Where passing denotes movement through space and general mobility,[77] the closet frames stagnancy. The image of "coming out" which so regularly interfaces with the image of the closet reifies the spatiality of the metaphor. For some, the closet is primarily a social space: one of isolation and withdrawal. For others the closet is primarily a political space: a space of reprieve from oppression and retribution. And for others it is primarily a psychological space: a space of self-loathing and/or insecurity. The closet is a construction of the heterosexual/homosexual binary, a result of the policing efforts of the 1930's, when behavioral markers associated with gayness were regulated as illegal.[78] The heterosexual/homosexual binary is a construction of late 19th century psychology and sexuality studies.[79] In the modern world it is often a community boundary marker, and the narrative of "coming out," as it relates to the closet, is its socially transgressive moment. It is arguable that the binary and the closet are forms of social regulation for all individuals. But it is particularly regulatory as the visibility/invisibility marker within the LGBT/Q community.

The closet has been a sustained source of study in queer literary theory. One of the most famous explorations is *Epistemology of the Closet* by Eve Kosofsky Sedgwick. For Sedgwick the closet is primarily about epistemology. Her work accentuates what the closet can tell us about the logics we use to make sense of identity. The gay/straight binary, she argues, that is predicated upon a minoritizing understanding of sexual identity as essentialist and separatist is ruptured by the space of the closet. The closet complicates the relationship between LGBT/Q and straight and illustrates many of the ways in which sexual identity is a product of social construction, individual rhetoric, public perception, etc. She asserts that the epistemology of the closet demonstrates the inherent instabilities surrounding sexual identity in the 20th century. She understands the closet to be universalizing, constructive, and transitive. She thinks that all 20th century sexualities are impacted and framed by the closet (hence the closet is universalizing). Whether you are heterosexual, homosexual, bisexual, or any shade of queer, your sexuality will at some point need to confront the closet or will be privileged and protected by the closet. The closet will construct the parameters of your sexual identity. The closet is also a necessary space between exiting a presumed heterosexual identity (given to all of us prior to birth by heteronormativity) and an authentic or chosen queer identity, and therefore is transitive. Even if one does not choose the closet, heteronormativity chooses the closet for us.

The closet reveals the limits of speech acts and individual rights over the expression of sexual self. She explains that closetedness can be understood as a speech act of silence, "not a particular silence, but a silence that accrues particularity by fits and starts, in relation to the discourse that surrounds and differentially constitutes it."[80] The silence of the closet circumscribes a space of ruptured knowledge access, where the unknown is subtly inserted for the uptake as known for some (who are sensitive to that silence—and can read into it) and to be rendered invisible to others.

Sedgwick seems to focus on speech acts (and particularly silences as a type of speech act) as the foundation for the epistemology of the closet given the larger aims of her work, which is specifically about the location of the closet in literary texts, and how to build a relationship of anti-homophobic inquiry between the texts and the reader of the texts. She sees this as an ethical prescription: that we should read the canon with an anti-homophobic agenda that seeks to expose the homo/hetero logic rupturing space of the closet.

Sedgwick's work covers many of these elements, but more can be said directly about the closet and how it is occupied and works with identity differently than passing. "The closet" is a socio-historical contingency. It is a regulating mechanism of modern sexual behavior, a psycho-social space that functions as an erasure of modern homosexuality. The closet, one might say, is a philosophical and ethical construct. It has a normative component. It occupies the boundary between heteronormativity and sexual perversity. It silences.

The closet is inescapable. All LGB/Q identities are constructed around its narrative. While in the closet, one is sectioned off from community (both heterosexual and homosexual). One is sectioned off from oneself, forcibly hiding certain aspects of identity, behavioral patterns, and human observations. Upon exiting the closet, through some variety of a "coming out narrative," one's remaining LGB/Q identity is structured from that moment forward ("I came out at twenty-one" or "I came out right after college" or "I came out during high school, was kicked out of my home, and forced to turn tricks to survive" etc.).

The coming out narrative is a pre-established identity constructor/construction. It is a narrative mold that structures relation to self and relation to others utilizing a few base components, examples include: 1) When one came out to self—and related psychic distress. 2) First same-sex sexual experience. 3) First articulation of a LGB/Q identity marker. 4) First articulation where some risk of loss was involved: to an unsympathetic parent, to an employer etc. There isn't space within this system to articulate an alternative, self-crafted narrative. The structure is inescapable and closes down possibility.

But there is also a double-bind ethical component to the coming out narrative. From an out-LGB/Q perspective the closet is a space of deceit and betrayal. From the perspective of the religious right it is a space of moral protection (protection of children, or the general social good). From the perspective of the mostly democratic, so-called liberal-heterosexual public it is either off the moral radar, or something that functionally works to keep homosexuality out of common moral discourse.

Conversationally, the emotive rhetoric behind the two terms, passing and the closet, can be distinguished in terms of the presumed psychological health of the agent. The closeted individual is still coming to terms with his/her identity, is having some difficulties with his/her self-acceptance, and has existential commitments to heterosexuality that keep an outward narrative expression of a subaltern sexual identity undesirable. The passing individual presumably has come to terms with his/her sexual identity, has certain existential commitments to being LGB/Q, but is utilizing a heterosexist rhetoric or style for personal or social gain. The distinction between a closeted individual and a passing individual could be categorized using intentionality, the binary of heterosexual/homosexual, and the engagement with homophobia vs. heterosexism. What remains a strong question throughout the latter part of this book is the ethical effect of these categories.

When I categorize an LGB/Q agent into the differing camps of "closet" and "passing" I am assuming that the agent has certain intentions. We could sketch this categorization along a continuum where a socially scripted and handed down heterosexual identity is in the center, the closet is to the left, while passing is to the right. The center position is neutral and might be said to be the identity location presumed for most human beings most of the time. It is the heterosexual narrative, with which we are all familiar: boy meets girl, boy falls in love with girl, boy marries girl, family and friends delight and celebrate, 2.5 children and some type of domestic animal follow.[81] When the LGB/Q agents engage this continuum, they are unable to rest in the neutral position, and their intentionality leads them in one of two directions. To the left, their intentions are consumed by a desire to self-protect. The internal narrative is one of stress and concern for one's safety and well-being. The existential commitments to the heterosexual narrative keep attracting the agent to the central neutral position, but the agent's internal struggle creates a repellent tension that continuously pushes the agent away. To the right, the agent has a healthier connection back to the neutral position. The tension has been relieved and the agent's existential commitments are to an LGB/Q identity. The intentionality of the agent is not directed to returning to the heterosexual neutral position, but rather is directed at appropriating the heterosexual narrative for certain positive social gains. The basic summation here is that the closet involves tension, negative-framed intentionality, and heterosexual existential commitments; while passing involves acceptance, positive intentionality, and LGB/Q existential commitments, both with the added performance of heterosexuality.

Another difference in the conceptual structuring of "closet" and "passing" is their connection back to homophobia and heterosexism. "Homophobia" refers to the fear or hatred of homosexuals or homosexuality.[82] Heterosexism refers to discrimination against homosexual persons by the privileging of heterosexuality. Homophobia constricts the LGB/Q agent through emotion, threat of violence, and physical safety, heterosexism constricts rights and visibility. Again there is a repetition of the rhetorical structure where guarding against homophobia involves guarding against negativity, and guarding against heterosexism involves guarding against the loss of positive rights.

Certainly LGB/Q moral agents can participate in homophobic behavior. This can be one of the most pronounced psychological markers of the closet: the internalized homophobia that creates the continual tension that reinforces the closet. But, by the very definition, an LGB/Q agent cannot participate authentically in heterosexism. However, in moments of passing the LGB/Q agent is attempting to engage the power of heterosexism, whether that is through appealing to the rights it offers, or allowing its assumptions to continue unquestioned. This is another defining distinction of the "closet" and "passing." The ethical associations with fear and hatred are different from those associated with discrimination. While the former is often foundational to the latter, the latter engages a more concrete socio-ethical analysis that I will take up in chapters 4, 5, and 6.

Note on the Down Low

I have argued that sexual identity passing is not the same thing as the closet. Also under consideration is the relationship between sexual identity passing and the "down low." The down low has gained recent attention in the popular media (beginning in the early 1990's) and refers to black men who maintain significant and serious relationships with women (often marriages with children) while sleeping with other black men in secret. These men dis-identify with traditional markers of queer sexual identity such as "gay" or "bisexual" and understand themselves to be full participants in the heteronormative structure of marriage and family.[83]

The popular media fascination with down low men uses rhetoric that frames the men as deceivers who put black women in danger through the spreading and carrying of HIV/AIDS. The anxiety that surrounds the sexual uncertainty of black men on the down low in the midst of the HIV epidemic means that most black presses that have written about the phenomenon have encouraged black men to "come out" of the closet and employ the homonormative terms of "gay" and "bisexual" to produce visibility and thereby allow black women to exercise extra sexual caution.[84]

The racial and sexual politics that surround the down low are such that this phenomenon participates in some of the politics and tropes of both racial and sexual identity passing, and is distinguishable from the closet. However, I argue that the down low is not in the same category of sexual identity passing that this book undertakes to explore, primarily because those on the down low dis-identify with LGB/Q culture and actively pursue not just the image of heteronormativity, but actual heteronormativity.

McCune argues that racial politics in the United States have always meant that black people have privileged discreet ways of being in the world, employing types of invisibility and quietness to protect "people of color's freedoms," spiritual health, and fragile dreams.[85] He argues that there has been a long tradition of black people circumventing social stigmas and avoiding "the gaze of surveillance" through lives of discreet behaviors.[86] This historical connection to racial politics as well as racial passing encourages McCune to see the down low as an historically informed phenomenon that must be understood along racial lines and through tropes of passing. I agree with him on this observation of racial passing. The down low exists clearly in relation to racial passing, more so, perhaps than sexual identity passing. At the same time he demonstrates the clear difference between racial passing and sexuality on the down low. In the former case, one must hide his or her racial past, in the latter case one must hide his sexual present.[87] He criticizes the black media for their inability to see the historical significance of secrecy in African-American life while still demonizing down low men and calling for them to "come out." He questions the praising and privileging of visibility.[88]

McCune argues that men on the down low cannot be understood as closeted, because the closet assumes a "prison-state and a place from which people want and need to escape."[89] Men on the down low do not wish to escape the secrecy that surrounds their same-sex sexual activity. Their positionality is one of permanence. It is the final destination along a continuum of sexual identity development. This is the key moment where McCune's understanding of the down low as passing falls apart. Passing always designates movement from and towards. In the case of sexual identity passing, the LGB/Q person passing for straight is moving away from gayness and towards straightness. The position of sexual identity passing is not a final destination in itself.

McCune sees the demand for those on the down low to make themselves visible to be in alignment with one-drop definitions of race. One-drop laws define the full racial identity of an individual based on very little African blood. The same principle is at play, he argues, when limited same-sex contact is said to define the full sexual identity of an individual. The binary thinking that limits racial identity to either black or white is the same binary thinking that makes one either queer or straight.[90] He argues that this puts undue pressure on all passing people to stay on the "down low," out of the gaze of surveillance and beyond oppressive definitions.[91] He also points to this binary thinking as a model that does not allow these men to occupy the position of the down low as a viable "true" identity. Instead they are seen as lying both about their heterosexual identity and their queer desire. The experience of being on the down low is rarely explored. The media interventions here also don't lift up the "physical and logistical nightmare" that would demonstrate the strained subjectivity of men on the down low, thereby showing the humanity in the down low. McCune argues that an exploration of this "double life" would more clearly demonstrate these men as seeking navigation of their desires and identities within a social structure that makes a fulfilling sexual life extremely difficult.[92]

McCune wishes to demonstrate through this historical connection that the context of the down low is steeped in modes of thinking that have historically done damage to black people. He talks about the "moral panic" incited by the popular press and the anxieties over HIV as denigrating same-sex behavior as simply disease prone and deceptive. He argues that the appropriate posture would be to address the matrix of heterosexism that necessitates secrecy and cheating on otherwise loved and honored spouses and significant others. He wants the focus to return to the genealogical.[93] I would continue his argument and say that the moral questions should be focused both on questions of interpersonal infidelity as well as on a social framework that encourages secrecy rather than openness surrounding sexual identities and practices.

Much like the categorization employed in one-drop kind of thinking, McCune questions the value of defining down low men as gay, bisexual, or queer men. Under one-drop definitions of race, whiteness could not tolerate even one drop of black blood. The down low demonstrates that definitions of heterosexuality are also currently conceived such that they cannot handle even small doses of same-sex desire or behavior. McCune questions why these down low men shouldn't be defined as heterosexual, and argues that they should be defined as such given the dominant visibility of their heterosexual lives, their lack of connection to the gay community, and their heterosexual values.[94] McCune argues that from this perspective, the down low could be instructive, even progressive in terms of our modern understanding of sexuality. It could help to expand the notion of heterosexuality, showing its inherent instabilities and its system of social constraint and enforcement.[95]

The historical politics and secrecy of the down low put the phenomenon in relationship with passing, clearly along a shared continuum. However, the down low remains a phenomenon separate from sexual identity passing, albeit in fascinating ways that are, and ought to be, the subject of complex scholarly interventions on its own. The main differences to be found between the down low and sexual identity passing as I explore it throughout this book includes the stationary location of the down low, the established parameters of its positionality as a "double life" that accompanies a heterosexual identity, the participants' subjective dis-identification with traditional sexual markers, and their full participation in heteronormativity.

How to Talk About Passing Narratives

Especially for those of us who are not passing, the primary way in which we learn about the subjective and identity content of passing is through narrative: sometimes historical, sometimes literary, at other times embedded in media. Historically, we are often removed from the subjective experience of passing when narratives are recounted—unless we listen to some of the rare voices of passers who tell their own stories. Third person and first person narratives are primary sources for thinking about passing, which has occupied history books, urban legends, memoirs, literature, and film.

An interesting aspect to the narratives of individuals who were famous for passing is that an individual can only be famous for passing because under some set of circumstances the person's passing was unsuccessful. Perhaps his/her true identity was exposed after s/he died, or a relative/friend/lover was able to tell his/her identity narrative, or the individual left behind a diary that disclosed the truth, and/or s/he was simply exposed. The truly great narratives of passing may well be the ones we don't know because they have remained or do remain successful cases of passing.

The way a narrative is framed also speaks to the agenda (or speaks through the agenda) of the narrator. Perhaps the narrator wishes to highlight the social demands that force an individual to pass (e.g., the emphasis might be placed on the professional motivations and the professional successes only to be had through a falsification of identity). Or perhaps the narrator wishes to be denogrative, i.e. forcing our attention on the moral or social failings of the passing individual, or the narrative might involve the motivation of assimilation on the part of the narrator. If, for example, an openly gay man tells the narrative of another gay man who passed for a woman in the streets in order to maintain a gay lifestyle in the bedroom under the appearance of heterosexuality, the gay male narrator might be telling the narrative to distinguish himself as living honestly, and thereby being more deserving of the right to assimilate into the rest of society. The narrative alternatively might take the form of a revisionist approach. This would involve using modern descriptive terms of/for identity and applying them to past historical periods. This is particularly common when describing gender deviance and gender passing using the modern categories of FTM, MTF, transgendered, or pre-19th century sexual identity passing using modern identity terms like "queer" or "homosexual."

Narratives about passing can also be told through a variety of lenses, each of which impacts the way in which the life of the passing individual is received. I think it is important to be aware of the ways in which the framing of the passing narrative impacts its uptake by the listener. I think it will serve my later critical analysis if I can get you, my reader, to think critically about the ways in which you have or will experience narratives of passing.

All of that said, narratives of passing fall minimally into the categories of explanatory, assimilationist, displacement, or sensationalist. Explanatory narratives of passing explain the person's life choices in terms of other initiating factors: "the individual passed as white to escape racial discrimination" or "the woman passed as a man so that she could have sex with other women." Assimilationist narratives emphasize the motivation to join dominant trends in society, and particularly in the case of sexual identity passing, assimilationist narratives emphasize the motivation to be normal. Displacement narratives read cultural anxiety into the passing lives so that the social categories involved are exposed as rupturable, and thereby constructed, all the while reinforcing the operative and organizational capabilities of those categories. Sensationalist accounts are told such that the deception and unbelievable escape from risk are emphasized. For literature and film we also need to add the tropes of comedy or tragedy. These categories can overlap. At times a film or novel is directed at exposing or recounting passing, at other times it is directed at exposing historical peculiarities or grave socio/political problems through the use of passing.

Chapter Summaries

Chapter 1: Passing in Abstraction: The Theoretical Organization of Passing

Chapter 1 categorizes the different ways in which writers, literary theorists, sociologists, philosophers, and other cultural critics have thought about passing. It begins with an ordinary/analytic definition of passing and its necessary relationship to a "successful" performance. Next is an exploration of how we think of identity: can we think of it as double (both/and), or must it be binary (either/or)? Passing suggests understanding identity through a double logic; ordinarily we think about identity in binary terms. The next set of questions will entertain how we produce identity. Is it embodied/corporeal? Or is it primarily about discourse, self-expression, and language? This chapter will also discuss some of the narratives of passing, the kinds of passing experiences, and the motivations involved in passing, primarily focusing on one schema: pleasure vs. protection. The rest of chapter 1 is dedicated to setting out the basic theoretical tension in understanding sexual identity passing through the most popular and contemporary rubric for gender and sexual identity construction: namely performativity.

Chapter 2: The Good, the Bad, and the Oppressed: Ethical Considerations

Traditionally, we think of passing as involving deception, lying, and pretense. When we think about identity in a social or community setting, passing involves socio-political questions about individual and collective responsibility and obligation. The beginning sections of chapter 2 organize the traditional moral concerns surrounding passing from the perspective of individual accountability as well as social location. The next section explores ethics under oppression, first by looking at political situations of horrifically abusive systemic power: the kind of power that is present in concentration camps. It explores what happens to ethics under extraordinarily corruptive and corrosive power, specifically in what Claudia Card has called "Moral Grey Zones." It also looks at what happens to our ordinary understanding of virtues. The exploration of morality in this section thinks about how it might be applied analogously to less horrific, but still corruptive and corrosive, situations of power (like heteronormativity). The final two sections explore ethics under first performativity and then under postmodernity more generally, exploring complications to our ethical analysis by thinking of identity as performed, unstable, and constructed.

Chapter 3: Thoughtfully Produced Sexuality: Sexology and the Queer Academy

Chapter 3 covers the history of sexual identity with particular emphasis on the production of the homosexual (and the heterosexual) by late 19th century sexologists. This is the constructive context for our modern employment of sexual identities as organizing categories of persons. I then take a look at traditional models of sexual ethics to capture some historical locations where queerness naturally fits and other locations where queerness is rejected as unethical. Then I turn to a survey of the postmodern body of literature known as queer theory. I argue that given queer theory's general lack of interest in ethics, it cannot supply us with a theoretical foothold for thinking about sexual identity passing through an ethical lens.

Chapter 4: Those Shoes Look Pretty Gay, Or at Least Bi-Curious: Style and Sexual Identity Passing

This chapter constructs a robust concept of style, drawing its initial framework and inspiration from French philosopher Maurice Merleau-Ponty to make sense of how we create identity and, I argue, is a concept that would be more useful in an analysis of passing than performativity. I argue that we should think of style as an ontological concept that is able to exemplify individuality, capture symbolic commitments, express emotion, demonstrate behavior, and function as a signature, and that requires constraint, has aspects of avoidance, and expresses a kind of ontological totality. The concept of style is explored in reference to bodies, narrative, and social relations. Style as a working concept of identity is put into dialogue with passing and ethics. The chapter closes by thinking about what theoretical resources we need to make sense of sexual identity and, by extension, sexual identity passing as a style. In particular, I emphasize that the concept of style allows for a constructive ethic—an ability that performativity is lacking—and that style is already present in our casual rhetoric and thinking about how sexual identity works.

Chapter 5: Political Perversity: Queer Sexuality and the Moral Majority

After all of this is said and done, I will try to convince you that there is something philosophically valuable about conceptualizing a moral ideal for LGB/Q individuals.[96] Is there a central moral core of LGB/Q life? If so, what should it look like? What particular moral considerations ought to structure LGB/Q life? Each of us is inculcated by a world that constructs our social obligations around the central relationship of the male-female reproductive couple. In crucial identity-forming ways, the homosexual moral agent is erased from ethical scopes of inquiry. Given the moral erasure of the homosexual agent, traditional philosophical ethical models underdetermine the complexity of LGB/Q life. The objective of these final two chapters is to determine the basic moral questions that apply to and result from same-sex sexual desire and relationships, critically thinking through what a functional homonormativity might look like.

This chapter begins with a critical look at the role of shame in the LGBT/Q communities, arguing that sexual identity is structured through a moral paradox: the liar vs. the pervert. I argue that shame must be infused into visible LGBT/Q identities and centrally featured in any productive model of LGBT/Q social ethics.

Chapter 6: Practicing to Preach: Gayness as a Practical Identity

I then posit the work of Christine Korsgaard and her model of practical identity as a framework for LGBT/Q social ethics, which I call "gayness." I argue that basing an ethic of gayness in a Korsgaardian practical identity allows us to circumvent basic questions about the nature of sexual identity: for instance, whether it is biological or a social construction, or even based in sexual practice. Gayness is a political identity with social implications. I argue for seven basic tenets of gayness: 1) a commitment to fighting sexual shame; 2) a commitment to fighting heterosexism; 3) a commitment to fighting internalized homophobia; 4) a dedication to rupturing the social conception of "normal"—in the heterosexual community; 5) a commitment to fighting the convention of "The Secret" in the gay community; 6) provision of role models and resources to subsequent generations of queer people; 7) willingness to step in on behalf of queer individuals when homophobia is being used against them. I conclude with an analysis of gayness in community and models of power conducive to the development of gayness.

Conclusion: Social and Legal Implications of Sexual Deceit

The substantive conclusion addresses some of the most practical social and legal implications for an analysis of the ethics of passing, as well as the proffered solution of gayness. I begin with the debate surrounding the ethics of outing oneself and other people, taking a critical look at the political rhetoric of privacy. Next is a set of questions and explorations of how "gayness" ought to configure our professional and public lives. I sketch out work for ethicists interested in role morality and professional ethics and consider an argument within gayness that LGBT/Q individuals ought to take on the responsibility of investing in the next generation. I conclude with a look at "don't ask, don't tell" as congressionally enforced sexual identity passing and the way same-sex sexual harassment poses a problem for sexual harassment law.

Notes

1. Note on the use of identity acronyms: LGBT/Q or Lesbian, Gay, Bisexual, Transgender/Queer will be my standard inclusive acronym throughout this book. When I am specifically focused on questions of sexuality, I will leave out the 'T' because transgender politics—while intimately intertwined with sexuality—are more significantly a matter of gender identity than sexual identity. Whenever I am quoting a different author I will maintain whatever nomenclature they have utilized. When I am referring to specifically and only gay men, I will employ the term "gay." However, when I begin to present

a new normative politic of "gayness," I will intend for that to include all of LGB/Q social ethics. I am symbolically representing the sometimes ideological tension between the queer community and the LGBT community by including a "/". This slash also represents the potential umbrella short hand of referring to all of the LGBT identity markers under the term "queer," which I will sometimes employ. I encourage my reader to use the nomenclature out loud, or silently, that best captures your personal sense of the best political term/acronym.

2. Cisgender is the equalizing term for transgender. The prefix *cis* means "on the same side as," and renders clear the assumption that someone was born in to the same gender as s/he is currently presenting.

3. This includes lesbian, gay, bisexual, queer, polyamorous, BDSM (bondage, discipline, sadism, masochism), and asexual persons.

4. Gunnar Myrdal, *An American Dilemma* (New York: Harper and Row, 1994), 683.

5. Myrdal, *An American Dilemma*, 683.

6. Myrdal, *An American Dilemma*, 684.

7. Myrdal, *An American Dilemma*, 685.

8. Myrdal, *An American Dilemma*, 685.

9. Rhinelander vs. Rhinelander (1925) is a very interesting and landmark legal case regarding racial passing and miscegenation laws. An excellent recounting of the trial and its legal/social implications is *Love on Trial: An American Scandal in Black and White* by Earl Lewis and Heidi Ardizzone (New York: W.W. Norton, 2001).

10. Myrdal, *An American Dilemma*, 687.

11. Myrdal, *An American Dilemma*, 686.

12. Myrdal, *An American Dilemma*, 687.

13. Myrdal, *An American Dilemma*, 688.

14. Anna Camaiti Hostert, *Passing: A Strategy to Dissolve Identities and Remap Differences*, translated by Christine Marciasini (Madison N.J.: Fairleigh Dickinson University Press, 2007), 79.

15. Myrdal, *An American Dilemma*, 688.

16. Rawls defines a primary good as "things which it is supposed a rational [wo]man wants whatever else [s]he wants." Anthony Kwame Appiah, *Ethics of Identity* (Princeton: Princeton University Press, 2005), 120.

17. R.W. Connell, "A Very Straight Gay: Masculinity, Homosexual Experience, and the Dynamics of Gender," *American Sociological Review* 57, no. 6 (December 1992), 743.

18. Connell, "A Very Straight Gay," 748.

19. Norah Vincent, *Self-Made Man* (New York: Penguin, 2006), 18.

20. Vincent, *Self-Made Man*, 223.

21. Vincent, *Self-Made Man*, 269.

22. Although early childhood might remain intact and general facts about family life and education can remain, large portions of adolescent and adult social life must be adapted.

23. A really good fictional work that includes an account of gender passing is *Stone Butch Blues* by Leslie Feinberg (Ann Arbor: Firebrand Books, 1993). The main character in the book is Jess, a butch lesbian who eventually begins to cross the gender line into masculinity. She begins to celebrate her experiences of passing at the barber and in the men's room (p. 172), she is outed as female by one of her well meaning colleagues and loses her job (p. 206), and she has an excellent conversation about the experience of passing where she describes both the pleasure of being read as a nice young man rather than a

perverted and degenerate female, but also speaks of the invisibility—"I feel like a ghost" (p. 213)—and the loneliness (p. 221) that results from passing.

24. Susan Stryker, *Transgender History* (Berkeley: Seal Studies, 2008), 33.

25. Stryker, *Transgender History*, 32.

26. Stryker, *Transgender History*, 34-5.

27. Stryker, *Transgender History*, 20-1.

28. Serano, *Whipping Girl*, 27.

29. Stryker, *Transgender History*, 16-17.

30. Stryker, *Transgender History*, 17.

31. Julia Serano, *Whipping Girl: A Transsexual Woman on Sexism and the Scapegoating of Femininity* (Emeryville, CA: Seal Press, 2007), 286.

32. Alice Domurat Dreger, "A History of Intersex: From the Age of Gonads to the Age of Consent," in *Intersex in the Age of Ethics*, edited by A. Dreger (Hagerstown, MD: University Publishing Group, 1999), 5.

33. Robert Crouch, "Betwixt and Between: The Past and Future of Intersexuality," in *Intersex in the Age of Ethics*, 31.

34. Sharon Preves, "For the Sake of the Children: Destigmatizing Intersexuality," in *Intersex in the Age of Ethics*, 53-4.

35. In 1993, Anne Fausto-Sterling argued that we need to recognize that there are five sexes in the human population: females, males, female pseudo-hermaphrodites, male pseudo-hermaphrodites, and true hermaphrodites. Dreger, "A History of Intersex," 20.

36. Sherri Groveman argues that there are about as many intersex persons as there are Jewish people globally. "The Hanukkah Bush: Ethical Implications in the Clinical Management of Intersex," in *Intersex in the Age of Ethics*, 24.

37. Stryker, *Transgender History*, 1.

38. Stryker, *Transgender History*, 18.

39. Christine Jorgenson made the popular press beginning in December, 1952, for a successful genital transformation surgery that took place in Copenhagen. She was not the first transsexual to have a successful surgery, but her "young, pretty, gracious, and dignified" demeanor helped to make her international news. This event was important in the social-political rights of the trans community. Stryker, *Transgender History*, 47.

40. Stryker, *Transgender History*, 13-4.

41. Stryker, *Transgender History*, 13-4.

42. As of the end of 2011, 16 states plus the District of Columbia have laws prohibiting discrimination on the basis of gender identity or expression, in addition 143 cities and counties also have such laws. Visit www.transgenderlaw.org/ndlaws/index.htm for updates on maps and numbers.

43. Serano, *Whipping Girl*, 12.

44. Serano, *Whipping Girl*, 13.

45. Serano, *Whipping Girl*, 15.

46. Stryker, *Transgender History*, 22.

47. Serano, *Whipping Girl*, 162.

48. Serano, *Whipping Girl*, 163.

49. Serano, *Whipping Girl*, 164.

50. Serano, *Whipping Girl*, 172.

51. Serano, *Whipping Girl*, 165.

52. Serano, *Whipping Girl*, 166.

53. Serano, *Whipping Girl*, 174.

54. Serano, *Whipping Girl*, 170.

55. Serano, *Whipping Girl*, 169.

56. Serano, *Whipping Girl*, 168.
57. Serano, *Whipping Girl*, 166.
58. Serano, *Whipping Girl*, 12-3.
59. Serano, *Whipping Girl*, 12-3
60. C. Riley Snorton, "A New Hope: The Psychic Life of Passing," *Hypatia* 24, no. 3 (Summer 2009), 79.
61. Snorton, "A New Hope," 86.
62. Serano, *Whipping Girl*, 27.
63. Serano, *Whipping Girl*, 177.
64. Serano, *Whipping Girl*, 177.
65. Serano, *Whipping Girl*, 178.
66. Serano, *Whipping Girl*, 178.
67. Serano, *Whipping Girl*, 178.
68. Serano, *Whipping Girl*, 178.
69. Quoted in Snorton, "A New Hope," 78.
70. Quoted in Snorton, "A New Hope," 79.
71. Snorton, "A New Hope," 79.
72. Snorton, "A New Hope," 87.
73. Snorton, "A New Hope," 79.
74. Snorton, "A New Hope," 82.
75. Snorton, "A New Hope," 88.
76. Snorton, "A New Hope," 89.
77. Much of chapter 1 will be is dedicated to all the ways that literary critics, philosophers, critical theorists, writers, and sociologists have thought about and organized the concept of "passing."
78. Although the term itself did not appear until the 1960's. George Chauncey, *Gay New York: Gender, Urban Culture, and the Makings of the Gay Male World 1890-1940*, (New York: Basic Books, 1995), 6-7. The introduction to Chauncey's work presents a different gay world in the early part of the 20th century. A gay world that people came into, not closets that people came out of.
79. The word "homosexual" is historically recognized as having been established and first printed in Krafft-Ebing's *Psychopathia Sexualis* (1886). Certainly this is the beginning of its popular usage in clinical medical settings. However, the word had been coined and used in an 1869 anti-sodomy pamphlet in Germany. The term homosexuality arrived on the scene also in the 1880's and 1890's, first in a work explaining homosexuality. The relationship between the terms was unstable until the early 20th century. See chapter 4 for a more detailed explanation.
80. Eve Kosofsky Sedgwick, *The Epistemology of the Closet*. (Berkeley: University of California Press, 1990), 3.
81. This last part is optional.
82. This definition is provided by the *Oxford English Dictionary*. I am immediately taken aback by the casual combination of "hatred" and "fear" and suspect that there might be some interesting philosophical work to be undertaken in outlining the conceptual relation of these terms.
83. Jeffrey McCune, *Doin' the Down Low, Remixin' the Closet: Black Masculinity and the Politics of Passing*. (Ph.D. Dissertation, Northwestern University, 2007), 10.
84. McCune, *Doin' the Down Low*, 11.
85. McCune, *Doin' the Down Low*, 15.
86. McCune, *Doin' the Down Low*, 17 and 37-8. McCune elegantly writes: "from the Middle Passage to the slave quarters, the experiences of freedmen and freedwomen

living under white surveillance, to the experiences of full citizens trapped between the confines of racism and its many injustices, black people have kept many secrets. They have hidden their religion, beliefs, thoughts, and ultimately, their spirits. In a sense, black mobility in America has always been predicated upon the agreement that we maintain codes. Black people, under the surveillance of whiteness and white people were often compelled to keep private those things they considered precious and in need of protection from those who potentially served as threatening forces to their humanity."

87. McCune, *Doin' the Down Low*, 58.
88. McCune, *Doin' the Down Low*, 21.
89. McCune, *Doin' the Down Low*, 13.
90. McCune, *Doin' the Down Low*, 28, 39, and 41.
91. McCune, *Doin' the Down Low*, 45.
92. McCune, *Doin' the Down Low*, 79.
93. McCune, *Doin' the Down Low*, 71.
94. McCune, *Doin' the Down Low*, 73-4.
95. McCune, *Doin' the Down Low*, 69.
96. Broadly defined with a primary focus on lesbian, bisexual, and gay but might readily include transgender, intersex, asexual, queer, and BDSM identified people.

Chapter 1
Passing in Abstraction:
The Theoretical Organization of Passing

Throughout the literature (philosophical and literary)[1] and in the media,[2] presentations on passing certain conceptual organizations reveal themselves. Scholars and writers envision and analyze passing through a variety of lenses including as self-creation, as experiential, as social protection, as omission, as a mechanism of control, as discourse management, through assimilationist strategies, and as human ornamentation (to name a significant few). Passing can also be understood as a performance or a practice; it can be viewed with moral disdain or as a necessary act of self defense in a morally corrupt world. It is always about transgression: cultural, legal, and/or social. Passing ruptures our common ordinary understanding of authenticity and natural identities. It necessarily functions on two levels: the individual and the social.

In this chapter I will begin with the ordinary and analytic ways of defining passing, followed by an analysis of the organizing conceptual themes of passing: identity, experience, and morality. This chapter will cover many of the inherent dichotomies that arise within those basic conceptual categories: double vs. binary logic of identity, experiential pleasure vs. protection, and individual vs. collective responsibility and obligation. It will cover some of the basic epistemic, non-moral tools of analysis we need to utilize in analyzing passing: how identity is produced in both discourse and the body; experiential modes of pleasure and/or protection; and the theoretical implications of passing for notions of identity. The chapter closes with two sections that discuss the most complicated theoretical space that sexual identity passing must confront—and also something I argue passing has the capacity to make the academy reconsider—namely, performativity as a postmodern way of understanding how identity inscribes itself on normative and non-normative bodies.

Definitions of "Passing" and the Standard of Success: Analytic/Ordinary Language

In her article, "'Passing': The Ethics of Pretending to be What You Are Not," Claudia Mills defines "passing" as either: a) pretending to be an x rather than a y, or b) trying in some artificial[3] way to make yourself into an x rather than a y, instead of simply accepting or affirming yourself as a y.[4] Mills specifies that it is key to her definition that the motivation to pass is grounded in conditions of oppression. One would not wish to be a x if the social conditions did not favor existing as x over y. She defines the most important instances of this phenomenon as light-skinned blacks trying to pass as white,[5] women as men,[6] Jews as gentile, and gays as straight. The condition and context of oppression is key primarily for an ethical analysis of passing. I will return to questions of oppression in chapter 2. For now, I will adopt a version of Mills' definition. My direct, straight-forward definition of passing is "socially presenting oneself as an X, when you know yourself to be a Y." This is a nice analytic philosophical definition of passing.

It is worthy to note that the philosophical definition includes some general assumptions about identity and access to self. First, there is an epistemological component, an ability to have self-knowledge about an identity marker, and secondly there is a performance component, an ability to present oneself to the world—or within a particular social world—in accordance with an identity marker that is recognizable on some sort of social schema.

Ordinary language dictionaries define passing as "to *identify* oneself or be *identified* as something one is not."[7] There is a conceptual shift in this definition, one that replaces the performance and epistemological components with self-association and ostensive definition by others. What comes to the fore is the receptive gaze of others as well as an ambiguous placeholder for how identity works for self. "To identify" might be a form of performance, it might be narrative, or it might simply be the self-application of an identity marker: such as declaring oneself a Yankees fan.

The *Oxford English Dictionary* defines "to pass for/as" with a different overt criterion, one of success. To pass for/as is "to be accepted as equivalent to; to be taken for; to be accepted, received, or held in repute as. Often with the implication of being something else." Acceptance by the Other, whether that other is singular or plural, is key for the phenomenon of passing to be what it is. This requires a successful social uptake.

What all three definitions share is the intentionality of the passing agent on the one hand, and the social accomplishment on the other hand. The intentionality must be centered on some type of social goal, whether that is professional advancement, an escape from repression or oppression, artistic or political freedom.

There are other things to keep in mind as we conscientiously move forward. Passing as a success term encodes its own erasure. While the effects of passing can be seen (i.e., the successful performance of an identity marker that is not one's own), the phenomenon itself is lost in the production of those effects. If one can identify a passing subject then that subject has failed to pass, although it should be noted that passing only encodes its own erasure in one temporal modality—the present. An after-the-fact self-disclosure of passing by an agent, or a historical narrative about passing, exposes but does not undo the phenomenal event. ("Event," here, is also temporally ambiguous. It could include the time span of a performance, an encounter, a period of a week, month, or years.)

Passing is also ambiguous in reference to space.[8] An agent can pass in one social sphere (examples include the professional sphere, familial sphere, friendship sphere, etc.) but choose not to pass in another. Or passing as a success term can be functionally applicable in one aspect of one type of social sphere (e.g., the classroom) and not in another (e.g., academic conferences). Judith/Jack Halberstam argues that the complexity of passing in social spaces is sufficiently complex for the gender deviant that "to understand such a process, we would need to do more than map psychic and physical journeys between male and female and within queer and straight space; we would need, in fact, to think in fractal terms and about gender geometries."[9] While it remains unclear to me how the practical application of Halberstam's metaphor would function, or what it would look like to map gender geometries and think in fractal terms, the articulation of this kind of complexity does adequately undermine simple explorations of passing in terms of agent intentionality and physical movement.

Passing has both a private and a public component. Some who choose to pass do so only for the public gaze. Others choose to pass primarily for their intimates and private life. Others allow the boundary between the two to fade and dissolve and choose passing as a thorough self-presentation for any and everyone. But passing, the decision to pass, and the intermediate phase just prior to successful passing is characterized by negotiating the gaze, perception, and identity knowledge of people who knew a prior identity or from whom knowledge of a "true" identity would threaten the freedom of individual self-creation. Public performance of a new identity can be a litmus test of the efficacy of passing, particularly in spaces of rigorous identity expectation where deviance from an expected identity produced deep and pronounced reactions: locker rooms/bathrooms for gender, bath houses or strip clubs for sexual orientation, places of segregation for race, houses of worship for religion, etc. Positive public reception of a performed identity, or even passive reception of a performed identity through a lack of reaction, can be a powerful and pronounced moment of success. It can even be a moment of substantial pleasure.

Double vs. Binary Logic of Identity and the Problem of Passing

One of the primary tensions to reveal itself through the multi-faceted exploration of passing is at the level of the basic schema of identity: is the logic of identity foundationally binary or double? There are at least two ways of interpreting the relationship between the two identities at play for any passing individual. The passing identity and the "authentic" identity can be seen as two identities layered on top of one another (a double logic) or they can be viewed as providing an either/or kind of option (binary logic).

There might be other ways of thinking about this, too. Both the binary and the double explanation of passing presume a dual aspect to identity under its conceptual confines. Social constructionism suggests that we should always think about identity through a singular logic where the binary is collapsed at the expense of the authentic identity: all identity is socially constructed, there is conceptually no difference between passing for male and being male. Both are the performance of a series of socially contrived scripts. Sex as the usual biological sorting mechanism for who should act in accordance with the scripts of masculine identity will be different for the passing individual and the non-passing individual, but according to social constructionism both will be performing the identity of masculinity in the same way. What is most significantly lost, here, is a placeholder for an authentic connection to identity. This becomes a problem if we wish to promote a social justice agenda where previously unrecognized social scripts are argued as necessary for the well-being of a class of people (e.g., freedom of gender identity and expression). By the standards of social construction neither the bio-male or the non bio-male has a greater right to demand the scripts of masculinity (which any sensitive feminist or queer analysis would celebrate), but at the same time any claims to the right to express a queer identity, camp or otherwise (high effeminacy in gay men, or low butch in lesbian woman, or displays of affection in public, or marriage), would also lose their foothold in arguments based in authenticity, happiness, or flourishing. What is also lost from the singular logic of the social construction position is the potential for a double logic that offers a better framework for a more sophisticated analysis of passing.

Of the theoretical and secondary writers on passing, Pamela Caughie, author of *Passing and Pedagogy: The Dynamics of Responsibility*, most thoroughly explores the double identity logic of passing. For Caughie, identity is something that we *do*, not something that we *are*. She thinks that an analysis of passing through a double logic helps to explain both the experience of passing and identity as activity. She also thinks that thinking through passing as a double logic clears it from its moral implications. She writes, "the passer does not relinquish one preexisting identity to move into another more highly valued one," this would have to be the case if passing truly happened under a binary logic. She continues, "rather passing participates in the cultural production of whiteness as 'racially pure' [in cases of racial passing] . . . and heterosexuality as 'normative' [in cases of sexual identity passing]." This is the beginning of her explanation of passing through a double logic. She says that "while the *concept* of passing is understood within a binary logic of identity the *practice* actually functions in terms of a double logic: it is both the problem and the solution. The passer adopts an identity that the act of passing in part constitutes."[10] I want to try to parse this out a bit. But, first it is helpful to see that she believes that the practice of passing offers a salvation of the moral variety. She argues that "the conception of passing as dishonesty, deception, or betrayal is produced by the very problem of identity to which the practice of passing is the solution." This produces a paradox for the passer. Someone who chooses to pass must implicitly declare that "there would be no need to pass if identity were not a problem, yet the passer must insist that identity is not a problem if he or she is to pass." The relationship between the problem of identity and the solution of passing is how Caughie retrieves passing from moral condemnation and demonstrates passing as a double logic. Choosing to pass demonstrates that some of the identities we live with are a problem for us. They subject us to ridicule, ostracism, oppression, and decreased financial resources. But from Caughie's perspective, choosing to pass also demonstrates that identity is a construct, something we can manipulate to achieve our desired goals. If identity is the problem, passing is at least a partial solution. It is also worth noting that a passing identity still remains as its own kind of identity: to be straight and to pass for straight are two different ways of interfacing with a heterosexual identity.

I do not agree with Caughie's analysis of passing as a solution to the problem of identity, particularly given the moral implications of granting passing the status of a solution. The moral story isn't as simple as she would like to make it out to be. However, her analysis of the double logic of passing, that passing suggests more than simply an either/or binary, that passing suggests layering, complexity, overlap, and exchange between the identities we exalt and show the world, is astute and will help us as we move forward.

Mechanisms of Identity Production: Discourse and the Corporeal

Passing demonstrates that when identity is produced, the mechanisms of its production differ based on the intended or wished for effect, or required elements for the uptake of identity as intended. Some identities, such as race and gender, are more thoroughly dependent on bodily or corporeal representations of certain skin tones (race), secondary sex characteristics (gender), and mannerisms. While other identities and their uptake can reside more fully in narrative descriptions, such as sexual orientation or religion. Most production of identity involves elements that are both steeped in discourse and reliant upon corporeal elements.

Passing exposes these mechanisms in a clearer way than does ordinary identity development.

Self as Narrative/Self as Discursive Production

Human beings make sense of themselves through narrative. We each tell and retell our own histories in hopes of gaining understanding from others, social connectivity, self-acceptance of our own plights and struggles. Our narratives construct images of self for others. In certain social spaces certain glosses on our narratives are presented, certain details accentuated, certain interpretations offered. Our narratives can be confessional, deconstructive, productive, attempts at honest exposure, or motivated at crafting a disguise. Identity, then, becomes trapped inside the narratives we tell and the narratives that are told about us. Narratives are collective endeavors that circumscribe certain behaviors, activities, lifestyles, and appearances to broadly implicative identity markers of social regulation and group association. It is important to remember, too, that passing can be an identity in this way: passing agents can tell a narrative about themselves *as* passing.

Kwame Anthony Appiah's book *The Ethics of Identity* explores the role of narrative in identity production and takes as a presupposition of its philosophical inquiry that all forms of identification share the same basic philosophical components. Given these shared philosophical elements, Appiah argues that all of us have ethical obligations that derive from our identities. He thinks that the ethical claims, or how we "ought" to live our lives in relation to our self-conception are basically the same regardless of the particular manifestations of those identities. Identities include "genders and sexual orientations, ethnicities and nationalities, professions and vocations." These identities make ethical claims upon us "because—and this is just a fact about the world we human beings have created—we make our lives *as* men and *as* women, *as* gay and *as* straight people, *as* Ghanaians and *as* Americans, *as* blacks and *as* whites."[11] In this section I will consider some of the discussions that Appiah has in his book, namely those on narratives and social identity that expand on the idea of the discursive production of identity.

Narratives

According to Appiah, one of the key creators of our individual identities is the narratives that we use in order to make sense of our experience. These narratives are drawn from collective identities, social scripts with a basic plotline that most people of a broadly defined social group make use of in framing their own individual experience.[12] For example, people who self-define as LGBT/Q often situate their adult romantic lives in terms of "coming-out" and the pain of remaining "closeted." Appiah cites Charles Taylor to establish that narratives are "'a basic condition of making sense of ourselves' that 'we grasp our lives in a narrative;'

narrative, then, is not 'an optional extra.'"[13] It is clear to Appiah that this idea of narrative configures our identity in terms of a collective, and that these narratives are basically the same for all identities. He gives two examples that parallel one another.

> An African American after the Black Power movement takes the old script of self-hatred, the script in which he or she is a nigger, and works, in community with others, to construct a series of positive black life-scripts. In these life-scripts, being a Negro is recorded as being black: and for some this may entrain, among other things, refusing to assimilate to white norms of speech and behavior. And if one is to be black in a society that is racist, then one has constantly to deal with assaults on one's dignity. In this context, insisting on the right to live a dignified life will not be enough. It will not even be enough to require that one be treated with equal dignity despite being black: for that would suggest that being black counts to some degree against one's dignity. And so one will end up asking to be respected *as a black*.

> An American homosexual after Stonewall and gay liberation takes the old script of self-hatred, the script of the closet, and works, in community with others, to construct a series of positive gay life-scripts. In these life-scripts, being a faggot is recoded as being gay: and this requires, among other things, refusing to stay in the closet. And if one is to be out of the closet in a society that deprives homosexuals of equal dignity and respect, then one has constantly to deal with assaults on one's dignity. In this context, the right to live as an "open homosexual" will not be enough. It will not even be enough to be treated with equal dignity despite being homosexual: for that would suggest that being homosexual counts to some degree against one's dignity. And so one will end up asking to be respected *as a homosexual*.[14]

Appiah thinks the same type of narrative could be set up for "An American White," "An American First Generation College Student," "A Canadian Deaf Person" or any other identity we might care to imagine. Of course, it would seem that we could participate in numerous social scripts until we have found just the perfect amalgamation that describes our individual situation and that perfect amalgamation will become one's personal narrative.

One problem with this set up is that we are left with one definition of "narrative": the combination of social scripts that intersect in our personhood. It seems to me, however, that this is altogether too coherent a description about the way narratives work for individual identity. Instead I want to build from Appiah's platform and offer a tri-partite definition of narrative which helps to capture the nuances of passing as identity more effectively. Narrative$_1$ is Appiah's definition: the perfect personal fit of any series of social scripts as they intersect a given individual at any given point in time. This describes a kind of authentic identity, one "true" to life's circumstances. Narrative$_2$ designates the *potential* combination of scripts that we utilize at any given moment to determine major life decisions. These are the paths that were not taken or perhaps are still yet to be taken. Narrative$_3$ is the biographical story that can be told about any given individual at any point in time, the narrative for public consumption. Narrative$_1$ is the story we tell the people in our personal circles: friends, lovers, perhaps our families. Narrative$_2$ is the story that we are constantly telling ourselves. Narrative$_3$ is the story of our lives meant for the general public.[15] For most of us narrative$_1$ and narrative$_3$ are not radically different from each other. Narrative$_1$ likely contains more intimate details and is messier than narrative$_3$. Elements of narrative$_2$ often make it into casual dinner conversation or talks with colleagues, friends, neighbors, family, or children, particularly when our narrative$_1$ is leaving us feeling less than satisfied in our lives. The counter-factuals and plan Bs that comprise our narrative$_2$ can provide profound hope and escape from daily pressures.

In situations of passing the interplay and relationship between narrative$_1$, narrative$_2$, and narrative$_3$ are significantly more complicated. For individuals who are passing, narrative$_2$ plays a unique role in motivating a performance at the level of narrative$_3$ that allows it to significantly deviate from narrative$_1$. For most people, the counter-factuals that exist in narrative$_2$ are other possible personal or professional worlds that do not rely upon a shift in basic identities. They are more along the lines of: "if I had gone to law school instead of graduate school, then I would have been an immigration lawyer." They might involve certain dreams about economic resource, like "if I had an extra $10,000 I would spend the summer living on the beach in the south of France." But the foundations of the person's identity are not altered. For individuals living under systemic oppression, the content of narrative$_2$ necessitates shifts in basic identity markers; even for ordinary dreams, basic elements of the person must change. A woman living in 1863 who had a narrative$_2$ about being a soldier during the Civil War would also have a counter-factual clause about being male, or at least passing for male. For individuals where the urge to live in accordance with the counter-factual is strong enough, the person chooses to model a narrative$_3$ to the world that presents masculinity. Narrative$_1$ remains true to the given aspects of identity—female, housewife, etc.—but narrative$_3$ becomes a polished script and performance for social uptake that is radically different. In this case: male, soldier, etc. Note that in the case of the passing individual, narrative$_1$ is a threat to narrative$_3$. For the rest of us, narrative$_1$ is simply a more intimate version of narrative$_3$ and while we might be embarrassed or hesitant to let aspects of narrative$_1$ come into the full light of narrative$_3$, the former is not a threat to the latter.

Social Identity
Many of the defining identity elements in narrative$_1$ and narrative$_3$ are what Appiah would broadly refer to as a "social identity." It is worth asking what exactly constitutes a "social identity." He recognizes that social identities are difficult to pin down, and for each social category there are relevant line-blurring examples that make it difficult to establish such identities with precision. Despite this, Appiah still thinks he can produce a list of necessary conditions for social identity. One necessary condition is that there is a "social conception of Ls." This

broadly means that society has a general understanding of an identification classificatory term (an "L"), e.g., Buddhist, Christian, Hispanic, transgender, etc. Accompanying the social conception will be stereotypes. "Stereotypes," Appiah informs us, "are rough-and-ready things," but it is "not necessary that the stereotypes or criteria of ascription be identical for all users of the term."[16] Stereotypes are a necessary condition for social conceptions, but they are not necessary for individuals who identify through a kind of social label. There must be stereotypes associated with Christians, but an individual does not need to participate in or adhere to those stereotypes to be a Christian. Appiah also tells us that "for a social conception to exist, it is enough that there be a rough overlap in the classes picked out by the term 'L,' so there need be no precisely agreed boundaries, no determinate extension."[17] This means that we don't need to worry about where one social identity begins and another one ends. We should expect that there will be overlap and blurry edges.

Social conceptions may also shift depending on the perception of the conceptualizing group or agent—whether he/she/ze[18] is in the group or outside of it. Appiah explains, "African Americans, for example, may well have characteristically different social conceptions of a black identity from others in the United States; and homosexuals may tend to conceive gay identity differently from heterosexuals."[19] This means that social conceptions are determined in part by those who participate in the social identity as well as by those who do not. The inside/outside forms of meaning-making do not need to be the same.

Why does "social conception" matter? Appiah conceives of it as one of the two necessary components of social identity. He states that "when a classification of people as Ls is associated with a *social conception* of Ls, [and] some people *identify* as Ls, we have a paradigm of a social identity that matters for ethical and political life."[20] Social conception plus identification equals social identity. According to Appiah, it matters to ethical life because we live *as* social identities, and it matters for political life because "it figures in treatment by others, and ... how others treat one will help determine one's success and failure in living one's life."[21] Appiah sees the connection between social identity and ethics and politics as straightforward and uncomplicated. While I agree that the relationship between social identity, ethics, and politics is a necessary relationship, I will argue (in chapter 5) that our social identity should change the very definitions of ethics that we utilize. So this picture that Appiah paints, is not complex enough yet, but the basic sketch is right.

A final thing to clean up regarding Appiah's conception of social identity is the degree to which we have or do not have control over the social identities that frame our lives. To say that individuals identify *as,* suggests that identity involves free will. It suggests that we could choose to identify with some identity markers but not with others. Appiah does not think this is always the case. Appiah specifies that there are certain identity markers over which the individual has no control, namely gender, race, and sexual orientation. In these situations individuals are "responding to a fact . . . that is independent of their choices."[22] In the case of African-American identity individuals are responding to a fact about their ancestry, in the case of gay identity individuals are responding to the fact of their same sex desire. These three types of social identity markers become necessary starting points from which we begin to configure our personal narratives. Given this necessary definition of social identity, I think it is fair to assume that Appiah would agree that passing is a kind of hiding and reaction to the political fallout of certain social identities.

Embodiment: The Corporeal Self

When language and narrative fail us or are unable to capture the full expression of self, we often rely on our embodiment to define us. The definition of self that comes from embodiment can also be prior to language, as it often is with gender, race, and other ways in which we are inscribed with meaning well before we can make our own, or even before we can communicate. The celebrated and critical employment of identity on the body has also been a strong part of the cultural politics of many different minority groups in the 20th century. Lisa Walker argues that "in the face of silence and erasure, minorities have responded with the language of the visible, symbolizing their desire for social justice by celebrating identifiable marks of difference that have been used to target them for discrimination."[23] Clearly these "identifiable marks" do not need to be visible or even embodied marks, but many are. The role of visible bodies in the creation of identity must be something we take into consideration for passing both theoretically and politically.

Walker argues that the history of visibility politics began with medical and scientific inquiry in the late 18th century that literally produced visible differences as a key marker of identities in its study to find anatomical differences to justify oppression and other forms of minoritization. This was true for race, gender, and, beginning in the late 19th century, also for sexual orientation. She writes,

> The history of visibility politics begins with the production of visible difference on the body, and the scrutiny of minorities by medical and scientific "professionals." In the late eighteenth century, natural scientists began using comparative anatomy to investigate the origin and nature of racial difference. Over the next hundred years, comparative anatomy became the principle methodology employed to study blacks, women, homosexuals, prostitutes, criminals, and the insane; the body had become the primary site of both identity and difference. It was during the late nineteenth century that sexologists such as Havelock Ellis, Richard von Krafft-Ebing, and Karl Heinrich Ulrichs proposed the theory of inversion, or cross-gender identification, to explain the origins of homosexuality. Today we rarely hear the term "inversion" used in anything but a historical context. But the stereotype that homosexuals exhibit characteristics of the opposite sex because they are "trapped" in the wrong bodies remains prevalent. Concentrating on the biological or congenital origins of sexual deviance en-

abled the medical community to "discover" manifestations of homosexual difference on the body—a presumably immutable object of study.[24]

So the body becomes a way in which the majority can identify the "true" nature of the minoritized subject. We can't be duped by the passing subject if we know the biological markers or the physiognomy of the people we want to be able to identify. Of course the built-in dependence on the visual manifestation of identity characteristics causes problems with identity politics, for some identities are more strongly marked by their visible recognition than others. Gender and race are commonly thought to be defined on the basis of visibility. Sexual orientation and religion easily come to mind as identities that do not have associated physiognomies.

Richard Dyer argues that a way we can understand visibility in identities that are not defined by elements of corporeal visibility (secondary sex features, or levels of melanin in the skin), is by thinking about "signs." He specifically uses the example of gayness (where I think we could also easily insert religion) to say that while there may not be a physiognomy associated with gayness, there are "signs of gayness, a repertoire of gestures, expressions, stances, clothing, and even environments that bespeak gayness."[25] We can still find visible signs on the body that suggest a minoritized identity, and these can be cultural products themselves, rather than socially constructed interpretations of visible difference.[26] Here arises issues of identity hierarchy, defined through oppressive forces within culture, in terms of what gets seen first and why. Sharon Lim-Hing explains that racial identity (because it is visible) will always trump sexual identity (because it is not visible). She writes, "the first thing many of you would think if you walked into a room and saw me is 'Asian woman.' Not young, old, badly or well dressed, intellectual, punk jock, diesel dyke, girlie girl, etc.—just 'Asian.' Whites get to play all the roles, while Asians are invisible or are stuck in a few stereotypes."[27] Visible markers of race and gender will supercede any other non-visible markers. bell hooks specifies this fact as the primary reason we cannot compare the oppression of homophobia with the oppression of racism. hooks argues that most homophobic attacks occur near places that are known as gay: gay bars, community events, etc. but that the normal "apparatus of protection and survival" (namely assimilation into the broader culture) is ready at hand for many LGBT/Q people everywhere else. Racism is a comparatively pervasive and inescapable for nearly all people of color.

Passing allows us to ask new questions about visibility and signs on the body. Passing, itself, can even become a sign of marginality. Carole-Anne Tyler argues that passing can be the "sign of the victim, the practice of one already complicit with the order of things, prey to its oppressive hierarchies."[28] The passing subject establishes the limits and the boundaries of visibility. And for that reason, some (myself included) argue that passing must fit centrally into an analysis of visibility. Some see passing as the thing that can be done with identity that "destabilizes identities predicated on the visible to reveal how they are constructed."[29] The question of the visible for passing is the most socially salient criteria of success. I simply don't think this can be overlooked, even if it can't tell the whole story. But not everybody agrees. Some regard the indeterminate figure of the passer to "exceed the categories of visibility that establish identity" and that therefore he/she/ze should be "regarded as peripheral to the understanding of marginalized identities."[30] The passer might well be the individual who understands the categories of identity better than the rest of us, the one who could do the best analysis of the social construction of identity and explicate what it means to have an authentic sense of connection with identity—especially the passing individual who feels burdened by his/her/hir[31] decision to pass.

Embodiment: Plastic Surgery as Passing

The most extreme intervention on the embodied self for the purposes of passing is to employ plastic surgery.[32] Corporeal passing usually happens without the added assistance of medical technology, but when technology is employed, the corporeal aspect of passing simply cannot be ignored.

Making the Body Beautiful by Sandra L Gilman is a cultural criticism of the origins of aesthetic surgery—better known as plastic surgery. Gilman explores the Enlightenment ideology of medical interventions into appearance and determines that a conceptual exploration of passing must be done in conjunction with a cultural exploration of aesthetic surgery.

Aesthetic surgery, Gilman argues, is centrally dependent on the enlightenment idea that happiness can be found in the autonomy of the individual to transform him/herself.[33] We expect autonomy over our lives, our careers, and in the ultimate form of control, aesthetic surgery allows us to have autonomy over our physical appearance. Gilman argues, "in a world in which we are judged by how we appear, the belief that we can change our appearance is liberating."[34] She talks about aesthetic surgery specifically in terms of passing because:

> "Passing" is a means of trying to gain control. It is the means of restoring not "happiness" but a sense of order in the world. We "pass" in order to regain control of ourselves and to efface that which is seen (we believe) as different, which marks us as visible in the world. Relieving the anxiety of being placed into a visible, negative category, aesthetic surgery provides relief from imagining oneself as a stereotype. This is the origin of the happiness generated by aesthetic surgery.[35]

And:

> It is the desire for control, for the face that existed "before the world was made," before we came to recognize that we were thrown into the world, never its master, that lies at the heart of "passing." ... Becoming aware that one is marked through one's imagined visibility as aging, or inferior, or nonerotic, concepts that become interchangeable, can make one long for the solace of the original fantasy of control.[36]

She says that this urge to be other than what one "is" is a common human desire. The ability to pass as something socially better, more highly valued, or more in line with a desired self is what we all want. She compares this to what Isaiah Berlin calls "positive liberty," or wishing "to be somebody, not nobody . . . self-directed and not acted upon by external nature or by other men as if I were a thing, or an animal . . . incapable of playing a human role, that is, of conceiving goals and policies of my own and realizing them."[37] Some of us take that want further than others, and the types of people who do that, Gilman argues, are the type of people who would choose to pass or simply choose to have aesthetic surgery. Plastic surgery does not always entail passing, but she thinks that the two choices about identity are clearly on the same continuum, even when they don't overlap. And when we analyze passing from the perspective of corporeal adjustments, it's clear that Gilman is correct in asserting this association.

Passing, for Gilman, is the natural "other side of the coin of our persistent and constant need to generate stereotypes in order to organize the world."[38] But even if it is something we all want, it doesn't come without its inherent tensions and contradictions, especially from the perspective of the people who don't have to "pass" or who establish the standards of beauty/identity that we are all trying to live up to. Gilman argues that there is "an inherent tension between the enlightenment promise—you can become one of us and we shall be happy together—and the subtext—the more you reshape yourself, the more I know my own value, my own authenticity, and your inauthenticity. You become a mere copy, passing yourself off as the 'real thing.'"[39] As we've been noticing in our evaluations of passing, the split between the sense of the real and the sense of the performed is inherent to an analysis of passing. Also associated with both passing and aesthetic surgery is the hope that by changing the outside—the body—there will be an associated change on the inside. If the body is an outward signifier of the soul, then for both the recipient of plastic surgery and the passer the hope is that a shift from a negative category to a positive one for the body will also improve the health of the soul. Clearly this does not always become the case; there are some people that will respond to the changes in corporeal features with a heightened sense of feeling like a fraud.

The origins of aesthetic surgery in the 19th century, and the ideologies that impacted and bolstered the profession demonstrate things about identity they have fallen out of favor in our early 21st century cultural milieu. One of the key elements to 19th century ideology was that identity was seen as "a real category defined in nature rather than a social contract." For those seeking aesthetic surgery it was understood, or thought, that if a "Jew" wanted to pass for a "German," both of those categories were real categories. The particular concern was that aesthetic surgeons were assisting criminals[40] and other degenerates in their attempt to pass for a respectable citizen of the state.[41] The pejorative associations with passing as a kind of social boundary transgression also became *the* pejorative association with aesthetic surgery.

Postmodernity and Corporeality

Postmodernity gives us a reason to think that there may be a more direct relationship between language and the body. The matter that comprises the body is often referred to as a "text" within postmodern criticism. This means something like that the ways in which we understand the identities and bodies of others are textual, comprised of language, and created as "real" through "fictions and fantasies, the myths and fabulous projections, of metaphoric transference."[42] Bodies hold scripts, or discourse, which is the way in which we make sense of ourselves and others. The most radical position of this kind suggests that there is nothing beyond the text of bodies. Bodies simply are texts, and therefore are the receptive site of cultural meaning—there is nothing pure, essential, or necessary beyond the text. This kind of postmodern position on the body means that my decision to separate out the preceding sections into a discussion about language and *then* bodies is to confuse you with an arbitrary distinction between two identical sources of identity meaning making. The Biblical phrase: "the word was made flesh,"[43] captures the basic understanding of the postmodern position. Not exactly that words make flesh, or that someone godly and powerful makes language into flesh, or that there is a divine process incarnated among us (although, this may also be true), but that it is the force behind our language that makes bodies into something that imports meaning.

Vicky Kirby gives a good account of what might be a middle ground between postmodernity's bodies as texts only, and a more commonsense idea of language as one form of identity production and bodies as another. She originally attributes this to Judith Butler's explanation of language and bodies in her book *Bodies That Matter* but goes on to retract this as an inaccurate presentation of Butler's work and position. Kirby's intellectual model seems to me to be one of the most productive for thinking about identity (and passing) in terms of language and bodies and also something that takes seriously the idea that language and bodies may be conceptually collapsible. Kirby argues that the connection between bodies and language could be

> likened to the enfolding overlap of a Venn diagram, wherein two recognizably different spheres are nevertheless involved in a mutual and constitutive relationship that comprises their integrity. In Butler's account, this figuring of the overlap between ideality and matter, or language and the body, allows her to deny that "the body is simply linguistic stuff" while at the same time insisting that "[the body] bears on language all the time."[44]

So we could think of bodies as one sphere in our diagram, and language as the other sphere. If this is the case, it would make the most sense that identity production would happen not only in the overlap between bodies and language, but also in the portion of the sphere that represents just bodies as well as the portion of the other sphere that just represents language. Passing, as something that we do with identity, could also be seen as occupying these three possible locations. For the types of passing that require bodies, or that involve identities that are specifically marked by corporeal features (namely, usually gender and race), passing could happen simply in terms of bodies. For types of passing that are not marked corporeally (religion and sexual orientation, perhaps) passing might happen purely in terms of language, self-ascription, and narrative. For many instances of passing both bodies and language are manipulated, covered, sheltered, or edited to present an identity that lacks a sense of history or authenticity.

Experiential: Pleasure vs. Protection

The phenomenon of passing has an experiential component. Some individuals who have passed have reported doing so with great cost to their personal sense of well-being. Others have declared that it is a significant source of pleasure. Some experience the success of passing as something that must be painstakingly sought after; others experience it as something that happens rather naturally, with some of those natural passers enjoying their freedom and others frustrated by their invisibility. This section will discuss four of the main experiential components of passing: pleasure, protection (with the range of primary and secondary emotions), active passing, and passive passing (with the range of primary and secondary emotions).

Pleasure: Primary and Secondary

As Marjorie Garber sensitively explains in *Vested Interests*, "passing is said to have both a secret pleasure and a cultural effect."[45] This description is certainly not applicable to all kinds of passing—some types of passing can and do involve substantial psychic distress on the part of the agent. But it does seem to adequately capture certain kinds of temporally and spatially limited passing. Garber highlights the public restroom as a site of pleasure for the performance of gender passing:

> The public restroom appears repeatedly in transvestite accounts of passing in part because it so directly posits the binarism of gender (choose either one door or the other) in apparently inflexible terms, and also (what is really part of the same point) because it marks a place of taboo.[46]

Transgression of *the* public space for gender segregation allows for secret access, a hidden epistemological viewpoint, a hindrance of self-as-other, but performance of self-as-same. The taboo is what allows for the pleasure. Halberstam, too, is interested in Garber's isolation of the space of the public restroom for exploration of gender deviance. In what she calls the "bathroom problem," she concurs with Garber that the perils and privileges of the bathroom are central to the experience of passing for transgender and genderqueer persons. It is a site of heightened cultural sensitivity to expressions of gender. It is a space of intimate vulnerability, it is a space of cultural anxiety, and it involves both pleasure and the cultural paranoia of being caught.

While gender deviance might make demands of theorists to think in sufficiently abstracted and complicated terms so that passing can only be mapped through gender geometries and fractal terms, these deconstructive methodologies must be discarded for the binary practicalities of the "women's" vs. the "men's" room.

Garber thinks through this paranoia/pleasure by isolating it as a kind of liminality. The liminal is a middle space, an intermediate, barely perceptible sensory threshold. It is the experience of a transitional space of being an X as Y in a space for only Ys, where X as Y isn't a recognizable category, and the discovery of X as Y status would produce social outrage. The phenomenological reality of the "passing" agent is one unrecognizable by those who can't, or otherwise haven't thought about passing. This is a unique isolation embedded in the social.

In expanding on her understanding of the liminal, Garber often conflates the term "masquerading" with "passing." Rather than a woman passing for a man, a gender deviant woman is masquerading as a man. Masquerading more clearly gestures towards a liminal space, and a temporary time period, while still maintaining the idea of disguise and an actively falsified self. It has resonances of a celebration (such as Mardi Gras), and it speaks of collusion. This might help to expand some of the considerations above.

Passing is not always about isolation from one's "authentic" identity. It can also be a social gathering centered around public subterfuge. Garber at one moment metaphorically describes passing as a diphthong—"inaudible as difference." This inaudibility allows for pleasure of passing as a successful performance and for the pleasure derived from the social access that would otherwise be unavailable.

Protection: Primary and Secondary

When people choose to pass out of a sense of protection and necessity, especially when it is not the choice they would have otherwise made, the emotional cost can be high. Passing can be chosen as a form of protection from individual circumstances (such as the film *Some Like It Hot*, where the characters were motivated to pass to escape the mob), or they can be social (to escape discriminating laws, social ostracism, oppression, or to achieve a status a person would otherwise be denied). The forced sense of needing to hide oneself from a hostile environment can have a range of emotional counterparts.

The best-case scenario: if the passing is successful and the protection is thoroughly felt, a sense of well-being and relief may settle in over the passing individual. This would erase the dissonance between self and society that is often the motivation for passing and would provide the individual with an integrated place and social role that the passing was intended to provide. Often, however, the sense of well-being accomplished by passing is accompanied by underlying tension and anxieties. There can also be a perpetual stress from deceit, or a stress that arises from deceiving some and not others, depending on one's sense of obligation to the individual or the intensity of his/her attachment. There can also be despair from isolation, or a building existential loneliness that arises from not being able to tell anyone else one's full life narrative, or to have spaces in which to process difficult or complicated elements of one's former identity, or the process of passing.

If someone is inclined to pensive self-examination, passing may have a different effect. The psychic toll of passing may require significant intellectual analysis: a continual sorting and examining of the social conditions that led to the hostility against one's original identity. There may also be an added level of socio-political awareness to all human interaction as well as a perpetual caution, fear, and/or lack of trust. There may also be a basic intellectual shift in the passing individual's understanding of identity and cultural influence.

Active Passing

A clear distinction that most people who have passed can readily draw is the difference between active and passive passing. Active passing is the primary focus of this book; it is the default mode of passing for our analysis. It is the easiest form of passing to analyze from a moral perspective, because it involves intentionality and full consciousness of the chosen behavior. Active passing involves an active assertion and a willful manipulation of self-styling or self-presentation. Most of the individuals who are famous for passing are famous for *active* passing. Any individual who chooses to actively pass will be able to articulate both the aspect of choice and the aspect of self-production, whatever that entails (corporeal changes, discourse management, personality affect, social restriction, or physical movement, etc.).

The underlying intentional structure and motivation for active passing is most likely some version of a psychological reaction to oppressive forces and institutionalized power (which will be explored in chapter 2). A common colloquial understanding of passing is that it is an internalization of the negative social messaging about the hidden identity and thereby a form of self-hatred or self-loathing. At least one author suggests that the practice of passing is motivated by self-loathing. There are some important political, existential, psychological, and emotional truths in this explanation that most thinkers on the topic of passing share: namely that positive authentic self-regard is neither enhanced nor evident in individuals that pass. Ian Miller in *Faking It* directly equates passing with "wishing you were what you are not." He says that the self-loathing is more of an umbrella explanation that includes emotions directed against oneself, like "contempt, or disgust, guilt, or shame." He offers the caveat that for the purely opportunistic passer this may not be the case, or that self-hatred may play a minimal role. But for most people who pass, the secondary level of emotions, the ones that motivate the original decision to pass, that arise from passing, and that motivate continual passing, will be emotions of poor self-regard.

Passive Passing: Primary and Secondary

Passive passing is a more complicated phenomenon. It *can* be intentional, but often it is not intentional. People who don't look like the identity markers that they wish the world to see are often frustrated by a world that assumes an identity other than the one they wish to be recognized as authentically their own. Passive passing is about the assumptions and perceptions of others. (The importance of the assumptions and perceptions of others is key in all kinds of passing; however, the role of perception, assumption, and uptake are all particularly interesting for someone who is unintentionally passing.) Passive passing means simply that one is commonly perceived as an identity they don't consider themselves to be, or that the identity they do consider themselves to be isn't recognized by the larger culture at a glance, at least without effort to correct assumptions. In a culture characterized by heteronormativity many queer people feel they passively pass for straight if they don't give verbal disclosure or adhere to stereotypes of gay culture. Ethnic identities, religious identities, and sometimes race and gender identities can be misconstrued through passive passing. For identities that are not easily readable through visual cues, passive passing can be as simple as verbal withdrawal, or a decision not to disclose. Resolving passive passing in these situations requires an awkward discursive revelation. Sometimes the social impact is minimal and is likely to cause minimal emotional distress (for all parties—and particularly for the passing agent). And at other times the disclosure can be received with immense emotional discomfort in a way that feels socially invasive.

For some, passive passing is a desirable side effect of a culture insensitive to the more subtle cues of an identity that would otherwise be a source of discrimination. For others, passive passing is a burden that requires continual counter-efforts and is a source of deeply unwanted political frustration. The reaction to passive passing that an individual has says a lot about his/her other political and moral commitments to authentic identity presentation and the way passing corrodes, obscures, or makes possible.

How Passing Demonstrates a Theoretical Problem of Identity

You will remember from chapter 1 that passing demonstrates a new way of thinking about the logic of identity. Common sense suggests an either/or (or "binary") model of identity. I am either a man or a woman, I am either gay or straight, etc. Passing suggests something that looks more like a double logic. I am a man passing for a woman, and therefore am both man and woman. I am gay passing for straight, and therefore am both gay and straight. Layers of identity are assumed under models of passing, with our ordinary logic telling us that the outer layer is performed, masqueraded, or otherwise constructed for the uptake of a social gaze, while the under layer is understood as the location of truth or authenticity. It's the under lying identity that is somehow something more significant than simple social construction. It is somehow essential, inescapable, yet still capable of being hidden. While the double logic description of identity sheds light on the ordinary understanding of how passing works, it does not give us much to explain how identity is formed. Rather, it runs counter to the popular social construction vs. essentialist debate in that it explains that it is possible for a mechanism of identity to be produced through both social construction and essentialist means, in the same individual at the same time, one wrapped around or on top of the other. It would seem that we should want something more streamlined, something that can instead explain passing and identity using the same kind of conceptual apparatus. In order for a concept to be able to do this, it seems to me that it would have to be able to contain both aspects of the double logic in relation to identity, as well as the ethical evaluations that are in tandem with identity. Particularly for the purposes of this book the concept will need to be able to explain sexual identity, in both its essential and culturally constructed aspects. As mentioned above, I will argue for a particular explanatory model of identity, but first I will discuss the most popular conceptual model of gender and sexual identity: Judith Butler's conception of performativity.

Identity as Performativity

One of the most common ways of articulating gender identity and its development in the tradition of gender/sexuality studies is through the concept of performativity. Originally developed by Judith Butler in her 1990 book, *Gender Trouble*, performativity is a concept designed to explain how gender identity adheres to corporeal bodies in the form of identity. Her discussion, briefly but famously (perhaps unfairly), takes into serious consideration how we can identify gender on bodies that do not match with their performance: namely drag performance. Thinking critically about this phenomenon (which is not quite passing, but certainly related on a continuum of passing), the idea of gender as performativity allows us to think about the way we learn to enact our "natural genders" in a way that is not the same thing as a cognitive construction, or performance, but reiterates cultural expectations of gender in alignment with pre-set norms in the same way that, for example, masculinity can be recognized on a female body in drag by the repetition of masculine norms. Biology is not at the root of the question for Butler when it comes to gender identity. What is at question is how the social norms predictably present themselves on bodies as though they were natural or naturalized genders. In short we perform our gender identity, without conscious participation. But, that is altogether too simple. What she is more fully interested in is an explication of the infusion of power and social convention and the resulting product of both discourse and embodied performance that looks like our socially contrived gender.

Performativity has its roots in speech act theory. Speech acts are events that alter identity through their very articulation. Examples include "I do" in marriage ceremonies, legal sentencing, baptisms, consecrations, ordinations, etc. The idea is that in these ritualized moments, when individuals in positions of power make certain invocations through speech, the participants in the ritual actually experience an ontological shift. Where one was once single, s/he becomes married. Where one was once a candidate for ordination, s/he becomes a priest. The weight of the normative force behind the speech act is so great that the expected result is an actual shift in identity. In these moments of ontological shifting, three elements are necessary: power, repetition, and normative expectations.

In the case of the ritualized speech act, the repetition of iteration at different temporal moments is the defining aspect of the ritual; it is what makes it ritualized. Power is of course difficult to pinpoint (please see chapter 2). But here we can understand it as an institutionalized phenomenon that grants rights to some and not to others, imbuing certain individuals with stature based on rules and rituals that give them certain social benefits like increased trust, influence, and access to resources. Speech acts can only be articulated under this kind of ritualized power found in repetition.

When it comes to questions of gender identity the kind of power and repetition of speech acts becomes something that is less containable, less definable. The norm-ing doesn't primarily happen during rituals (although it certainly does take place there); it happens throughout childhood (where nearly all adults have some degree of power), and throughout adulthood with predictable normative force still surrounding the gender socializing. The power still takes place in social structures that institutionalize identity through reiteration. In fact, it is necessary that social structures institute the definitions and implications of our gendered concepts and that the repetition of the speech acts infuse our very sense of selves. Examples include a father's repetitive verbal declaration of "good girl" to the female child that enacts behaviors in accordance with our social norms of femininity. These kinds of ordinary speech acts become the paradigm instances of how gender identity inheres to corporeal bodies through repetition, favoring certain behaviors over others.

The example of the father becomes a kind of paradigm case for how gender identity can be understood through performativity. Judith Butler argues that the statement at birth of "It's a girl!" anticipates the iteration of "I pronounce you man and wife."[47] The interweaving of the iterations of gender throughout life begins in the first moments. The gender identity contains within it a historicity that neither the subject controls nor in which s/he can voluntarily choose not to participate. The iterations sustain a full relationship of gender identity until death.

Please note that in the example of the father, the role of socially sanctioned authorial approval—along a moral continuum of good and bad—is playing a crucial role. The concept of performativity is about social norms, but it is descriptively normative from a third person perspective. It explains how our normative values construct our senses of self. This is my biggest critique of Butler: what is missing in performativity is room for something prescriptively normative, or a conceptual apparatus that allows us to rework the norms we've been given, or to construct a new normative system. The key restrictive component to a prescriptively normative interface with performativity is what it does to our sense of agency within the structure it describes. All individuals are subjected to the system of repetitive speech acts. Indeed all individuals become subjects in this system. But, as currently envisioned, the individual does not retain the agency to fight, invert, or reinterpret the system. This is theoretically unsatisfying, and also politically melancholic.

In her essay, *Critically Queer*, Butler argues that this conception of performativity also applies to queer identities. In order to do this she specifically links performativity with discourse. "The performative," she writes, "is thus one domain in which power acts *as* discourse."[48] She must make this connection because "queer" is historically a term of hate speech; it is a maneuver of the dominant culture to shame individuals through ostensive identification of personhood with sexuality. She borrows the concept of interpellation[49] to describe the way this ostensive definition creates identity and positions "queer" within her concept of performativity. Butler writes,

> The term "queer" emerges as an interpellation that raises the question of the status of force and opposition, of stability and variability, *within* performativity. The term "queer" has operated as one linguistic practice whose purpose has been the shaming of the subject it names or, rather, the producing of a subject *through* that shaming interpellation. "Queer" derives its force precisely through the repeated invocation by which it has become linked to accusation, pathologization, insult.[50]

If I understand Butler correctly she sees that "queer" shows us a way into performativity where we discover that its normative parameters are not equally predictable for all subjects in all circumstances. Gender demonstrates room for variation and instability, it shows the limits of its force—or at its limits it shows the true hostility of its force—and the opposition of proper gender manifestation with improper or sub-proper gender formation. Something that should be duly noted about the way the term "queer" creates a subject through ideology, is that it does so through a negative moral framing that adheres to the subject through emotional negativity, namely shaming. Gender adheres to the subject through a continuum of moral shame and praise ("good boy," "bad girl") but "queer" firmly sits in the negative end of the moral spectrum, as a source of continual judgment. Butler identifies the ideological interpellation as accusation, pathologization, insult.[51]

54   CHAPTER 1

The power of Butler's concept of performativity has demonstrated itself in its pervasive acceptance across disciplines within the academy. Its intuitive appeal as a model of gender theory is attractive to those with gender trouble and those without. The implication of moral norms in performativity seems balanced as a regulating mechanism. Moral norms create gender through performativity in the same way that moral norms create or control behavior in every other aspect of our lives. However, performativity is about *identity* and not about behavior and its use of the moral in constructing identity through the regulation of behavior should give us pause. Performativity only gives us a descriptive model of identity formation. We should consider what a concept of identity formation would look like if it was also prescriptive, i.e., norm producing through agential commitment and identity uptake. What if we had a theory of identity that would allow us to consciously choose to participate in certain identities and at the same time shape the normative demands of those identities.

Perfomativity and Passing

While working on this chapter, I had the fortunate experience of having an audience with Butler during a visit to Northwestern University. I asked her what work she thought the concept of performativity could do for explaining the concept of passing. She admitted to not have spent time thinking about performativity and passing together, but thought performativity could do something to explain what happens to identity construction in passing although she didn't specify how.

She did have a number of other things to say about passing more broadly.[52] First she wanted to voice caution against the true and false dichotomy that underpins passing: the idea that one identity is the "true" identity, namely the one that is hidden from view and that one identity is the "false" identity, the one that is placed for consumption and uptake by others. She thought instead that passing is better understood as a kind of "instrumentalized mobility" that plays on ambiguities in relation to discreet identity categories. She took the case of the mulatto to illustrate her point. A mulatto is both black and white, but neither black nor white. This ambiguity gives the individual the opportunity to choose, or instrumentalize the identity categories available to him/her so as to achieve whatever other goal is attainable. Another example she employed was a Jew during the holocaust. If someone were to inquire about a Jewish individual's ethnic/religious heritage and s/he had the opportunity to pass, Butler thought s/he certainly should do so. Butler's exact words—with perfectly timed humorous intonation—were "this is not the time to go Kantian." Given this analysis of passing, and her understanding of it as instrumentalized mobility, Butler argues that passing is not a moral issue; it is a political issue. She thought that it was reasonable to understand that people could live into an ethical tension when making decisions about whether to pass or not, but, that in the end we should interpret passing as primarily being about the exploitation of discreet identity categories that are not fully capable of containing the ambiguities that are inherent to identity.

The idea of instrumentalized mobility suggests a moral hands-off approach to an analysis of passing, which will be of concern in the next chapter. For now, I'd like to fill in a bit of the gap that Butler left in her minimal analysis of passing and the use of performativity. I am sensitive to her caution of fictionalizing one idea and glorifying the other as 'true,' but for the sake of better consideration, I'd like to focus on individuals who do not lie naturally in between the binary of two identities.

The most difficult aspect of performativity in explaining passing is that it does not include an understanding of interiority, but rather only ever suggests what Vikki Bell calls "coextensivity."[53] Individual subjects are seen as not having an interior space or *cogito* that is developed through self-examination. Rather, individuals are seen as coextensive, meaning that any given person who is "existing within power, within certain temporal and spatial coordinates, within certain ways of speaking and knowing, is also a coexisting with others."[54] The presence and effects of thinking cannot tell us anything more about an individual than that s/he lives in a discursive world and that the language and discourses that surround him/her have been internalized.[55] This means that the norm-ing network of human relations of which we are all part is the perpetual extension and creation of our sense of self. Butler refers to the function of interiority in explaining human behavior simply as a "trope," a metaphorical linguistic term used to ostensively define a locus of internalization of one's discursive and linguistic surroundings, but without intentionality, or a unique output created and controlled by a unique subjectivity. What we will always find instead is the trace of power-effects.[56] This lack of interiority and focus on coextensivity suggests that identity cannot have two aspects during passing: a subjective interior sense, and an objectively projected and received exterior sense, but rather, all we have during passing is a movement through one coextensive state (in which we are framed and received as one kind of identity) followed by a movement into another coextensive state (in which we are framed and received as a different kind of identity). While we might want to alleviate the moral burden on some who choose to pass in an instrumentalized mobility kind of way, eradicating interiority can have a disastrous impact on our understanding of self and its role in moral responsibility. This moral complexity is the focus of the next chapter—which explores and seeks to understand where we can affix moral responsibility under systemic oppression and in instances of coerced or otherwise necessary passing.

Notes

1. The philosophical literature on passing is woven throughout this book. I direct my reader to the bibliography for an exhaustive list. The novels and biographies about passing are numerous and each interesting for its own humanizing story of varied forms of passing. Novels include: Phillip Roth, *The Human Stain* (New York: Vintage, 2001); Nella Larsen, *Passing* (New York, London: A.A. Knopf, 1929); Emma D.E.N. Southworth, *The Hidden Hand* (London: Ward and Lock, 1859); James Baldwin, *Giovanni's Room* (New York: The Dial Press, 1957); Sinclair Lewis, *Kingsblood Royal* (New York: Random House, 1947) and Leslie Feinberg, *Stone Butch Blues* (Ithaca: Firebrand Books, 1993), and Elizabeth Lewis, *Sunbathing in Siberia* (Minneapolis: Consortium, 2003). Biographies include: William Craft, *Running a Thousand Miles for Freedom*, (London: William Tweedie, 1860); Julie Wheelwright. *Amazon and Military Maids* (London: Pandora, 1989); Jim McGreevey, *The Confession*, (Los Angeles: Regan Books, 2006); J.W. Johnson, *The Autobiography of an Ex-Colored Man* (Boston: Sherman, French, & Co., 1912); John Howard Griffin, *Black Like Me* (Boston: Houghton Mifflin, 1961); Norah Vincent, *Self-Made Man* (New York: Penguin, 2006); Honor Moore, *The Bishop's Daughter* (New York: W.W. Norton, 2009); Bliss Broyard, and *One Drop: My Father's Hidden Life* (New York: Back Bay Books, 2007).

2. The films about passing, or that include a character who is passing, are each a fascinating and entertaining dramatization of these issues. I recommend that my reader view at least a few, particularly if the issues of passing are not embedded in one's own life experience. The films about passing—broadly defined—include: *Boys Don't Cry* (1999), *The Brandon Teena Story* (1998), *Some Like it Hot* (1959), *Tootsie* (1982), *Mrs. Doubtfire* (1993), *M. Butterfly* (1993), *Mulan* (1998), *Yentl* (1983), *Victor/Victoria* (1982), *Soul Man* (1986), *The Human Stain* (2003), *Europa Europa* (1990), *Angels in America* (2003), *The Talented Mr. Ripley* (1999), *Imitation of Life* (1959), *Pinky* (1949), and *Gentleman's Agreement* (1947).

3. Techniques of artificiality (such as plastic surgery) will be discussed later in the chapter. The complexities of how we might think of "artificial means" will engage directly with the theory of performativity, so much so that artificiality itself will begin to blur with naturalness.

4. Claudia Mills, "'Passing': The Ethics of Pretending to be What You Are Not," in *Faking It* (Cambridge: Cambridge University Press, 2003), 1.

5. As characterized in Nella Larsen's novel *Passing*.

6. It is clear, also, that a man might successfully attempt or wish to pass as a woman. But given the motivational requirement of passing for social gain, this particular reversal of her example seems to fail her criteria. Mills clearly thinks that men hold the position of social privilege in modern society. There might, however, be a way in which we could circumscribe a social setting to arrange passing as a woman to achieve socially desirable results: e.g. where the sexual attention of heterosexual males is the social reward desired.

7. This definition is from the online Merriam-Webster dictionary.

8. Spatial ambiguity is not of primary concern for this chapter. But, it does mark itself as worthy of mention. Temporal ambiguity is of primary concern. If the Kantian metaphysical paradigm is correct, then it is impossible for us to think through the temporal problem of passing without referencing its spatial problem. While I think Kant is probably correct, this brief mention of spatiality will have to do.

9. Judith Halberstam, *Female Masculinity* (Durham: Duke University Press, 1998), 21.

10. Pamela Caughie, *Passing and Pedagogy: The Dynamics of Responsibility* (Urbana: University of Illinois Press, 1999), 22.
11. Kwame Anthony Appiah, *The Ethics of Identity* (Princeton: Princeton University Press, 2005), xiv.
12. Appiah, *The Ethics of Identity*, 22.
13. Appiah, *The Ethics of Identity*, 22.
14. Appiah, *The Ethics of Identity*, 109.
15. Perhaps an example is in order: Say that I am currently living my life as endocrinologist, with a wife and 2.3 kids. (My wife is 3 months pregnant). I am a devout orthodox Jew (from my mother's side of the family, but only after meeting my current wife who is also an orthodox Jew), and am an avid tomato grower in my spare time. *This is my narrative$_1$.* Each day as I head to work, a job that often demands seventy hour work weeks and constant rational mental attention, I think about the other possible careers that I could have that would perhaps be more gratifying. Everyone on my father's side of the family is devout Catholic, and until the age of 16, when I met my current wife, I was convinced that my life calling was to be a man of the cloth. (After meeting my future wife, I couldn't imagine a life of celibacy.) My plan was to graduate from my small Midwest Catholic high school and high tail it to the local Catholic seminary. There are days when I day-dream about celebrating the Eucharist and hearing confessions. My primary hobby, growing tomatoes, is truly a passion. For months out of the year I think about how to perfect the health and flavor of all of my basinga, roma, kaki coing, black krim, purple calabash, azoychka, banana legs, cherry, hess, manyel, green zebras, brandywine, elbe, faribo goldheart, limmony, beefsteak, stor gul, marvel striped, tonnelet, plums, ananas, and Armenian tomatoes, producing new cross-pollinations every year, all the while avoiding rotten tomatoes as best I can. I often think about what life would be like if I made that my profession. Yes, the money would be less—but I could spend my days talking about my life's passion. *This is my narrative$_2$.* My life's work, in the career that I actualized, has been researching menopause and treating menopausal women. I am at the top of my field, and recently a feminist biographer approached me, wanting to write the story of my life. There is a lot of investigation into my childhood and the relationships I had with my mother and nine aunts that spawned my initial interest in helping women through their menopausal years through drug therapy. There are a couple of chapters that span my education, a chapter on my personal life (wife, 2.3 kids), a chapter on my tomato passion, and two chapters summarizing my professional career. *This is my narrative$_3$.*
16. Appiah, *The Ethics of Identity*, 67.
17. Appiah, *The Ethics of Identity*, 67.
18. "Ze" is a gender-neutral singular possessive personal pronoun. Because the English language does not have a non-gendered pronoun, activists have attempted to introduce a number of different versions of one. No non-gendered pronoun has made it into popular vernacular to date.
19. Appiah, *The Ethics of Identity*, 67.
20. Appiah, *The Ethics of Identity*, 69.
21. Appiah, *The Ethics of Identity*, 69.
22. Appiah, *The Ethics of Identity*, 70.
23. Lisa Walker, *Looking Like What You Are: Sexual Style, Race, and Lesbian Identity* (New York: New York University Press, 2001), 1.
24. Walker, *Looking Like What You Are*, 2.
25. Quoted in Walker, *Looking Like What You Are*, 9.
26. Another way of thinking about minoritized identity is through the marked/unmarked trope. When using the language of marking, it is understood that iden-

tities in positions of power are unmarked, while minoritized identities are marked (e.g., white = unmarked, black = marked) and is common language in feminist and cultural criticism. Marking can refer to a kind of designation by the broader culture and the people in power, or refer to qualities that manifest in a person because society designates them as "lesser than". Self-loathing, or internalized misogyny or homophobia, would be good examples of marking that are not corporeal but still a product of the cultural standing, nevertheless.

27. Quoted in Walker, *Looking Like What You Are*, 210.
28. Quoted in Walker, *Looking Like What You Are*, 8.
29. Walker, *Looking Like What You Are*, 10.
30. Walker, *Looking Like What You Are*, 8.
31. "Hir" is a gender-neutral singular possessive personal pronoun.
32. Given the key role of surgical interventions in gender transitions and trans politics, I wish to remind the reader that my exploration of sexual identity passing and its varied significations is not meant to be a direct exploration of the logics of gender passing. For the purposes of this section, I want to emphasize the extremity of corporeal passing through artificial means by rendering clearly its most direct case.
33. Sander Gilman, *Making the Body Beautiful: A Cultural History of Aesthetic Surgery*, (Princeton: Princeton University Press, 1999), 18.
34. Gilman, *Making the Body Beautiful*, 1.
35. Gilman, *Making the Body Beautiful*, 331.
36. Gilman, *Making the Body Beautiful*, 333.
37. Gilman, *Making the Body Beautiful*, 25.
38. Gilman, *Making the Body Beautiful*, 330.
39. Gilman, *Making the Body Beautiful*, 18.
40. Two interesting pop cultural media items that explore the role of plastic surgery in criminal passing ("innocent" criminals who alter their identity through plastic surgery to escape retribution) include the pilot episode of the LAPD detective show *The Closer* and the 1947 film *Dark Passage* starring Humphrey Bogart and Lauren Bacall.
41. Gilman, *Making the Body Beautiful*, 27.
42. Vikki Kirby, *Telling Flesh: The Substance of the Corporeal* (New York: Routledge, 1997), 88-89.
43. Kirby, *Telling Flesh*, 55.
44. Kirby, *Telling Flesh*, 103.
45. Marjorie Garber, *Vested Interests* (New York: HarperCollins, 1992), 9.
46. Garber, *Vested Interests*, 14.
47. Judith Butler, *Gender Trouble* (Routledge: New York, 1990), 22.
48. Butler, *Gender Trouble*, 17.
49. First coined by Louis Althusser, "interpellation" refers to the process by which ideology brings a subject into being by addressing the pre-ideological subject. The naming of a pre-adolescent effeminate boy as a "fag" by peers would be a perfect example. The insidious homophobic element gets applied to a subject before the subject can be said to have a sexual identity, creating his sexual identity in light of a pre-established and hostile ideology.
50. Butler, *Gender Trouble*, 18.
51. Clearly within the queer community, the interpellation of "queer" can be positively intoned signifying inclusiveness, acceptance, community, and political solidarity. But, within the larger society "queer" remains a shaming mechanism. This becomes the locus of political hope: if the ideology of queer can be change, then the interpellation of the subject through queering can be a positive experience.

52. Butler has written one article, "Passing, Queering," that explores issues of passing. It's in reference to Nella Larsen's novel *Passing*. It explores the sexual tensions in the novella, and argues that it explores both racial passing, and sexual queering which she sees as two different kinds of inquiry and evaluations of the novella.

53. Vikki Bell, *Culture and Performance: The Challenge of Ethics, Politics, and Feminist Theory* (New York: Berg, 2007), 101.

54. Bell, *Culture and Performance,* 20.

55. Bell, *Culture and Performance,* 11.

56. Bell, *Culture and Performance,* 11-12.

Chapter 2
The Good, the Bad, and the Oppressed:
Ethical Considerations

The problem of sexual identity passing does not make sense in a world without power.[1] There would be no implicit or explicit benefits to be derived from hiding an aspect of one's identity. There would be no hierarchy of preferred behaviors in relation to sexual identity, gender, religious belief, class status, or race without a structure of power to define who and what constitutes privilege. Moreover, passing involves a certain ethical posturing to power, one that is complicit with the dehumanizing flaws inherent in the structure of passing. An understanding of the ethics of sexual identity passing will be one that considers power and its effects on our moral lives and decision-making. But, as the lived experience of most sexual minorities will demonstrate, power is most actively felt through its ability to oppress. First, I will explore the ethical judgments and analyses of passing, asking if and how we might think of passing as a form of deception, lying, and/or pretense. I will then explore what our political and social commitments ought to be to each other. The chapter will close with a closer look at the ethical problems exposed by a theory of identity as performativity, and the ethical problems associated with identity under the contemporary theorizing of post-modernity.

The Traditional Role of Morality: Deception, Lying, and Pretense

Traditional morals suggest that the primary problem with passing is that is entails some form of lying or deceit, or at the very least pretense. By traditional morals I am referring to a common sense morality in the United States that is broadly based on a secularized Judeo-Christian framework, one that judges that "bearing false witness against your neighbor" is morally wrong. The traditional ways of analyzing passing from a moral perspective involve asking questions about the deceit of the identity performance. Included are questions of assumed trust, incomplete disclosure, required disclosure, active vs. passive, and the moral distinction from pretense.

In the most direct forms of passing, where we could unequivocally identify a type of lying at work, there remain philosophical questions about the nature of lying, what types of lies are involved, and what might be the reduced responsibility under a corrosive or coercive environment. This section will primarily focus on deceit, lying, and pretense without a sophisticated engagement of power and oppression. What will be assumed is that the individual who is passing is doing so with the alternative option of presenting an "authentic identity." This section will explore how passing interfaces with some of the basic moral theories of what constitutes lying and deception. It will ask if and how passing is at times a form of lying and at times a form of deception. It will look at the moral structure of lying and deception (especially the perpetrator-victim model of the intersubjectivity of lying/deception) to help understand the social peculiarities of passing as an intersubjective phenomenon. At the end of the section I will argue for a more complicated understanding of the moral, epistemic, phenomenological, and categorical elements of passing that should continue to leave the question of the ethics of passing open. I will also point to some thoughts about pretense under pressure that might explain the general moral ambivalence or even positive moral sympathies regarding passing.

Is passing a form of lying? On an initial and superficial analysis passing appears to be a form of lying. St. Augustine defined lying as "having one thing in one's heart and uttering another with the intention to deceive."[2] This definition, which is both historical and colloquial, captures a basic Judeo-Christian understanding of lying. It is also the same structure as the basic colloquial understanding of passing, where one holds one identity in one's heart and presents another to the world in order to deceive (or gain certain social goods). A more involved analysis suggests, of course, greater and deeper complexity.

Most moral philosophers who have defined "lying" have done so by arguing for at least two elements: 1) that it is a form of intentional deception and 2) that it is packaged in a statement.[3] Sisela Bok argues that the statement need not be verbal, but it must be actively communicative.[4] For others, there are at least three elements to lying: the semantic (a statement), the epistemic (an untruth), and the metaphysical (an intentionality).[5] The fourth element clearly to be added is the moral.[6]

For some, lying falls along a moral continuum where it is the most morally problematic form of communicative human interaction. Along this continuum lying is on one end and truth-telling is on the other. In between the two are shades of half-truths, incomplete disclosures, circumlocutions, falsely implicating, and intentional deceptions. This is the traditional breakdown and established relationship between lying and truth-telling: they are along the same continuum, and deception lays between the two. As an alternative to the traditionally modeled relationship between deception and lying, lying can also be thought of as under the conceptual umbrella of deception. Under this model it is seen that lying is a form of deception, but a more narrow form in that it involves something that is both literally false and in statement form. This is a conceptual relationship rather than a moral one, or a relationship that is driven by conceptual considerations rather than moral considerations. The continuum is helpful for making sense of the moral comparison between lying and deception, the umbrella is helpful for understanding the conceptual connection. There is also another way of thinking about the relationship between deception and lying, and that is in regards to the experience of the "victim" of each.

Morality of Lying

People who evaluate the moral values and implications of lying usually do so from one of two perspectives. There is the deontological approach and the consequentialist approach. The consequentialist approach judges lying based on the socially problematic outcomes of the lies. The deontological approach defines lying as problematic outright. Immanuel Kant, the classic deontologist, argues that "by a lie a man throws away and, as it were, annihilates his dignity as a man" (*Doctrine of Virtue*).[7] Lying is viewed on this model as problematic in terms of human dignity and respect for self and others. Philosopher Polycarp Ikuenobe argues definitively from a deontological perspective that "the liar loses her dignity and respect, in that she is not to be trusted, and she also fails to respect the dignity of the person being lied to, in that she uses the person as a tool or a means to an end. Lying vitiates the bond of trust and moral dignity or respect, which are the basis of our moral and social relationships."[8] Lying is corrosive to self, to others, and to the relationship between self and others.

There are also deontological-esque absolutist perspectives outlawing lying because it is a violation of nature, or will result in the eventual "death of the soul." Augustine and Thomas Aquinas have both argued, inspired by Aristotle, that lying is a violation of nature. They argue that God endowed each of us with the power of communication for the sole purpose of expressing our thoughts. So, if we misuse our capacity for speech by expressing thoughts we do not believe, then we have violated our God granted capacity, which makes lying "inescapably sinful, regardless of motive or effect."[9] Presumably the definition of sin being employed here is against the will of God. Augustine also took the argument further that lying literally kills the soul.[10] It is difficult to translate this declaration out of religious language, but putting it back into Kantian speak it suggests something akin to the annihilation of dignity, or the eradication of our basic life force and fuel.

Legal interpretations of lying (and deception—the law makes no distinction here)[11] center on consequentialist attitudes. If lying results in concrete measurable harm to another person or persons, usually economic harm, then it is deemed a criminal act.[12] Utilitarians (and other various consequentialisms) assess lying based on its harm. Usually this is understood to be problematic because it leaves the act of lying morally neutral outside of its consequences and furthermore could support a lie if its impact promoted happiness or well-being. Both of these conclusions run counter to our moral intuitions about lying and the social damage done purely by the act of lying itself through the corrosion of trust and communication.[13]

Epistemic Elements of Lying

The epistemic element to lying has two components. There is the "internalist" epistemic and intentional states that are not accessible by an outside party, and there is also an "externalist" condition which is the objective condition of truth or falsity which under ideal conditions all would have access to.[14] There is also an epistemic excess to lying compared with truth-telling. Lying requires a reason, something beyond ordinary communication, information exchange, and community building. Truth-telling, as an ordinary experience, doesn't require a reason.[15] However, it does require certain virtues. This lead to some basic questions about what is "truth-telling." For Bernard Williams, truth-telling requires the virtues of accuracy and sincerity. He states that you must "do the best you can to acquire true beliefs, and what you say reveals what you believe."[16] Sincerity is directly focused on the communicative action and uptake. Williams argues, "sincerity consists in a disposition to make sure that one's assertion expresses what one actually believes... so a speaker will not only have expressed his belief, but, if he is trusted, he will have led his hearer to have some beliefs."[17] The use of sincerity, it is clear however, is a disposition that liars must be able to mimic. And in this mimicry liars reveal an imbalance in reciprocity that they expect to exchange with the world: they wish to be believed because of their false sincerity, while also wishing to believe others correctly when others sincerely present themselves.

Sisela Bok argues that there are two kinds of liars: there is the 'free-rider' and the 'strategist.' Both the free-rider and the strategist share the desire with the general population not to be lied to. The trust that others will generally tell the truth allows them to navigate through society and social relations in the same way we all do. The free-rider and the strategist, however, are different in their justification for lying. The free-rider would simply like to reserve for themselves the right to deceive others. This gives "them the benefits of lying without the risks of being lied to."[18] For the strategist, they derive their justification for lying from the fact that others lie in society. Bok describes the psychology of this liar as being rooted in a conviction of "survival in a corrupt society."[19] It will be helpful in our exploration of passing *as* lying to recognize that this strategic psychology can also be based in oppression and prejudice, and not based on the understanding of others as liars.[20]

Passing *as* Lying

When asking if passing is a form of lying, we need to determine if we are looking for a conceptual relationship or a moral equivalence. Does passing fit one of the definitions of lying? Are the things that are morally questionable about passing the same things that make lying morally condemnable? As this book demonstrates, passing is a multi-valenced phenomenon, which might mean that some instances are clearly lying, some are not quite so clearly lying, and some instances are simply not lying. But when we apply the criterion of lying to passing some questions directly emerge. Is the passing intentional? If the answer is no, such as in the case of passive passing, then it has failed to meet a criterion of lying. In the case of active passing then the criterion of intentionality has been met.

The next criterion is semantic. Does the type of passing under consideration take a propositional form? Usually passing is a significantly more complex set of actions, presentations, and appearances than simply a statement. But often it entails articulations that would qualify as a false statement of fact (e.g., "I am straight"). Of course, in many instances of passing the phenomenon is entirely about making a show of identity that does not require a counter statement of fact.

When it comes to exploring the moral equivalence between lying and passing there are a few questions we might choose to ask ourselves: is it helpful to analyze passing through the lens of deontology or consequentialism? How do we want to think about dignity and respect in relation to passing? What about the claim that lying destroys the soul (or one's emotional/psychological health)? Presumably many individuals whose lives are marked by systemic oppression have thought about the possibility of passing. Surely when they do so, moral questions arise: What would this do to my family? My career? To my financial security? To my reputation and popularity? (These are all questions that suggest consequentialist analysis and thinking.). Or the questions might have something more to do with self and the implications of passing qua passing: Will I be able to respect myself? Will I be able to express my truths? Will I be able to form authentic friendships? What will passing do to my sense of dignity?

Passers share with liars the epistemic imbalance of needing a reason for their actions. For people who do not think about how to alter a basic identity, the connection between self and the world is comparatively unmitigated by questions of identity and self-presentation. For both active and passive passers there is an extra epistemic element. For active passers, it is the reasoned motivating factor for a different identity presentation. For passive passers, they have the added epistemic burden of considering when, why, and how to correct incorrect perceptions of identity. Passers, however, as a general rule—if they are indeed liars—are strategists rather than free-riders. Their choice to lie is driven by the understanding that society is corrupt, and that the oppression experienced in light of their identity is something they should not have to shoulder. It does not seem to be the expectation of passers that there are not others that pass, nor does there seem to be a desire not to have others pass. It is a personal decision based on complicated strategies of maneuvering through complex and unfair social structures.

Passing *as* Deception

In instances when passing is not a semantic expression and/or when it is not intentional, and therefore does not meet the criteria of lying, we can ask if passing is simply a form of deception. Depending on the answer to questions regarding the relationship between lying and deception (continuum or umbrella) it is worth asking if it is better that passing be understood as a form of lying or deception.

First, what is deception? What is the moral status of deception? What are its defining qualities? Sisela Bok defines deception as communicative efforts to mislead people. To mislead is to try to get people to "believe what we ourselves do not believe." But, unlike lying, deception does not require a direct statement of false fact. Bok argues that we "can do so through gesture, through disguise, by means of action or inaction, even through silence."[21] Clearly, Bok wants to open deception to include more of the behaviors that we are used to associating with passing. The idea that deception must involve effort or be intentional is a definitional element of deception that many moral philosophers agree upon. Some have also argued that intentionality is a necessary condition.[22] Not everyone agrees. Some have argued that the key element in deception is a kind of "invitation." In lying, the false conclusion is fully crafted and handed to the victim. In deception, a space is left open. Certain conditions and/or premises are outlined and organized in such a way as to suggest a false conclusion. But the deceiver issues an invitation to the deceived, inviting him/her to draw a false conclusion. This invitation implicates the deceived in his/her own deception.

An added element of deception that distinguishes it from lying is its ambiguity, its liminality, its metaphorical excess, and its associated characteristics. Traditionally, those who lie are known as "liars." Their definition is concrete, and they are not to be trusted. But the deceiver is many more things: "sleazy, misleading, sneaky, underhanded, greasy, cunning, euphemistic, manipulative, sly, seductive, distorting, slanderous, evasive, deceitful."[23] Deception comes in many forms and in many personality traits. Lying is comparatively morally cut and dry.

For some, deception is an ordinary part of healthy social interaction. Adler, for example, thinks this is an ordinary observation. He writes,

> Deception generally, of course, need not be intentional or voluntary, as lying must. Even when it is, though, deception does not violate a simple, fundamental moral rule or principle, as does lying. Intentional deception is a constituent of many acceptable forms of everyday social life, such as tact, politeness, excuses, reticence, avoidance, or evasion, which are ways to protect privacy, promote social harmony, and encourage interest.[24]

Deception, under ordinary social constraints, can promote good social relations (compare this with lying: where it is argued that only white lies can produce positive effect, all other lies have a corrosive quality). This is the precise moral location where judgments about the deceptive nature of passing become complicated. Clearly there are positive social gains to be achieved by passing. There are ways in which passing makes social relationships and opportunities possible. If we are to evaluate passing on a consequentialist model and there is no deontological reason to question the morality of passing, then under many circumstances the outcomes could easily justify the decision to pass.

Only under certain conditions (e.g., where a statement is involved) can passing be construed as participating in lying, and perhaps more accurately, only the statements that provide false information about identity are a kind of lying. While a passing individual might be a repetitive liar in regards to one aspect of who they are, they might at the same time be quite honest about every other aspect of who they are. The phenomenon of passing is not co-extensive with lying. For those who think of passing as a form of social mobility, with neutral or perhaps even positive moral outcomes, this kind of social deception is implicit in their thinking. When considering passing as a form of deception, it feels intuitively frustrating to think that the moral evaluation can suggest either sociability, or manipulative, greasy, slanderous cunning.

Neither Lying or Deception

So maybe what we need is another category of not quite truth-telling that is not equivalent to deception. Recently, Henry Frankfurt wrote a short book: *On Bullshit*. He declares that he is interested in the subject because most people seem to think they have the tacit ability to recognize bullshit, and because of this there is little conceptual clarity about it. This observation is interesting and helpful, because it circumscribes an area of non-truth-telling that has gone under the radar of moral philosophers.

The first thing he notes is that both lying and deception are in relationship with the truth. He writes,

> telling a lie is an act with a sharp focus. It is designed to insert a particular falsehood at a specific point in a set or system of beliefs, in order to avoid the consequences of having the point occupied by the truth.... [A person must know the truth because] in order to invent an effective lie, he must design a falsehood under the guidance of truth.

This becomes one of the key differences between lying/deception and bullshit and may be the best place for finding a moral evaluation (or part of an evaluation) of passing. We have seen that passing shares some of the dual structuring of lying, but it may not be the case that the person who is passing is focused on truth and the manipulation of truth in the way that the liar is focused on the same thing. Critical for Frankfurt, and other moral theorists in regards to lying and deception, is that there must be the *intention* to deceive. So what do we do in a situation where the person who is passing is not concerned with deceiving?

I could easily imagine a case in which someone was passing purely to manipulate a corrupt system or to acquire knowledge or information that would otherwise be unavailable.[25] This individual, if psychologically healthy, would realize that the passing also entails deception. This might be an undesirable side-effect, and something that causes the individual great stress (e.g., Norah Vincent, the author of *Self-Made Man*, needed to go into psychiatric care after her year long experiment passing as a male). Under a circumstance like this, an analysis of the identity deception must take a background in the moral assessment. Of greatest moral concern should be the intended and achieved consequences of manipulating the corrupt system. If the consequences are indeed positive or intended to be so, we have a sympathetic moral case for passing. For Frankfurt, the bullshitter (albeit an unsympathetic character) may have some resonances with our sympathetic passer. The BS-er has a freedom and a creativity that allows him to pick and choose from the truth, but only insofar as it serves his interest in achieving some sort of social good through use of his bullshit. The idea is that the behavior is intended to produce certain desired effects but it is not meant to produce deception and lying.

Frankfurt does not think kindly of the moral value of the bullshitter. So while the equation I describe above between the bullshitter and the passer leaves us morally sympathetic towards the passer, I don't want to give a false impression of Frankfurt's position towards bullshit. He describes the bullshitter in terms that has resonances of moral condemnation. He says that the bullshitter "does not reject the authority of the truth, as the liar does, and oppose himself to it. He pays no attention to it at all. By virtue of this, bullshit is a greater enemy of the truth than lies are."[26] It would seem that if Frankfurt were to morally assess the passing individual who chose to do so with no regard for the truth, he would see them as more morally corrupt than the actively deceiving and lying passer for the added reason that s/he disregards the truth all together. Frankfurt doesn't articulate this, but it seems that bullshit involves two layers of lying: the first is the disregard for truth, and the second is the disregard of the importance of gesturing as though truth matters. Truth receives double violence under bullshit. At least the liar knows that truth is important and only does violence once. The intersubjectivity of lying and deceit is the next traditional problem with passing that needs to be addressed.

The Intersubjectivity of Lying and Deceit

The social harms passing poses to trust and intersubjectivity are catalogued again and again in memoirs of passing. The concrete harms of passing are very real, both to the passing individual and to the people with whom they are in community. The idea of moral violence is not solely a conceptual problem. It is also an interpersonal problem.

Trust is an interpersonal phenomenon that makes many things possible, including economic efficiency, social achievements, and human love. It has been argued that "the insufficiency of [mutual trust] does more than any one thing that can be named to keep back civilization, virtue, everything on which human happiness on the largest scale depends."[27] The violation of trust is usually the most readily announced problem with lying or deceit. The moral core of lying and truth-telling happens at the level of trust: whether it is corroded or nourished. So is it fair to argue that passing does moral damage in the same way? First a closer look at the intersubjectivity of lying and deceit.

When we are lied to we rightly feel angry. There is a sense of being victimized, manipulated, and/or violated. Two separate authors—Adler and Green—specifically use the word "brutalized" to explain the sensation. This is often where the locus of moral blame is located in an analysis of lying. All of this is of course dependent on the trust that is inherent in human relationships. Bernard Williams argues that the existence of trust means that we should encourage people to a have "a disposition of sincerity which is centered on sustaining and developing relations with others that involve different kinds and degrees of trust."[28] The mere existence of trust and its sensitivity becomes the impetus for the development of virtue. The maintenance of trust can become the basis of the character and moral development of an individual. And the worthiness of trust is often how we judge the character of others.

In situations where we've been lied to some of the richest frustrations happen because of our lack of control. Lies have a ubiquitous opportunity to take root and flourish and this can be an additional source of frustration. Adler notes "unless we renounce communication, there are few effective ways to immunize ourselves against the liar. The means to lie are readily at hand and the opportunities coeval with normal conversational assertion."[29] So we are always wide open to the possibility of betrayal and brutalization from the people we rely upon in our business transactions, personal lives, and maintenance of our daily existence. This makes lies all the more unwieldy and dangerous.

The basic form of the argument that exposes the intersubjectivity of lies is centered on the concept of autonomy with an emphasis on the victim's autonomy. When a lie is successful it "distorts the reasoning process of the person lied to, displacing his will and manipulating his action for the speaker's ends. The liar thus fails to respect the victim's capacity for reasoned self-governance."[30] So the victim experiences the onslaught at the level of his/her reasoning ability. The abuse of lying is experienced as mentally violating as well as willfully manipulative. Because our natural social dispositions are such that we are inclined to trust others in our interactions: the abuse that lying afflicts on individuals begins to corrode the underlying support that is necessary for a healthy functional human community.

We may want to argue that lies under certain circumstances are more justifiable than lies under other circumstances. Or we may even want to argue that under certain corrupt circumstances lies are the only proper way to behave or handle a situation. Sisela Bok wants to warn against this kind of excusing. She argues that lies are not something that can be "*aimed* only at others with the precision of many forms of violence"[31] meaning that lies can reverberate beyond and extend out further than they were intended. She argues that there is a direct correlation between the size of a deceptive scheme and its likely hood of backfiring on the deceptive party. Certainly backlash and retaliation are a potential fallout of any scheme of punishment or perpetrated violence. But the time delay between lie and discovered truth, or the hopeful projection that a lie will rest uncovered make the violence of lying uniquely prone to unforeseen backlash or reverberations. Bok also warns that lies (even to enemies) create the additional risks of self-harm and severe injuries to trust.

For deceit, as opposed to lying, the details of the argument are a little different. Where the victim of lying feels righteous indignation at the unprovoked violation of her reasoning and trusting good nature, the victim of deceit finds herself more involved, even participatory in the deception. Adler argues that "depending on the nature of the deception, the victim feels anything from foolish or tricked to corroded. Not only has he been misled, but the embarrassment or horror of it is that he has been duped into collaborating on his own harm. Afterward, he cannot secure the relief of wholly locating blame externally."[32] The partial involvement of self-blame in deception gives the moral intersubjectivity of deceit a different flavor than lying. Some want to argue that the partial self-blame that occurs in deception lessens it as a moral crime comparatively to lying. I think the peculiar intersubjectivity of deception might suggest otherwise. Self-blame is an unpleasant self-regarding emotion. It diminishes positive self-esteem and positive self-regard. On the occasions of being lied to, one's self relation is left intact. It is the external relations that become the subject of suspicions. To have someone else hijack your trusting relationship with yourself seems a bigger moral crime that someone destroying your trusting relationship with them.

Green describes this same intersubjectivity of deceit (or misleading) in terms of responsibility rather than self-blame. He writes, "when *A* merely misleads *B*, *A* invites *B* to believe something that is false by saying something that is either true or has no truth value. Any mistaken belief that *B* may draw from *A's* misleading statement is, at least in part, *B's* responsibility, and (other things being equal) *A* should be regarded as less fully culpable than if she had lied."[33] This is the basic moral argument that suggests that the deceit is a less blameworthy crime than lying. But, again notice that the shared responsibility for the deceit is still the result of the corrupt actions of one party, solely initiated and intentioned by one party. Despite the two that tango, the one that is leading must take responsibility for leading the tango, and initiating the dance under false pretenses with the other party. While the intersubjective responsibility may be lessened, the culpability for the entire deceitful scenario must still rest squarely on the shoulders of the deceiver. As I suggested above, the involvement and corruption of another individual's moral integrity might actually place deceit as more morally bankrupt than lying.

Green also distinguished lying and deceiving through the emotional reactions of both the victim and the perpetrator. He argues that the primary emotions experienced by one who is deceived are foolishness and embarrassment, "presumably because he believes he has contributed to his own harm by drawing an unwarranted inference from misleading premises." The embarrassment arises from a reflection on one's reasoning skills and a poor assessment of the implementation of those skills. The person lied to, however, feels brutalized. Green draws an analogy here with the emotions one feels when they have been subjected to threats or coercion. He also argues that the emotions of the perpetrator are significantly distinguishable. He writes,

> one who lies is likely to feel a different degree, or at least different kind of guilt than one who merely misleads. The non-lying deceiver will be much more able to rationalize his conduct that the liar—a fact that may explain why people go to such considerable lengths to avoid the need to lie.[34]

Likely because the blame for deception can be distributed amongst both the deceived and deceiver the perpetrator can maintain a relationship with his/her self-esteem and rational good will. The liar must either admit moral corruption or irrationality and therefore must distinguish themselves from humanity as less than fully capable of honesty or reasoning. The deceiver has an accomplice as close to the situation as s/he is, and may therefore maintain a better sense of self. But, again when we look at the intersubjectivity of lies and the intersubjectivity of deception we find that lies attempt to brutalize someone else's rational capacities, but that deception actually attempts to corrode the other person's rational capacities. Lying involves better boundaries, the externalization of hurt, and the opportunity for quicker healing. Deception involves enmeshment, the personalization of victimhood, and self-reproach.

Problems with These Accounts of Lying and Deception

If we focus on arguments against lying that are primarily grounded in an analysis of the intersubjectivity of lying and in particular the violation and corrosion of trust that is the primary social moral locus of lying, we are left with a problematic result. Bernard Williams argues that "it has always been a problem for those who ethically explain truth-telling and promise-keeping in terms of abusing people's trust that such accounts seem to let the known liar and promise-breaker off the hook. Since no-one trusts him, no-one is damaged or let down."[35] Let's call this "the paradox of the liar." If lying is only ethically corrupt because of the advantage it takes of trust, and all the trust is corroded between two people because of all the lies, then the liar can continue to lie with no moral failing past the point when all the trust was dissolved. Of course, our natural moral intuitions want to say that this paradox must be wrong. We want to still be able to hold the pathological liar accountable for his/her lies beyond the point when we've identified him/her as a pathological liar. The understanding of an individual as unworthy of our trust may be a practical tool to help us in managing our attachment, retrieval of information, and implementation of what another says. But, it seems wrong to suggest that if we maintain communication, or if we must maintain some kind of relationship (work, family) with our pathological liar that the interpersonal damage they can do will be negligible because we know them to be a liar. This criticism and observation suggests two things: 1) that we need an additional element to our ethical analysis of lying and deception that does not limit our judgment purely in terms of trust, and 2) we would be hard pressed to determine a situation in which no more intersubjective damage can be done by a liar as long as we are still in relationship with that person. Both of these observations have implications for an ethics of passing.

The emphasis on the intersubjectivity of lying is also sometimes stated in the form of a positive duty. Here the argument against lying becomes: "we owe each other the truth as an unconditional obligation, which also derives from a social expectation and desire not to be deceived."[36] We enter into human relationships under the hope that we will be dealt with honestly. As a general rule, people of good character engage in relationships honestly and expect the same in return. But, difficulties arise when we take into consideration how lies and deception can be and are used as a part of good social relations. Alexander and Sherwin argue that "well-socialized people engage in deception, regularly and skillfully, not only for altruistic reasons but also to gain advantages over others. We know how to suggest false facts through words, conduct, and concealment."[37] But, the fact that well-socialized people engage in deception does not dismiss the moral complexities or problems with deception. David Nyberg on the other hand argues that lying can make a positive moral contribution. He argues that lies and other forms of deception can make positive contributions to "civility and effective moral teaching; to privacy, self-confidence, and emotional comfort; and even to trust, if trust is understood as the expectation that another will act in one's best interests."[38] Given this observation about lying and deception, that it can actually function as a means to good ends, Nyberg advocates particularistic evaluation of lies and deception that firmly take into consideration the circumstances, outcomes, and intentions of the deception and lies. This observation and orientation has important implications for passing.

Something More Interesting to Say About Passing

Even if common sense morality seems to suggest that passing is a form of lying or deception, both the discussion above and the nature of passing warrant a closer look at the relationships between passing, lying, and deception. To begin there are conceptual confusions in declaring passing to be a form of lying or deception. Lying is a moral category; its corollary of untruth is an epistemological category. Passing, however, is something we do with subjectivity: philosophically it raises questions that fall both into the category of phenomenology and ontology. To equate passing directly with a category of moral failing is to ignore the different categories that are at work in each half of the equation.

What does passing do to social relationships? Does passing corrode trust? Does passing fundamentally misuse the social expectation that we will not deceive or be deceived by others? Under what kinds of circumstances or in what kinds of relationships are we under obligation to disclose identities that may not otherwise be visible? Should we take into consideration the goods that can be achieved through passing (professional success or family unity, as examples)? Should we take into consideration the potential harms (violence, economic hardship, isolation)? Should we take into consideration the moral virtues that would be aided and employed by denying the people the right to pass (authenticity, honesty, dignity)? Nyberg, I strongly suspect, would argue that these kinds of considerations are exactly the particularist elements that will help us determine whether an incident or a life-time of passing is morally reprehensible or sanctioned. This kind of particularistic approach to the ethics of passing would allow us to both acknowledge the deceptive elements inherent to passing, while also finding the moral room to acknowledge the value of passing.

The intersubjectivity of sexual identity passing is particularly complex. Under the normative prescriptions of heteronormativity few if any people are expected, in public or even private discourse, to reveal a queer sexual orientation. This means that there is no trust or faith in the disclosure of gayness. Ikuenobe argues "if there is no faith or a right to expect the truth, there cannot be a lie. This implies that you cannot lie to someone who is not expecting the truth from you or someone who does not trust or have faith in you."[39] If heteronormativity does not make room for gay disclosure, then sexual identity passing simply can't fall into the intersubjective framework of lying vs. truth-telling.

There is also a certain strong moral sympathy for people who choose to pass. Green argues that "although we admire people who take responsibility for their wrongful acts, we are nevertheless sympathetic to those who not only fail to do the virtuous thing but actually compound their wrongdoing by attempting to conceal it." We can appreciate the very human urge to minimize shame, negative consequences, and the poor self-regard that can be the conclusion to owning up to wrong-doings however significant or insignificant. Green continues on to say that "the basis of this moral sentiment, I believe, is an implicit recognition of the right to self-preservation—a right not to cooperate with those who would seek to bring adverse consequences against oneself."[40] Under circumstances where passing is a legitimate solution to violence against the self, I find that I have deep moral sympathy with the decision to act in deceptive ways about identity for protection. But moral sympathy and exoneration from guilt are not the same thing. We can understand the poor or difficult decisions of loved ones or strangers. But, still find the space to determine that passing is in violation of some of the virtues and interpersonal practices we are well-advised to revere.

On occasion passing is morally implicated as lying, other times it is deception, some times it is simply bullshit. But, the intersubjective damage and corrosion of trust that occurs from passing is mitigated by the social expectations of heteronormativity, and of course those expectations of heteronormativity are shifting as our culture moves towards greater political inclusion of LGBT/Q identities. Before focusing on the shifting ideological context of sexual identity in the public sphere and its direct implications for a theory of sexual identity passing (chapter 3), I will now turn to the philosophical and moral questions surrounding our obligations within community.

Socio-Political: Individual vs. Collective, Responsibility and Obligation

The intersubjective components of lying and deception strongly suggest that irreparable damage is done in relationships where trust is corroded by deceptive actions. But a broader social question arises when we think of passing in its social-political context. Do we owe others who share our identity the honest disclosure of our own? Does systemic oppression increase or decrease that obligation? What if tangible social goods can be reached for a community of minoritized individuals by the passing of one individual who can achieve a greater status, and thereby do greater things for the oppressed community? What if our self-elected passing can protect someone else from significant harm? What if the person to be harmed is a dependent? What if the person who is passing is also someone who is abusing his/her professional or personal power?

For philosophers who think about the socio-political arguments and moral considerations for the LGBT/Q community, two types of norms come into view when arguing positively for passing: norms of responsibility and norms of repression. Norms of responsibility are directed at serving the well-being of others or at aiming for a greater good. Norms of repression argue that certain aspects of self and behavior should be repressed or hidden because they are understood to be detrimental to others or society. For those who argue that their passing, especially in terms of sexual identity, is justified for the protection of others, either norms of responsibility or norms of repression (or both) are going to come into play. Norms of repression then often become the site of political confrontation for people who argue for the visibility of LGBT/Q people. Michael Warner, for example, argues that norms of homophobia are norms of repression that asymmetrically constrain certain portions of the population and not others. He further thinks that if we are to talk about morals in practice then we must talk about norms that consider all subjectivities equally, or we are not acting in the moral interest. Therefore the norms of repression with their asymmetrical privileging of heterosexual subjectivities cannot be moral.[41] Norms of responsibility remain standing.

Under systemic oppression an individual may want to argue that his/her responsibility to self, children, or others justifies passing. Philosophers who argue about the ethics of the closet and outing most often deal with both phenomena through either the lens of virtue ethics, or the lens of social and political obligation to others who are LGBT/Q identified. The focus on virtue ethics is something I will discuss at greater length in chapter 6. The socio-political arguments are usually motivated by their consequences. Group liberation and progress on gay causes (HIV/AIDS, marriage equality, non-discrimination in employment) are usually cited as the primary end points/goals of self-disclosure, or even the outing of other people. It is also cited that most of the progress made for the LGBT/Q community happened because a few individuals held true to their sexual identities at great personal cost, sometimes even death. For those who justify outing (3rd party disclosure of someone else's sexual identity, when that disclosure is unwanted), often do so on more deontological claims. There becomes a baseline claim that gay people have a duty to out themselves so that more people will be exposed to gayness which in turn will reduce homophobia, so that young gay people will have role models, and so that out gay people will have more social support and dating options. Many people who advocate outing also do so by arguing that it will have important personal benefits for the person who was outed: namely the opportunity for honest and authentic relationships with friends, family, lovers, and colleagues; as well as increased opportunities for happiness. This last concern is clearly more individual centered. But if we are to take the role of intersubjectivity seriously in both questions of passing and deception more broadly, then it can also be seen that this is an important socio-political concern because it affects some of the most intimate relationships in the community. There have been counter deontological concerns that claim outing is a form of using an individual as a means to an activist end. The argument against the consequentialist approach claims that sometimes coming out does not have the best results, particularly in conservative environments.

For sexual identity passing, or any other kind of passing, if an individual affirmatively decides to rid themselves of the trappings of their old identity, do they have an obligation to uphold the social commitments of that former identity? For example, if an individual converts away from a religion, we think they are no longer responsible for upholding its traditions, respecting its authority, celebrating its rituals and holidays, tithing or otherwise financially investing in the institution. Do we want to think this is also the case for bisexual individuals who decide to enter a life-long monogamous partnership with someone of the opposite gender? This is a practical question that members of the bisexual community struggle with in particular. But, is there something morally distinguishable from converting religions, entering into a heterosexual relationship, or lying about a racial identity? Clearly our perspective on this question will differ if we find ourselves as part of the abandoned identity group, or if we are assessing it from an out group identity.

Again for sexual identity passing, philosophers have argued that "closetude" (this is a term I am borrowing from James S. Stramel who defines it as: "the term for one's letting others believe that one is heterosexual"),[42] even when it happens at the individual level, is a social phenomenon. When an individual chooses to stay in the closet s/he is reinforcing the idea that gayness is shameful and immoral, which in turn encourages more closetude. This has lead some to argue (most notably Richard Mohr) that gay people have a duty to be out and also have a duty to out everyone that they know to be gay. For Mohr this is an issue of self-respect and dignity. To allow others to pass is to capitulate to anti-gay values.

There are a few lingering positive social arguments in favor of passing. In our professional spheres many of us want a kind of public separation from the turmoil and nuances of our private life. Having this separation allows us to function better in our professional sphere and frees up our energies to stay focused on the tasks at hand. When our personal lives are something that might detrimentally impact our professional perception we are keenly willing to leave it at home. For some, this justifies passing in regards to major aspects of their identity in their professional lives even if they are living more fully and authentically in private. There are other times when our intimate relationships force us to pass to protect a shared identity with someone else. Examples might include gay lovers who pass as straight friends at family functions where one of them remains closeted, or a light-skinned African American man who asks his white looking children to deny the full spectrum of their racial identity so that he can pass for white in his employment. Under conditions where the well-being of someone we love is at stake the agreement to pass may be driven by interpersonal sentiment that transcends political commitments.

The intentions behind passing and aims for which it is a side-effect or a necessary employment are varied. Depending on the intention or aim (to escape oppression, to seek out a better life or more opportunities, or to find satisfaction in the systematic deception of others), and the values we employ (to fight injustice, to live honestly and with dignity, or to cultivate authentic and healthy human relationships) we will find, uncover, or deliberate very different moral outcomes.

Ethics Under Oppression

Oppression is the systematic employment of power-over particular communities in line with cultural ideologies of privilege. For those who are oppressed, oppression creates a sense of alienation from the broader culture and those who are in power. Passing can mask this alienation, as passing can attempt to mitigate the insidious psychological effects of oppression, and especially in the case of sexual identity passing can mitigate the experience of shame.

Frantz Fanon's *Black Skin, White Masks* exposes the experience of psychological alienation; it is an alienation that has immediately recognizable social and economic realities. This psychological alienation manifests itself as an inferiority complex that is comprised of two components: primarily economic, and secondly the internalization, or what he says better yet, is the epidermalization[43] of this inferiority.[44] I found three basic themes in his exploration of alienation: relation to self inside the structure of power, relation to whiteness through language and desire, and the experience of lack of reciprocity that defines subjugation in all its emotional and psychological discomfort. I will briefly mention two alongside their insight into the case of the sexual identity passer.

The dominant power relation for Fanon is the white power-over black race relationship, which constructs the subjectivities of black men through white privilege. The man is the Other of his white counter part. This relationship to the Other, and the capitulating of self to the gaze and the power of the Other is thematic throughout his text and the clearest of motivations for the passing individual. Attempting to construct one's soul for the happy uptake of one's oppressor and ignoring one's sense of self-esteem in contorting this image of self has deep ethical implications that run counter to existential virtues such as authenticity.

The experience of reciprocity (or more accurately, the lack of reciprocity) is that which produces the psychological and emotional discomfort of subjugation. The experience of reciprocity that the black man can find with others of his race differs from the reciprocity he finds with the white Other. This can take the form of different behavioral modalities, objectification, ontological resistance, continual conscious awareness, or an enduring but futile plight for recognition. In accordance with the title of his work, Fanon announces "the black man has two dimensions. One with his fellows, the other with the white man. A negro behaves differently with a white man and with another negro." These two behavioral modalities illustrate that certain aspects of his persona the black man knows he can not experience reciprocity with the white man. So he must alter his behavior for sociality and social recognition. Black skins under white masks is a perfect image for racial passing. An attempt to regain the psychological benefits of reciprocity would explain why those of sexually minoritized status, particularly given their increased access to instrumentalized identity mobility through the relative invisibility of queerness (compared to race), would choose to pass.

What Fanon calls "psychic alienation" is the most pronounced experience of minoritization as the internalization of the socializing forces that define, produce, and maintain the power differentials between groups of people. Subordinates must appropriate a society's perspective—engaging their subordinated role, with minimal psychic investment, or they must, alternatively, maintain a critical perspective on the sociological pressures, constantly combating the urge to submit. This is to say that one's sense of self-results not from an internal source, but rather through the appropriation of the gaze of the other, the oppressor. So oppression is the product of a more fundamental subjective phenomenon: psychological oppression.

Psychological oppression is the appropriation of and dominion over the self-esteem of an individual. It is the capacity of the narratives of a broader society to produce the experience of self and self-regard in a way that is destructive, either subtly or overtly. Psychological oppression, Sandra Bartky argues, is "institutionalized and systemic," it reinforces the structures of power that keeps it in place by making the domination easier. It breaks "the spirit of the dominated by rendering them incapable of understanding the nature of those agencies responsible for their subjugation."[45]

Psychological oppression blinds people to the forces that replicate and inscribe the sociological structures that maintain the oppressed subject's location within a system of oppression. The myth of inferiority is just that, a myth: but the forces of psychological oppression instantiate the myth through its literalization within the subject.[46] The oppressed subject must engage the system for the oppression to operate.

Very much related to this concept of psychological oppression is what we might think of as a pervasive sense of shame. Not the shaming that occurs in a moment of moral failure, but the shaming that helps to construct someone's entire sense of self. It's the kind of shame that Bartky describes as having "boundaries [that] are blurred; [because] it is less available to consciousness and more likely to be denied. This shame is manifest in a pervasive sense of personal inadequacy that, like the shame of embodiment, is profoundly disempowering."[47] One way that she wants us to begin thinking about, and categorizing shame is as a "species of psychic distress" that is "occasioned by a self or a state of the self apprehended as inferior, defective, or in some way diminished."

When we think about psychological oppression, and shame as constructing of identity we think about it in relation to socially recognizable identities. Both Fanon and Bartky considered their model of psychological oppression to be applicable in cases of transparent identity markers: namely, gender and race that are easily readable by others in society. Of course, there are few forms of shaming as powerful as forms of sexual shaming.

Passing, by the very nature of its phenomenon, erases the readability of the identity markers involved. This, I think it is fair to argue, complicates the psychological pressures experienced by the subject. Perhaps, for some, it magnifies the psychological pressure given the inherent isolation that passing demands, and perhaps alleviating pressure for others given that passing inhibits the subject from experiencing the psychological pressure directly.

Passing, one might argue, doubles the experience of isolation: isolation from the group in power and isolation from one's subjugated community. Passing, one might also argue is only singularly alienating in that one sustains a connection to the group in power by building distance from the subjugated group. But in the second argumentative structure, distance from self must also be inserted if we can assume a common sense understanding of an authentic self.

If power based relations are constructive and destructive of human psychology, subject embodiment, and social relations, it also makes sense that power can be constructive and destructive of our moral lives. In this section I am interested in exploring ways of thinking about our sense of morality under systemic oppression, and will primarily draw from writers thinking about the moral lives of prisoners in concentration camps in Nazi Germany. I will try to draw connections here with sexual identity passing, that while under more ambiguous regimes of power, also must thrive within significant oppression. There is no ambiguity regarding the totalizing systemic nature of oppressive forces inflicted upon by the Nazis on the Jews.[48] In this regard (its totalizing nature) I think it is the cleanest model to establish a theory of what happens to our ethics under oppression. I will be working with two theories: 1) Claudia Card's adaptation of Primo Levi's moral grey zones and 2) Trvestan Todorov's understanding of heroic and ordinary virtues. Both theories work with different aspects of life in the camps, and at face value seem to be incommensurable with each other. In the end, however, I will argue that the concept of supererogatory duties helps us to bring both models together, and that this might be the best way to remove the theories from the concentration camps and apply them to our lives under ordinary oppression, and will begin to articulate a normative structure of the moral responsibility of LGBT/Q people under ranging degrees of oppression.

Moral Grey Zones

Claudia Card appropriates the concept of moral grey zones from Primo Levi[49] to describe complex demands of morality under systemic oppressive structures, like the ones found in concentration camps. She wants to apply this moral framework to help us think through ethical problems under ordinary (non-war) states of systematic oppression: namely, regimes of gender oppression under patriarchy, racial, class, and sexual identity oppression. The guiding premise of her exploration is that "oppressive social structures are an unfavorable context for flourishing or developing good character, whether we are favored or disfavored by those structures."[50] This is not a guiding premise of all writers on ethics under systemic oppression. Trvestan Todorov, for example, argues nearly the opposite, that under systems of extensive oppression ordinary virtues are amplified and extended to the level of the heroic. I will return to Todorov in the next section. Levi and Card both agree that under systemic oppression moral agents are necessarily subject to moral compromise, moral ambiguity, and complicity. Card, at least, does not present us with another option.

First a bit about Primo Levi's grey zones. The grey zones he discusses have three definitional features: 1) "their inhabitants are victims of evil," 2) "these inhabitants are implicated through their choices in perpetuating some of the same or similar evils on others who are already victims like themselves," and 3) "they act under extraordinary stress."[51] Levi's grey zones primarily refer to Kapos, or camp guards that were selected from the population of prisoners. These individuals served the interest of their captors, while in turn receiving favors and pardons. A significantly higher percentage of Kapos survived the camps then did traditional prisoners. What is clear in the case of grey zones, is that Kapos are both innocent in that they were victims of unbelievable oppression that they did nothing to deserve, and also implicated in evil they have chosen to perform given the degree of voluntariness in their actions. Here, perhaps we can begin to see the moral paradox of the sexual minority passing for heterosexual. The analogy is even more effective if we consider that individual as living in one of the seven countries[52] that currently has the death penalty for homosexuals. For Card, grey zones are "neither gratuitously nor willfully evil but nevertheless implicate choosers in perpetrating, sustaining, or aggravating evils."[53] In a non-war context, individuals in a moral grey zone for Card would include women who under extreme patriarchy inflict wounds on other women,[54] or closeted gay politicians that vote in anti-gay legislation.

Card wants to be perfectly clear in the ability to still place moral blame on individuals in grey zones. She argues, "we lose innocence in becoming responsible for other's suffering, even when we make the best decision under the circumstances."[55] The loss of innocence demands responsibility for our actions, even when the extraordinary stress pushes us beyond our natural sense of right and wrong. But, this blame is mitigated. Card argues, "the involvements of grey zone inhabitants are not of the same order or extensiveness as that of perpetrators who are not victims."[56] Hence why the zones are grey. She does seem to want to place the displaced blame somewhere. And does so by condemning oppression. "One of the greatest evils," she says, "threatening victims of oppression is the danger of becoming evil oneself, becoming complicit in evils perpetrated against others."[57] The oppression is the instigator of the evil, and the locus of its origin.[58]

Moral grey zones, at a considered glance, appear to be a functional analytic tool for an ethics of passing, if a sensitive mitigation of moral responsibility is what we desire. Passing suggests a hostile (oppressive) context, where the damage inflicted on oneself (if it can be argued that passing inflicts damage on the self) and on others, is rendered less severe—in terms of our moral judgment—in light of the compromising circumstances. Systemic pressure on a certain aspect of identity that encourages the individual to forge a new identity that can more easily maneuver (or even survive) within a social context shares this ethical structure. I do not, however, think that this model of ethics under oppression (and therefore as an ethic of passing) captures the full extent of the moral story, nor what should be the full range of intuitions about the moral complexities that arise. Resolving to adjudicate the oppressed subject in light of his/her experience of oppression is not the only ethical option, nor is it the only way that the impact of oppression on the ethical subject has been theorized.

Heroic and Ordinary Virtues

Trvestan Todorov's book *Facing the Extreme: Moral Life in the Concentration Camps* explores the impact of oppression on the ethics of individuals under a totalizing system. It does so in the manner of a theorizing historian, taking into consideration memoirs and personal accounts of the ways in which moral lives were shaped under the influence of daily pressures and horrors of life in the Nazi Germany concentration camps. His basic argument is that ordinary virtues, and ordinary vices are amplified to the realm of heroic and monstrous, respectively.

For Todorov, the ordinary virtues are: dignity, caring, and intellectualism. Under extreme oppression, such as the circumstances of the camps, these ordinary virtues become amplified. Dignity, for example, might refer to the acceptance of corporeal punishment or starvation or even death for the sake of protecting oneself against humiliation. Caring might involve the sacrifice of well-being for the comfort of others. The ability to maintain this virtue is one that Todorov argues is "to render oneself especially vulnerable, for in addition to one's own suffering, one takes on that of the people one cares about."[59] Suffering is ample and to maintain caring connections is to leave one's emotional self open to amplified suffering. Where intellectual pursuits are considered valuable under circumstances of ordinary social relationships; under circumstances of oppression (extreme or otherwise) the tenacity to pursue a life of the mind demonstrates its heroic quality. The scholar is just as easily terminated as the most inconsequential prisoner in the camps, but the persistence of the mind becomes notable by withstanding the oppressive regime. Here we have a moral analogy to the type of heroics we see in LGBT/Q activists who are currently living in regions where they are facing potential death. Take for example David Kato, the martyr/activist of Uganda who was assassinated for being openly gay and seeking equality for his people. His displays of dignity, caring, and intellectualism were all heroic.

The ordinary vices include: fragmentation of behavior (or the disconnection of conduct from conscience), depersonalization, and the enjoyment of power. In any given profession, Todorov argues, professionals are required to accomplish a certain amount of fragmentation from the work that they do. And while he defines this as a "vice" one might readily counter by arguing that this fragmentation is necessary, and when contextualized is often one of the most virtuous things that professionals can do (think for a moment of a doctor who can—without conscience—cut open another person in a professional capacity, while clearly doing so under any other context would seem appropriately abhorrent). But in the context of extraordinary oppression, or in a scenario of extreme dehumanization, the fragmentation of behavior can be viewed in a light that is truly monstrous. This would include the types of camp roles that Card alludes to: prisoners that are employed to implement torture or death upon their fellow prison-mates. Depersonalization and enjoyment of power (in its insidious manifestations) become the corollaries of the fragmentation of behavior that can result in truly monstrous consequences. Stepping into "professional" responsibilities within a war camp that employ the abilities to depersonalize and enjoy positions of power was evidenced to produce millions of deaths. Here we can imagine an analogy with the closeted despot, or more commonly—the closeted preacher, who condemns to death, or at least eternal damnation of his/her brethren, while likely at the same time enjoying sexual concubinage with one or more members of the same sex.

Clearly in the application of an analogy of Nazi War Camps to ordinary social regimes of social oppression, hegemony, and other structural inequities, we must be careful in too readily assuming the same type of moral corrosion, even in lesser degrees.

But the dual interpretations of the moral life of prisoners: on the one hand as positioned within a moral grey zone where ordinary judgment must be mitigated, and on the other where all moral qualities (both virtues and vices) are amplified presents us with a basic incongruity of how to conceive of the impact of oppressive or hostile circumstances on our moral lives.

What I wish to suggest is that this incongruity doesn't necessarily force us to choose one model over the other. There might be compatibility if we blend our understanding of moral grey zones and heroic virtues while thinking about the latter as supererogatory. First, a definition of supererogatory.

David Heyd argued that an action is supererogatory if and only if all the following four conditions hold: 1) The action is neither obligatory nor forbidden, 2) its omission is not wrong and does not deserve sanction, 3) it is morally good, 4) it is done voluntarily for the sake of someone else's good.[60] Let's take a look again at Todorov's "ordinary virtues turned heroic" of dignity, caring, and intellectualism. In a moral grey zone, all three virtues (particularly the last one) are beyond what the situation demands. Given that the grey zone presents a scenario where ordinary expectations of human morality is lessened, ordinary virtues are no longer obligatory and their absence no longer wrong. (Therefore, the first two criteria are met.) They remain virtues (therefore criteria 3 is met) and they must be done voluntarily in accordance with the second virtue[61] primarily for the well-being of others. (Therefore, the final criteria is met.)

Why is it valuable to think in terms of ordinary virtues turned supererogatory virtues in moral grey zones? As a result of serious considerations on the varying degrees of genuine social hostility that encourages scenarios of sexual identity passing, the result can not simply be to reduce moral culpability for passing individuals, nor can the increased cost of ordinary virtues of the openly queer individual under the same degree of oppression be overlooked either. So what the combination of Card and Todorov allows us is a model of ethics under oppression, where we must on the one hand think of moral culpability as somehow mitigated and on the other hand be able to lift up instances of ordinary virtue as supererogatory.

Performativity and Ethics

As I mentioned previously, performativity doubts the presence of an interior self. I want to bring up this particular difficulty of performativity as a theory, now that sustained conversation about ethics and passing have been undertaken. Vikki Bell argues that "the doubting of interiority, of 'identity,' is simultaneously a doubting of ethical judgment."[62] We assume that the individual, in making judgments of an ethical nature, engage an interior self that is reflexive and capable of independent judgment. Indeed, this assumption of interiority is what allows us to hold people accountable for criminal and other unsavory ethical behaviors. Essentially, under performativity as the descriptor of the process of identity formation, there can be nothing that we can identify as a "conscience." Instead what we have is a folding of power into the body, which is "simultaneously an objectification and a subjectification,"[63] and which cannot result in an independent moral voice of assessment. What happens, more accurately is a taking of the inward folding of moral power and judgment, and then a shift to send it outward as moral power and judgment. Individuals re-assert the normative claims they've been subjected to, thereby simply subjecting others to what they themselves have received.

Butler was not blind to this ethical and political difficulty associated with performativity. And the result of her model of identity creation was not meant to be an abdication of all ethical agency and sense of self to the interiorization of power and social construction. Instead she meant more thoroughly for performativity to specify the "foreclosures or exclusions that constrain the possibilities of the subject even as they enable that subject to emerge." Vikki Bell describes this as the paradox Butler was attempting to disclose: on the one hand the constraints of a cultural system of identity which supplies all of the possible intelligibility of identity under which a person can become a subject, which paradoxically creates the possibilities for becoming and emergence but at the same time significantly limits the possibility for becoming and emergence.[64] In particular, any instance of looking inward is also an instance of looking "up" at the institutions of power. In conjunction with pondering one's interiority, one is also simultaneously "compar[ing], measure[ing], and chastis[ing] her[or him]self against prevailing abstract norms, be they social, scientific, moral, or developmental."[65]

This is the foreground under which a model of ethics can come into view, and clearly has profound ethical implications.

Butler's concern with ethics came much later; significantly after the publication of *Gender Trouble* (1990) and her initial exploration of performativity. Where she takes on the questions of ethics is in *Precarious Life* (2004) and *Undoing Gender* (2004), although she utilizes some of the intellectual material she developed in *The Psychic Life of Power* (1997).

In *The Psychic Life of Power*, Butler argues that our primary form of subject development is through what she calls "passionate attachment." The most illustrative example is that of a child's initial unconditional love for a parent or significant care-giver that is driven by a primal set of needs that must be met. The passionate attachment guarantees that the child will internalize certain character traits and positive or negative senses of self in alignment with the treatment s/he received. This process of attachment and internalization is one of the earliest forms of subject formation, with its basic pattern under significant repetition through different passionate attachments, sometimes motivated by caregivers and other times motivated by institutions or other cultural phenomena. Based on this development of self, Butler argues that the subject or self can no longer be viewed as the foundation for ethics, but rather the self must be viewed as the problem of ethics.[66]

Traditional models of the self/subject hold that essential characteristics will remain through the passing of time—even though non-essential characteristics may change. It functions as a foundation upon which accidents and qualities rely. This suggests that while the particulars of my life may be contingent to the historical time, physical region, political climate, and class culture; there is something underneath those particulars that is firm and unchanging, which would be reliably identifiable despite the particularities of my current condition. This concept of the subject dates back to Aristotle[67] and is the understanding of self up through the post-modern period. Under this model, despite the course of action chosen in rational deliberation of the good, or the right thing to do, the self or subject would remain unchanged. This is not Butler's understanding of self and therefore it cannot be her understanding of ethics.

Butler's concept of self is a product of the cultural discourses that surround it, in conjunction with the speech acts employed by the individual. The individual engages a social construct by speaking itself into the construct; by identifying 'as' something. This means that the self also cannot be presupposed to have any of characteristics as fixed entities (reason, understanding, knowledge of oneself, etc).[68] Please note that this also de-centers the psyche and psychic processes as the location of imperfections and incompleteness in the subject.[69] The room for ethics that Butler leaves is in the deliberations upon the socio-cultural conditions of the self that enable its identity, and more importantly the ways in which the socio-cultural conditions make the life of the subject unlivable.[70] Loizidou argues that for Butler the subject becomes agentic through resistance to the socio-cultural conditions after this kind of deliberation.[71] But this kind of resistance should not be viewed as running counter to the power structures.

Rather, it should be understood as always "working with and even along the lines" of the different cultural discourses in place.[72] This means that first and foremost our moral wills are not something that we can maintain as a product of ourselves, but something that is established in the relations prior to our development of will—of how we are seen and addressed by others.

Butler argues,

> what binds us morally has to do with how we are addressed by others in ways that we cannot avert or avoid; this impingement by the other's address constitutes us first and foremost against our will or, perhaps put more appropriately, prior to the formation of our will.[73]

This means that any sense of moral authority we find within ourselves must be understood as having both "radical complicities and radical indebtedness."[74] Our morality is necessarily pre-constructed through global and local interdependencies and any kind of moral progress must start from this understanding and build forward, either looking for new possibilities in the "nascent forms" of our current moralities, or by looking for "new arrangements" within the system of ethics we already have.[75] And this is where we can, for Butler, find a place of moral responsibility. Although we are not the individuals responsible for the framework of moral norms we have been born into, we are responsible for the consequences of these frameworks once we begin to transmit these norms to others.

This outcome of morality for Butler, under her initial identity model of performativity is something I find appealing, and its general understanding of the development of and agentic shift within ethics is a basic model I will employ both implicitly and explicitly in chapter 6. The counter intuitive aspect of her theory, however, is the shift from a model of identity that has no interiority, only coextensivity, into a responsibility-bearing model of agentic resistance and engagement with a pre-constructive ethical framework. For me, this counter intuitive shift demonstrates the need for a new concept and way to think about identity so that we have a better model of how the construction of selves occurs from the environment and resources around us, but still (from the beginning) makes room for an interiority and self-directed engagement. This will allow us to produce both a descriptive, and more importantly a normative sense of ethics in relation to identity. A better model for describing this kind of identity development, I will spend a good portion of the next part of this chapter arguing, is through the concept of 'style.' I think this will be more fruitful that re-working Butler's performativity with its Foucaultian roots. The primary philosopher who has been my inspiration in thinking about style as constructive of identity is Maurice Merleau-Ponty.

The Postmodern Ethical Dilemma: The Radical Instability of Identity

Passing is clearly dependent on an understanding of collective identity as demarcating real categories of persons. For many postmodern thinkers, identity is an unstable notion: it is primarily or entirely a social construct. Passing, as an ostensive phenomenon, suggests that individuals can use one socially constructed identity to hide something underneath that is more "authentic" or at least more firmly rooted in the emotional and psychological aspects of the individual or the individual's history/memory. Postmodernism would be inclined to dismiss this possibility, given its general inclination to deny an essential or authentic aspect to identity. Postmodern philosophy and its identity theory raise significant questions about the nature of passing.

The self has undergone significant theoretical transitions under postmodernity's focus on social influence and technology's intervention into production of selves. As a point of comparison, Hostein and Gubrium, authors of *The Self We Live By: Narrative Identity in a Postmodern World* lift up the European Enlightenment self which was the dominating model of self prior to postmodernism. They write that the self was "once viewed as an idealized, abstract platform from which concepts and judgments emanated, the self transcended society, standing prior to, apart from, and philosophically above the everyday hubbub of life. This was a lofty—even haughty—*transcendental* self."[76] This conception of self was one that could be understood outside the context of social influences, and without an analysis of things like power, discourse, hegemony, or psychoanalysis (as examples). The postmodern self is a socially and technologically embedded self. Psychologist Kenneth Gergen refers to the postmodern self as a "saturated self." He claims that the world we inhabit is so full of meanings, "that it risks saturating the self," it leaves the self "filled to overflowing," to the point where the self "loses any distinct identity" and can not distinguish its actual self from all of the potential selves it could become. Gergen explains that this is in part due to the "proliferation of 'technologies of social saturation'—including print and broadcast media, rapid transit, computers, electronic mail, and diverse languages of identity" all of which pull us in so many different directions that it is hard to maintain a center, a trajectory, or bearings that can anchor a self.[77]

So the self under the most radical model of postmodernism becomes an entity that is present everywhere and has broad global access, but at the same time is nowhere in particular. With the new popularity of "second lives" or virtual identities (avatars) that have a social sphere, community, and life of its own, we can see even more pronounced that the digital revolution has disintegrated the parameters and boundaries of the self. Theorists of postmodernity amplify this cynicism towards the self. Jean Baudrillard, for example, argues that the self lives in "hyperreality" rather than reality "where the self is an image, among myriad others, for conveying identity."[78] This means that for Baudrillard "self-references, self-concerns, and definitions of self-worth are not more authentic than the ostensible realities of television commercials."[79] Clearly this poses a problem for an ethical analysis of passing. If the production of identity is no more real than the production of a commercial than we hardly have firm footing to assert much about the ethics of the authenticity of identity—although we might have the right to say something about the content of the production and its appropriate or inappropriate content for communicative uptake from the viewers.

For other postmodern theorists such as Jean-François Lyotard, postmodernity doesn't need to have such a deep skepticism. It can be simply about a skepticism towards overarching narratives of identity. Lyotard thinks that postmodernity should give us an "incredulity toward meta-narratives" which in terms of identity would include a "breakup or delegitimation of the grand narrative of self constancy."[80] What this means is that we would be unable to fairly articulate a life trajectory or narrative that would be able to sustain an "authentic" identity under the guise and pressure of a passing narrative. Both identities would represent different multiplicities of self, but neither would be able to claim legitimacy over the other under any kind of rubric.

So the closest thing we will have left is a self that is a "particular set of sited language games whose rules discursively construct the semblance of a more or less unified subjectivity centered in experience."[81] If the self has authenticity at all it is plural or "authenticities." This means that as individuals we engage in a kind of "interpretive salvage operation" where we create selves from what ever resources are available and at hand, resulting in a contingent product that is circumstantially defined.

But the knowledge that we employ the resources around us in our efforts to create a self does not exclude the possibility that there are important ontological elements involved in that self-creation that might serve as the locus of our authenticity. What I will do with the remainder of this section is talk about ways that we can understand both the social construction of identity on one level, but also expose the mechanism of production that is beyond the contingencies of the social location and what this does to our understanding of morality and ethics for the postmodern self.

Olav Bryant Smith argues that the best way to understand the self is "through an integration of a postmodern ontology and a narrative theory of identity."[82] Smith grants a clear acknowledgement that individuals are sign-bearing texts in the way postmodernity likes to think about bodies and selves. He follows this by a claim about the ontological make up of the world: that it is comprised of experiential, interpretive, creative, and expressive acts of which the self is part. The most important aspect of this determination of self for a moral interpretation of passing is an inclusion of a statement about the self that it "partially determines itself through a series of decisive and communicative acts." If the self can partially self determine, then it maintains agency, and we can still ascribe to it responsibility. This kind of hybrid postmodern model of self is the best way to defend against a dismissive claim of social construction at the expense of a responsibility to an identity that best represents one's location in the experiential, interpretive, creative, and expressive communicative network of the world. The self can be reflexive about its own expression and location, or as Charles Taylor argues we are "self-interpreting animals" meaning that our identities are a "matter of interpretive practice, of putting forth the effort and engaging in the everyday work of orienting to each other *as selves.*"[83] This defends the self from being a "mere reflection of social responses."[84] But it also frees up the self to be multiple rather than only integrated, meaning that the social construction and cultural forms that help to create the individual also allow that individual to (re)self-interpret depending on the environment in which it finds itself. This explains both how the process of passing might work, and also safe-guards the self from becoming saturated through the process of simple social/cultural reflection.

These conception of self, both the radical instability of identity that the most radical version of postmodernism suggests, and the more tempered hybrid model of self-interpreting multiplicity pose certain problems for our moral analysis and ascription. Some of our most basic underpinnings of punishment and retribution rely upon a conception of a unified subject. Olav Bryant Smilth argues,

> We punish criminals on the assumption that we are punishing in a present moment the individual who in some past moment perpetrated the crime, and we do this in the name of *justice:* i.e., to restore balance. Such a balance requires a unity in such a series of occasions. We punish individuals on the further assumption that this is the best protection society has from a repetition of such actions by the same individual in some future moment.

Whether we are considering a multiplicity of possible selves, or no self at all but rather a radically unstable social receptacle of cultural norms of identity, what we lose is a basic sense of person and coherent agent able to receive and learn from punishment. This should return us to much of the anxiety expressed around aesthetic surgery and the possibility for criminal passing. Social anxieties rise with the understanding that dubious figures could blend back into society with medical help that will allow them to pass. This idea of escaping moral responsibility through passing might be the very basis for the moral intuitions that suggest passing could involve grave potential harm to the social order.

Given the proffered hybrid models of self under postmodernity, there appear to be two potential moral outcomes. Again think back to the possibility of the saturated self, the one who is under constant barrage of technology and other media based cultural inputs. The moral danger for the saturated self, it is argued, is a loss of self along the way of one's "moral career." The self becomes exposed to too many different and compelling trajectories so that one's moral core or "internal grandly decisive beacon devolves into a thousand possible I's and me's, whose local articulations scatter us every which way. Buffeted about the self-construction terrain by diverse narratives, the self's compass spins wildly out of control ostensibly losing its ability to pick and choose its own moral course."[85] If the guiding light of our inner consciousness is dependent on certainty of identity we run the significant risk of losing that light under the multiplicity of pressures from our modern world. This is of course the most pessimistic interpretation. On the other hand, what we might have is a more robust sense of ethics for a self with more options at its finger-tips for development. Under this interpretation of the pressures of postmodernity, the moral self is found through its movement in the discursive practices of everyday life. The self must find and articulate its own compass through the multiplicity of options and this articulation becomes its most crucial moral aspect. The greater possibility for self-creation puts considerable responsibility on all of us, and shapes the potential discourses for future selves. Smith argues that the final judgment of an act as moral is "an act that brings us closer to harmony with our fellow actors, creating a better worldly environment that is the ultimate stage for all future acts."[86] This understanding of morality could provide us with a moral lens through which to interpret passing. Postmodernity makes passing easier, it provides us with infinite resources to create selves that will maximize our accomplishments in a less than morally ideal world. But if we take into consideration social justice, and improving the lives of the next generation, or maximizing expressions of self through modeling our own expression, especially those aspect of selves that are currently under regimes of oppression, then we have exactly the moral compass we need to argue for some identity expressions over others.

The postmodern lens on the self, with the role of multiplicity and self-creation through discourse production/management and its harkening to personal responsibility in self-creation creates its own kind of moral obligations and constraints. Our new awareness of the potential of selves places us in a new agentic position to make decisions in our trajectory of identity. While it may be the case that postmodernity will force us to abandon enlightenment notions of authentic self, or cultural givens of essential identities, it does *not* force us to abdicate morality in its wake. In fact, it may have the opposite effect, where it opens up the choices we can make in terms of self construction and promotion, and in that demands that we choose—unaided by necessity—but nevertheless very wisely.

Notes

1. For an extended essay on my position of the concept of power necessary for a theory of passing—an original extension of this chapter—see "Power Over the Passing Subject: Creating Ethics Under Oppression" in *Passing/Out: Sexual Identity Veiled and Revealed*. London: Ashgate Press, 2012.

2. Sisela Bok, *Lying: Moral Choices in Public and Private Life* (New York: Pantheon Books, 1978), 33.

3. Bok, *Lying: Moral Choices in Public and Private Life*, 15.

4. Bok writes, "Such statements [i.e., lies] are most often made verbally or in writing, but can of course also be conveyed via smoke signals, Morse code, sign language, and the like. Deception, then, is the larger category, and lying forms part of it." Bok, *Lying: Moral Choices in Public and Private Life*, 13-14.

5. Isenberg as quoted in Polycarp Ikuenobe, "The Meta-Ethical Issues of the Nature of Lying: Implications for Moral Education," *Studies in Philosophy and Education,* (2002), 41.
6. Ikuenobe outlines these four elements to lying. Ikuenobe, "The Meta-Ethical Issues of the Nature of Lying: Implications for Moral Education," 52.
7. Bok, *Lying: Moral Choice in Public and Private Life,* 32.
8. Ikuenobe, "The Meta-Ethical Issues of the Nature of Lying," 40.
9. Larry Alexander and Emily Sherwin, "Deception in Law and Morality," *Law and Philosophy* 22 (2003), 397.
10. Ikuenobe, "The Meta-Ethical Issues of the Nature of Lying," 40.
11. Alexander and Sherwin write, "Law prohibits deception in very broad terms. The modern tort of deceit (or fraudulent misrepresentation) cuts through the distinctions drawn by philosophers, encompassing words and conduct, active deception and passive non-disclosure, false suggestions and concealment of truth. It covers deception about facts, opinions, or law, and treats evasive half-truths and intentional ambiguities as equivalent to false statements... Deception is also a crime." Alexander and Sherwin, "Deception in Law and Morality," 405.
12. Alexander and Sherwin, "Deception in Law and Morality," 408.
13. Ikuenobe, "The Meta-Ethical Issues of the Nature of Lying," 53.
14. Ikuenobe, "The Meta-Ethical Issues of the Nature of Lying," 38.
15. Bok, *Lying: Moral Choices in Public and Private Life,* 22.
16. Bernard Williams, *Truth and Truthfulness,* (Princeton: Princeton University Press, 2002), 11.
17. Williams, *Truth and Truthfulness,* 96.
18. Bok, *Lying: Moral Choices in Public and Private Life,* 23.
19. Bok, *Lying: Moral Choices in Public and Private Life,* 23.
20. However, the relationship between oppression, prejudice, and this strategic psychology was not one that Bok intended.
21. Bok, *Lying: Moral Choices in Public and Private Life,* 13.
22. Green writes, "...there is no deception unless the communicator intends to deceive." Stuart Green, "Lying, Misleading, and Falsely Denying: How Moral Concepts Inform the Law of Perjury, Fraud, and False Statements," *Hastings Law Journal* 53 (2001-2002), 163.
23. Adler, "Lying, Deceiving, or Falsely Implicating," 442.
24. Adler, "Lying, Deceiving, or Falsely Implicating," 435.
25. Walter White is an excellent example of this kind of information seeking passer. He was light-skinned, blue-eyed, w/ blonde hair, but 5 of his 32 great great great grandparents were black, so he legally qualified as African-American. He used his Caucasian appearance to "pass" and attend and investigate lynchings and race riots. He eventually became the executive secretary of the NAACP, and held the post for 24 years (1931-1955).
26. Henry Frankfurt, *On Bullshit* (Princeton: Princeton University Press, 2005), 61.
27. Alexander and Sherwin, "Deception in Law and Morality," 398.
28. Williams, *Truth and Truthfulness,* 121.
29. Adler, "Lying, Deceiving, or Falsely Implicating," 439.
30. Alexander and Sherwin, "Deception in Law and Morality," 397.
31. Bok, *Lying: Moral Choices in Public and Private Life* 142.
32. Adler, "Lying, Deceiving, or Falsely Implicating," 442.
33. Green, "Lying, Misleading, and Falsely Denying," 160.
34. Green, "Lying, Misleading, and Falsely Denying," 168.

35. Williams, *Truth and Truthfulness*, 120.
36. Ikuenobe, "The Meta-Ethical Issues of the Nature of Lying," 39.
37. Alexander and Sherwin, "Deception in Law and Morality," 393.
38. Alexander and Sherwin, "Deception in Law and Morality," 399.
39. Ikuenobe, "The Meta-Ethical Issues of the Nature of Lying," 51.
40. Green, "Lying, Misleading, and Falsely Denying," 172.
41. Raja Halwani et al., "What is Gay and Lesbian Philosophy?," *Metaphilosophy* 39 (October 2008), 438.
42. Stramel in Halwani et al., "What is Gay and Lesbian Philosophy?," 439.
43. Epidermalization is medically defined as "the transformation of glandular or mucosal epithelium into stratified squamous epithelium." Glandular/muscosal epithelium is the sensitive, porous, and moist skin that constructs internal cavities like the mouth, esophagus, vagina, or anus. Stratified squamous epithelium is the skin that constructs the external body. As a metaphor, one might think of this as literally transforming the sensitive interior into the rough exterior.
44. Franz Fanon, *Black Skins, White Masks*, (New York: Grove Press, 1967), 14.
45. Sandra Lee Bartky, *Femininity and Domination: Studies in the Phenomenology of Oppression* (New York: Routledge, 1990), 23.
46. I conceptually borrowed the literalizing of a productive myth from Judith Butler's *Gender Trouble*. See p. 89.
47. Bartky, *Femininity and Domination*, 85.
48. Although it should be noted that most of the prisoners whose moral lives will be considered entered the camps as fully morally mature adults. Morality under totalizing systemic oppression where the individuals where raised under the regime, might change the models we have to work with. It should also be noted, that perhaps this is a good working model for LGBT/Q people, given our exit from heterosexual privilege in our adult years, while this might be a more problematic model for other identity markers such as race and gender.
49. For Levi a grey zone is the moral space in Nazi concentration camps and ghettos occupied by prisoners in positions of responsibility and administration.
50. Claudia Card, "Groping Through Moral Grey Zones," *On Feminist Ethics and Politics* (Lawrence: University of Kansas Press, 1999), 3.
51. Card, "Groping Through Moral Grey Zones," 9.
52. As of the end of 2011, with two additional African countries proposing the death penalty: Uganda and Liberia.
53. Card, "Groping Through Moral Grey Zones," 14.
54. An example here would be women, who in regions of Africa and the Middle East perform clitoridectomies on girls and other women.
55. Card, "Groping Through Moral Gray Zones," 7.
56. Card, "Groping Through Moral Gray Zones," 9.
57. Card, "Groping Through Moral Gray Zones," 3-4.
58. It seems problematic to attribute "evil" to an ideological structure and regime of power with the human origins out of sight. Religious thinking participates in this abstraction of evil. I wish to leave this as an open question for now, but does it make sense to use a humanistic concept, namely evil, and apply it to an intellectual concept?
59. Tzvetan Todorov, *Facing the Extreme*, (New York: Henry Holt and Company, 1996), 90.
60. Ann Cudd, *Analyzing Oppression*, (Oxford: Oxford University Press, 2006), 199.

61. Caring is the most unambiguously definable virtue in terms of our relationships with others. Dignity and intellectualism, particularly in moral grey zones outside of the camps, demonstrate a commitment to the enhancement of an oppressed identity that can be understood in terms of our relationships with others, even if the virtues are primarily a commitment to self.

62. Cudd, *Analyzing Oppression*, 13.
63. Cudd, *Analyzing Oppression*, 15.
64. Cudd, *Analyzing Oppression*, 19.
65. Cudd, *Analyzing Oppression*, 15.
66. Elena Loizidou, *Judith Butler: Ethics, Law, Politics* (New York: Routledge, 2007), 46.
67. In the Physics and the Metaphysics. Loizidou, *Judith Butler: Ethics, Law, Politics,* 47.
68. Loizidou, *Judith Butler: Ethics, Law, Politics,* 46.
69. Vikki Bell, *Culture and Performance: the Challenge of Ethics, Politics, and Feminist Theory* (New York: Berg, 2007), 114.
70. Loizidou, *Judith Butler,* 77.
71. Loizidou, *Judith Butler,* 82-3.
72. Bell, *Culture and Performance,* 28.
73. Judith Butler, *Precarious Life: The Powers of Mourning and Violence,* (London and New York: Verso, 2004), 130.
74. Carolyn Dean, "The 'Open Secret,' Affect, and the History of Sexuality," in *Sexuality at the Fin de Siecle: The Makings of a Central Problem,* ed. Peter Cryle and Christopher Forth (Newark, NJ: University of Delware Press, 2008), 121-2.
75. Bell, *Culture and Performance,* 25.
76. James Holstein and Jaber Gubrium, *The Self We Live By: Narrative Identity in a Postmodern World* (New York: Oxford University Press, 2000), 4.
77. Holstein and Gubrium, *The Self We Live By,* 58-60.
78. Holstein and Gubrium, *The Self We Live By,* 57.
79. Holstein and Gubrium, *The Self We Live By,* 63.
80. Holstein and Gubrium, *The Self We Live By,* 69.
81. Holstein and Gubrium, *The Self We Live By,* 70.
82. Olav Bryant Smith, *Myths of the Self: Narrative Identity and Postmodern Metaphysics* (Lanham: Lexington Books, 2004), 1.
83. Holstein and Gubrium, *The Self We Live By,* 11.
84. Holstein and Gubrium, *The Self We Live By,* 12.
85. Holstein and Gubrium, *The Self We Live By,* 222.
86. Smith, *Myths of the Self,* 177.

Chapter 3
Thoughtfully Produced Sexuality:
Sexology and the Queer Academy

To claim that someone is passing in relation to his/her sexual identity, we must also be able to claim something substantive about sexual desire as constituting an identity. The contours of sexuality and its import into identity have different valences along gender lines. To be male and to have non-normative sexual desires is socially and politically different that to be female and have non-normative sexual desires. The question of sexual identity is historically embedded. The socio-political sexual identities that have developed in the post-Stonewall Era are significantly different that those arising before 1969 but after the mid-1860's and the rise of sexology and psychoanalysis. And of course there are significant trajectories of sexuality and identity across cultural boundaries and also prior to the 1860's in the Western world. My discussion of both sexual identity passing and sexuality as a style (in chapter 4) and an identity will focus on the modern manifestation of sexuality in the post-Stonewall era. The discussion, however, will weave in considerations of past eras of theorizing about sexual identity.

The etiology of sexual orientation remains unknown. There is scientific research and inquiries into biological factors such as genes, prenatal hormones, and brain structures. No conclusive biological cause has been found to date. There are a significant number of modern studies into the psycho-social elements of sexual orientation, including numerous studies into and theories of the personal development of a sexual identity. There are cultural studies into the predictable patterns of behavior found in the gay community. There have been empirical studies of sexual behavior. There is a historically peculiar science known as sexology that has sought out to identify and name sexual deviance creating the basis for our modern categories of sexual identity. There have been intellectual critiques that have sought to critically examine the thoughts and assumptions present in our modern sexual identities.

This chapter will discuss a sampling of the classic theories of sexuality alongside some of the (post)modern intellectual critiques associated with theories of sexuality, identity, and deviance. After both a discussion of the classic models of sexuality and the intellectual critiques of sexuality (queer theory) I pause to discuss the ethical implications or associations relevant to each.

Classic to Modern Theories of Sexual Identity

Our modern intellectual history regarding homosexuality and sexual "deviance" began in the late 19th century. Sexology was beginning to gain popularity as a science, and researches such as Richard Von Krafft-Ebing (1840-1902) and Dr. James Kiernan (who worked on questions of sexuality in the 1880's and 1890's) began to catalog and study "perversions" and homosexuality; both employed the term "heterosexual" in different ways, heralding the start of heterosexuality as an identity. Other major early figures include Karl Heinrich Ulrichs (1825-1895, who is considered a pioneer of early gay rights), and of course Sigmund Freud (1856-1939).

A common theme of sexuality studies towards the end of the 19th century is the medical categorization of bodies into categories of deviants. Carolyn Dean has argued that this time period could be described as a "medicalization of sinfulness."[1] Richard Von Krafft-Ebing's book *Psychopathia Sexualis* (1886) is a 436-page text categorizing what he thought to be an exhaustive list of the "perversions" of human sexuality, some of which he considered to be biological anomalies, and some of which were considered acquired anomalies. All were defined in terms of their deviation from a procreative sexual instinct. The word "homosexuality" was already in use at this time, having made its first public appearance in Germany in 1869 in a pamphlet against anti-sodomy laws published anonymously by Karl-Maria Kerbeny.[2] By the time the term was employed by Krafft-Ebing, the term homosexuality clearly referred to same-sex sexual behavior and attractions. The behaviors and attractions were being associated with a type of person, a deficient human subject. This identification of a perversion with a type of person began to spur conversations about the social function of these individuals. Were they to be viewed as a social menace, or as something to be humanely tolerated?[3] Tolerance began to mark the bodies of these perverts as unnatural and Carolyn Dean argues, allowed the "benevolent profession" of sexology to consider the fate of the homosexual or the invert as "pathetically distinct from that of the majority." This rhetoric of tolerance, she argues, became the way in which sexual identity was formed around the turn of the century, with certain types of sexual persons receiving favor over others, and the creation of what she calls the "open secret" of homosexuality where the behavior was known to exist, but the intimate lives of these individuals were expected to be kept private, rendering a class of people into a place of isolation, loneliness, and shame.[4]

The identity of heterosexuality had a more complicated beginning. Historians of sexual identity will be quick to remind you that the identity of homosexuality was invented *before* the invention of the identity of heterosexuality. Prior to the late 1800's, the dominant thought surrounding sexual behavior privileged reproductive behavior as moral with all other types of behavior as immoral. After the invention of the homosexuality as an identity and the significant efforts of sexology to understand the contours of sexuality; opposite-sex sexual desire that privileged—but did not exclusively expect—procreation became not only the definition of natural sexual development, but the types of persons who developed these opposite-sex sexual urges began to be understood as the healthiest of citizens, the ones who are natural and worthy of moral and psychological respect. Sigmund Freud, in his *Three Essays on the Theory of Sexuality*, had a strong influence in developing the contours of healthy psycho-social development, mostly through his work establishing the pathologies that could arise along the way to healthy psycho-social development.

The word "heterosexual" made its very first public debut in Germany in 1880 in a work defending homosexuality. In 1892 it appeared in an article by Chicagoan Dr. James G. Kiernan, for the first time in the United States. Dr. Kiernan originally used the term to mean a kind of "psychical hermaphroditism": a mental condition where a patient exhibited both male erotic attractions to females and female erotic attractions to males. What we would now think of as bisexuality. After a bit of time and some debate, the word settled into its modern day meaning of opposite-sex sexual desire.[5] Especially given the work of Freud and other sexologists, heterosexuality began to be seen as a healthy developmental possibility for all persons, which gave rise to a fear of rooting out homosexuality. Heterosexuality became normative.[6]

So before we assume that the identity of heterosexuality has always been around (because humans have always been procreating), and that its normative elements have always been celebrated as institutional and ethically normative, it is important to slow down and recognize that heterosexuality as an identity and class of persons is only just more than one hundred years old. It is now a positive identity encouraged by the medical profession and the state, and if we note how widespread it is advertised in our schools, media, religious, and public institutions, we might be able to clearly understand Wilkerson's argument: "If anything is obviously socially constructed, it would be heterosexuality since the pressure to be straight is everywhere."[7]

After the construction of heterosexual and homosexual identities, people began to theorize about what it means to be a homosexual. Originally there were concerns about how heterosexuality masked on to homosexuality. For example, sexually aggressive males were often contrasted with sexually indifferent females. So in a same-sex pair bonding, the only way that two individuals of the same sex could "recreate" this pair bonding would be if one of the women showed markedly masculine attributes and if one of the men showed markedly feminine attributes. The only homosexual, then, would be the masculine woman who desired sex with a normal woman, and the effeminate man who received the sexual advances of a masculine man. These distinctions still remain in other countries—Mexico, for instance, is only concerned with the male homosexuality of an effeminate "bottom"; as well as in the study of sexuality in other mammals—the only gay rat, for example, in a same-sex female pairing is the female rat who does the mounting.[8]

After 1950

Up to the 1950's, the struggle over homosexual identity remained mired in questions of psychological and biological health.[9] But, as progressive intellectuals began to take up the idea of sexual identity, positive critiques began to be produced, and the pathologizing efforts of the medical and psychological professions began to fade, which allowed the modern era of identity politics to bloom in full force by the end of the 1960's. The rest of this section will highlight some of the important intellectual and philosophical writing that has happened in regards to sexual identity as well as some of the psychological theories that began to support homosexuality as an identity that could provide a person with a sense of integration and actualization. More importantly, theories about homosexuality began to be produced by homosexuals and other varieties of sexual "deviants."

Intellectual Critiques

In 1949, Simone de Beauvoir published *The Second Sex*. She began her chapter on lesbians by calling to mind the stereotypical image of a lesbian as a woman who wears mannish clothes and has a rough demeanor. She discounts this stereotype and seeks to normalize the lesbian in terms of the life of most women. She argues that the attraction to males is one laden in fear for most women: "every adolescent female fears penetration and masculine domination" but the lesbian takes this fear further as "she feels a certain repulsion for the male body."[10] She states that due to the adolescent experiences of a female, "it is perfectly natural for the future woman to feel indignant at the limitations imposed upon her by her sex."[11] She argues that the lesbian also displays acceptance of femininity through the desire of another woman, and that the more masculine characteristics are outward expressions that help to counter-balance the intimate feminine nature of her erotic life.[12] Beauvoir writes about lesbian sex with a positive poetic tone:

> between women love is contemplative; caresses are intended less to gain possession of the other than gradually to re-create the self through her; separateness is abolished, there is no struggle, no victory, no defeat; in exact reciprocity

each is at once subject and object, sovereign and slave; duality becomes mutuality.[13]

She attributes the mutuality and freedom of lesbian sexuality as the causal factor for the number of female artists and writers who choose the lifestyle.[14] Simone de Beauvior presented the lesbian life from the standpoint of a bisexual woman.

Approximately thirty years later, another feminist thinker, Adrienne Rich addressed the issue of lesbianism. This time, however, the perspective is that of a lesbian and the framework seeks to critique the very structure of society: namely its compulsory heterosexuality. Rich's major complaint is with the feminist literature available. By the time Rich was writing (the early 80's), second wave feminism was under full swing, book after book was being published on women's experiences in modern society, but:

> in none of them is the question ever raised, whether in a different context, or other things being equal, women would *choose* heterosexual coupling and marriage; heterosexuality is presumed as a "sexual preference" of "most women," either implicitly or explicitly. In none of these books, which concern themselves with mothering, sex roles, relationship, and societal prescriptions for women, is compulsory heterosexuality ever examined as an institution powerfully affecting all these.[15]

Rather than positively exclaiming the power of lesbian relationships in undermining the patriarchy, Rich focuses her gaze on heterosexual women, asking why they cannot see through the ubiquitous power of heterosexual society. There is a shift from an analysis of the individual woman who identifies as a lesbian, to a critical deconstruction of the external forces that keep many more women from identifying as lesbian.

As second wave feminism subsided and the third wave began its rush towards the academy, the critical gaze turned almost solely on the socio-culture pressures that create not only sexuality, but also gender. Third wave feminism, with its postmodern influences and overtones, calls into question every assumption about the naturalness of heterosexuality and femininity. Within the discipline of philosophy Judith Butler remains the most prominent postmodern feminist theorist.

In "Melancholy Gender/Refused Identification" Judith Butler hypothesizes about the formation of gender within a culture that only allows for expressions of heterosexual desire. The inter-psychic forces that create a personal sense of gender identity are internalized from our interactions with those around us. Butler appropriates the Freudian notion of melancholy (as a sense of sadness over something which can not be grieved) to explain how this internalization works. In a heterocentric/homophobic society, we are only socially sanctioned in our intense attachments with people of the opposite sex. When we lose attachments to people of similar gender, the social structure we find ourselves in does not support grieving out the pain of those attachments. This is what Butler calls the "never-never" structure of modern society, the idea is that when we lose a close attachment to someone of our own gender we deny that the attachment was ever really there. In other words, we find ourselves saying "I never loved her, I never lost her." But the residue of that loss is still present. This residue, Butler claims, is what creates our gender identity. Rather than mourning the loss of the individual, we appropriate some of her character traits. Our entire sense of gender identity is the remnants of losses of others of our own gender.

Within psychoanalysis, Freud began theorizing about homosexuality in terms of stunted development, inverted desire, and psychological malfunction. As psychoanalysis has developed over the last hundred years through the work of Jacques Lacan, the focus on the structure of the psyche has shifted to a focus on language and the way it mirrors the unconscious. For Lacanian psychoanalysis, sexuality and gender are questions of language.[16] Not surprisingly, feminist thinkers have undertaken numerous critiques of psychoanalysis, both Freudian and Lacanian. Lesbian feminists see psychoanalysis as "culturally linked to phallocentrism and patriarchy, [it] is . . . the Law that defines and oppresses lesbians."[17] When undertaking a critique of Lacanian psychoanalysts, feminists turn to the nature of language itself, its control and structuring by men, and seek to theorize about what a female language would look like. Psychoanalysis has often focused on the causes of homosexuality. It is worth asking why psychoanalysis has spent so much time looking at the causes of homosexuality, rather than looking at why society harbors so much fear, anxiety, and hatred towards homosexuals.[18]

In his book length essay "What Do Gay Men Want," gay historian David Halperin argues that the inner worlds (the subjectivities) of gay men (and lesbians) have occupied a negligent position in modern conversations regarding LGBT/Q identity politics. He outlines a historical relationship between sexuality and psychology/psychoanalysis that demonstrates a need for disdain of subjective exploration from a community that has been medicalized and pathologized. Halperin explains,

> In the wake of more than a century of medical and forensic treatment of homosexuality as a psychiatric pathology or aberration, lesbians and gay men of the post-Stonewall era directed much political effort to undoing the presumption that there was something fundamentally wrong with us.[19]

He argues that in order to establish itself as a respectable community worthy of ethnic or racial minority style rights, the LGBT/Q community had to distance itself from articulating its subjectivities both to escape the charge of sickness and to make gay people appear as much like straight people as possible thereby reducing fear and otherness. So, in the post-Stonewall era of LGBT/Q politics, to be gay was not to participate in or display any kind of subjectivity, rather it was based on the membership within a certain social group. The political efficacy of this move means that homosexuality no longer refers to an "individual abnormality but [rather] to a collective *identity*."[20] This shifts the understanding of homosexuality from a "psychological disorder" into a "social disqualification". Now the socio-political move is to grapple for group rights that are justice based in light of social ostracism, genocidal oppression, social hostility, irrational and intense prejudice, and unjustified discrimination.[21] This "foregrounding [of] gay identity and backgrounding [of] gay subjectivity" has had political efficacies in ways that any LGBT/Q activist must pause to appreciate.

The difficulty remains, on the other side of Stonewall, of how to find ways to articulate queer subjectivities without finding ourselves once again embedded in the psychological language of sickness and abnormality. Halperin suggests that we could look at the literature of gay men at the time of the rise of psychology and psychoanalysis. Examples include Walter Pater, Oscar Wilde, Andre Gide, Marcel Proust, Jean Genet, and Roland Barthes. The exploration of subjectivity in their works explore the psyches of gay men without the condemning rhetoric of psychoanalysis. A primary concept that he zeros in on is "abjection." Abjection, in this context, signifies a kind of "pleasure in being the lowest of the low, in being bad, in being outlaws, in betraying both our own values and those of the people around us."[22] For Julia Kristeva an early theorist of abjection, who wrote a book on the subject: *Powers of Horror*, argued that it is

> a kind of splitting or crisis in the self, whereby one violently casts out of the self something that is so much a part of the self that one can never succeed in getting rid of it . . . The abject is neither subject nor object, but something of one's own for which one feels horror and revulsion, as if it were unclean, filthy, rotten, disgusting, spoiled, impure.

It seems difficult to interpret, or find the space for pleasure in abjection with a description of the phenomenon as something inherently opposed to the integration of the subject. But this paradoxical relationship to the abject is exactly the defining quality that makes it constitutive of gay (and particularly gay male) subjectivity. Halperin argues,

> homosexuality itself can be a perennial source of abjection for some gay men, a source of horror and revulsion, because it is universally abominated, considered abnormal and perverted, and some gay men take those judgments against homosexuality to heart from a young age. Indeed, even to recognize oneself as being named, described, and summed up by the clinical term *homosexual* (or *faggot* or *queer*) is to come to self-awareness and to recognition of social condemnation at the very same instant . . . Gay subjectivity is divided against itself, formed in stigma, in rejection by others—especially by those whom one desires—and by oneself. ***Our very loves and pleasures are causes of irredeemable shame in our social experience of them. In the era of gay pride, moreover, such shame is occasion for further shame.*** This is what Warner meant when he referred to abjection as our "dirty secret."[23]

The double aspect of abjection, which resides as a force within us, is a product of the social stigmas that by necessity we must inhabit. The internal state is not one of psychic disrepair, or agent centered damage, it is the healthy result of unhealthy circumstances, and despite our politically savvy attempts to overcome the social stigma, our subjectivities remain caught up in its residue, or in what Halperin calls "the annihilating experience of exclusion from the world of decent people."[24] This isn't the end of the story of abjection, however.

Abjection can also have a transformative aspect to it. Jean Genet, a French gay male literary figure in the mid-20th century, argued that abjection can transform its most incriminated subjects into figures of saintly stoicism. Genet argues,

> In the unpredictable course of its efforts to abject the pariah, society suddenly loses its annihilating power over its victim; his fear and horror are turned into resistance, even into desire.[25]

For Genet, the overpowering force of abjection with its moral abasement can result in exaltation, a feeling of social transcendence, and "subjective escape from persecution." There is an internal shift where the judgment and condemnation can no longer be internalized. The recognized and accepted erotic source of abjection within becomes the spiritual fuel for transformation. This is not to say that all individuals will transcend the degrading influence of abjection to reach greater virtuous heights, but the suggestion remains that one healthy alternative in the subjective response to the social stigma of sexual abjection is a transforming freedom of its isolating pressures.[26] Halperin begins to call this the "paradox of abjection":

> The more people despise you, the less you owe them, and the freer and more powerful you are. The contempt in which you are held, and the isolation it imposes, also open up rare but precious opportunities for love and solidarity among the outcast. The social drama of abjection . . . consists in its amplification of the individual's importance—in the way it endows him with an inverted glamour, an antisocial prestige. Contempt is the price of publicity, the trade-off for personal transfiguration. Abjection registers the paradox of social violence, with both degrades and glorifies.[27]

The essay by Halperin is an extended analysis of a shorter piece of writing by academic and political scholar Michael Warner on risky sex and the HIV/AIDS epidemic in the gay male community. So the search for an intervention into the internal workings of gay men, their desires, their drives has already been framed by a question of why do gay men have risky sex, which contains a problematic and inherent assumption that there is something wrong with gay men. He is looking for a way to discuss and reflect on queer subjectivities without resorting to psychology or psychoanalysis; an account of gay [male] subjectivity that is "neither individualizing nor psychically empty, neither normalizing nor politically defensive."[28] The concept of "abjection" is the primary resource that he uses to argue such a model. While he doesn't think it is necessarily the only answer to the problem, he does think it is one potentially fruitful way of thinking through it. In his essay Warner argues that "abjection continues to be our [gay men's] dirty secret."

It is also important to note that since the 1980's HIV and AIDS have also had an important influence on the collective identity of the (particularly male) gay community. Michael Warner argues that "positive men have developed a culture of articulacy about mortality and the expectations of 'normal life.'" In addition the pace of their lives are heightened and their humor mordant.[29] The socio-political impact of AIDS on the gay community cannot be overstated. While I won't pursue such an analysis here, I acknowledge a significant deficit in recounting the intellectual and socio-political history of the LGBT/Q community by only giving it a brief mention.

Psychological Theories

When the academy began to theorize about sexuality, gender was considered to be dichotomous: male *or* female, and sexual attraction was considered unchanging: healthy if directed towards the opposite gender, and unhealthy if directed towards the same.[30] The first major change in this dichotomous thinking was the Kinsey model (1948), which developed sexuality theory along a seven point scale—on one end falls the pure heterosexual, on the other the pure homosexual. Most individuals fall somewhere in between.[31] The Kinsey model was an attempt to break away from the heterosexual/homosexual distinction and evidence that same-sex desire is natural and common amongst most people. Also interestingly, Kinsey found a way to once again talk about sexual behavior without the burden of identity. His studies focused on questions of arousal and orgasm of individuals and ignored relational terms like affection or marriage. And so he studied sexuality as a phenomenon of persons; not as a phenomenon that is produced or developed within human relationships.[32] But this new type of sexology did not take hold in the medical or particularly in the psychological communities. Instead the new way for psychologists to talk positively about same-sex desire was to embed it more deeply into identity and then to theorize about how those identities form in healthy and unhealthy ways.

Vivienne Cass was one psychologist to produce a popular stage model of sexual identity development. She developed six-stages to explain gay identity development. The six stages are as follows:

1. Identity Confusion: homosexual thoughts, feelings and attractions emerge, which can lead to both anxiety and confusion.

2. Identity Comparison: there is acknowledgment of some aspect of possible LGBT/Q identity. This leads to feelings of isolation from family and friends and possible seeking of other LGBT/Q individuals.

3. Identity Tolerance: The acknowledgement of stage two is solidified and the individual begins to actively seek out socialization with other LGBT/Q individuals.

4. Identity Acceptance. Deeper friendships are formed with other LGBT/Q individuals. Public identity at this stage may be either heterosexual or homosexual, but private identity is established as the latter.
5. Identity Pride. This is a political stage. Anger is felt at non-gay individuals and issues.
6. Identity Synthesis. Being gay is seen as one aspect of one's identity and not all encompassing.

Cass' Model offers an explanation of the shifting and unstable nature of sexual identity. Its six stages suggest a uni-dimensional development. But she did not think that identity development moved neatly from one stage to the next. The process of coming to terms with one's sexual identity could mean that two steps forward might sometimes include one step back; and at other times a devastating romantic loss might throw someone all the way back to stage one.

Based on his clinical work with gay men, Alan Dowds argues for a three-stage model of identity development.[33] Stage one is characterized by a sense of feeling overwhelmed by shame. In this stage life is lived in an attempt to deny or hide one's sexual orientation in order to hinder the overt shame that society inflicts. Damaging and traumatizing relationships are common in this stage, as well as what Dowds identifies as "psychological splitting" where the individual separates and compartmentalizes his personality based on the sphere he finds himself in (work-sphere vs. family sphere vs. friendship sphere). Stage two is characterized by compensating for shame. Dowd associates this stage with the stereotypes of the out gay man, where extensive effort is expended to maintain high praise and lead a fabulous lifestyle. Dowd argues that this stage is directed at receiving continual social validation for financial accomplishments, home décor, physical beauty, career achievements, and sexual prowess. All of these accomplishments, however, receive inauthentic validation because they are motivated by a hindrance and covering of shame. Relationships in this stage can be unstable, because the slightest invalidation by a partner unleashes the buried shame. Stage three is characterized by cultivating authenticity. Not all gay men reach this stage of development, some Dowds argues, remain in stage one or two for their entire adult lives. In stage three, gay men directly confront the shame they have internalized from society and work through the emotional wounds and self-esteem issues the social shaming has caused. Often stage three involves a reassessment of career choices, relationships (friendships and romantic), and behaviors that inhibit achievement of genuine joy. It is worth noting that Dowds three-stage model coheres with but is a simplified version of other stage models of sexual identity development. In his clinical work, Dowds only deals with gay men, and for this reason declares his three stage model to be exclusively in description of the gay male experience but still applicable to the gay female experience. The most notable aspect of his three-stage model is its focus on the emotional, psychological, and political aspects of shame.

Not all psychological theories about sexual identity development are in the form of a stage model. Anthony D'Augelli developed what he calls a "Lifespan

Model" which he says is a fluid holistic life long process of identity development that involves five recognizable behaviors and are interwoven together, and can occur at different and multiple times. These behaviors are: exiting a heterosexual identity, developing a personal LGBT/Q identity status, becoming an LGBT/Q offspring, developing an LGBT/Q intimacy status, and entering an LGBT/Q community.

Finally, there do continue to be sex researchers who approach sexuality on a more complicated grid. Ritz Klein for example, used seven variables on grid to measure sexuality: sexual attraction, sexual behavior, sexual fantasies, emotional preference, social preference, self-identification, hetero/homo lifestyle; all of which are superimposed on a time scale (past, present, future).[34] This kind of approach to sexuality mirrors the Kinsey approach, thinking of sexuality as an attribute of an individual, rather than a product of society, or as an identity to be achieved. It is hard to contest, however, looking at our modern state of sexual politics that questions of identity are still at the center of a complicated political and ethical debate.

Queer Theory as Identity

Recent scholarly literature and intellectual analysis of sexual identity—queer theory—centers on the socially constructed aspects of both gender and sexuality, exposing the mechanisms of production and critically examining assumptions of gender or sexuality as essentially present in the core of each individual. This theoretical rhetoric has focused on the production of discourses that have turned sexual acts into sexual identities, examining the influences of power and institutional forces, and thinking through (or around) the political implications of utilizing destabilized concepts of gender/sex identities. The body of literature that can be referred to as queer theory was originally founded by Judith Butler, Teresa de Laurentis, and the recently deceased Eve Kosofsky Sedgwick with strong influences by Michel Foucault (who it can easily be argued created the intellectual roots of possibility for queer theory).

The phrase 'queer theory' was introduced by Laurentis, a feminist film theorist, in 1991. She employed the phrase to describe her intellectual work as something that allows space for the voices of women and desire in a system of language that is patriarchal in a culture that signifies women as object rather than subjects of desire.[35] She liked the word 'queer' as something that indicated an open and undecided definition of identity, she thought it left room in sexual identity definitions for other markers of self: things like class, age, race, or anything else.[36] This was the beginning of the use of the phrase, but the body of literature has grown to signify an analytic model of inquiry into the unstable relationships between chromosomal sex, sexual desire, and gender. The primary mode of inquiry (or primary tool of questioning broad based cultural assumptions about the relationship of sexed bodies to desire and gender identity) is the use of genealogy. The starting point for much of the inquiry is in the experience and social realities of gay, lesbian, bisexual and transgendered people; although, it is presumed from the onset that these identity markers are themselves unfinished and unstable. The term "queer" is to be "a means for enabling and describing certain political and discursive conjunctions without relying on the assumptions of a settled definition or identity."[37] But the allowance for a political conjunction between queer theory as identity and rights-based discourse becomes tenuous, we will see, insofar as the conceptual work of queer theory is at odds with the political clout it would need to employ under modern liberalism to provide us with a foundation for a libratory politic.

The basic intellectual approach within queer theory is the genealogical deconstructive investigation into foundational concepts that become the foothold for gender and sex discrimination or more broadly for the complex hegemonic matrix known as heterosexuality. The investigation turns a keen critical eye to the historical development of the concepts and the political assumptions that are imported with the concepts' development. So, for example, a queer theorist might ask about a concept like "matter" (this is a concept that Judith Butler explored). S/he might ask how the ancient Greeks thought about matter (they privileged masculinity in its investigation), and demonstrate how the concept has developed into the modern era to create disparities of power amongst identities and individuals.

The term was selected as a rhetorical gesture meant to hold ground against institutions of identity dissemination based on categories and binary demarcations between particular opposing subject locations: e.g., gay/straight, male/female, etc. The resistance of queer theory to the institutions of identity politics was not so much directed at the expected white patriarchal institutions, but instead aimed at the limitations of feminism and the lesbian and gay political movement. At the same time, many of the conceptual roots can be traced back to feminist scholarship much more so than lesbian and gay scholarship. The most basic turn against these two camps of liberationist and identity consciousness raising camps is in their assumption of rational, dispassionate categories of identity.[38] The idea is that when these communities unite under the rubric of a shared identity for political results there are "inevitably, if inadvertently" a sense of "exclusion, delegitimation, and a false sense of universality"[39] for those that lie on the boundaries and peripheries. So queer theory becomes focused on the historical and institutional production of identity with two particular regimes of Western discourse fully in view: knowledge and power. Common questions become: "how have the intellectual pursuits of science and psychology pathologized and medicalized sexual identity and sexual orientation to produce subjects under its purview? How has the wielding of institutionalized distributions of power found its installations among subjects? The over-arching thought is that these investigations will be ultimately more libratory than seeking greater distribution of rights or goods to minoritized stable identities under our modern democracies. 'Queer,' under this type of libratory hope, becomes a beacon of the future without directly signifying something specific or direct on the horizon, and without the reliance on false universals constructed through suspect and insidious hidden forces it also turns the tables for the discomfit individuals by specifying that the problems lie within the categories available, not within the persons unable to fit those categories.

The most substantive question for queer theory is how sexuality and gender operate in the lives of persons. The second most substantive question pertains to how to describe sexuality and gender within personhood more generally. Psychoanalysis becomes a particularly wrought source of theoretical debate because it is both the primary tool of explication as well as a source of genealogical suspicion.[40]

Queer theory, as with psychoanalysis and feminism, seeks to revise the western philosophical ideal of humans as fully rational subjects to occupy the starting position of philosophical analysis and political theorizing. Instead the intellectual move is to look at subjects of philosophical inquiry as embedded in cultural and historical locations with the hope that queer theory will neither reproduce a universalized location in queerness or create new "disciplinary requirements for conformity."[41] But, of course the difficulty has become that queer theory has established itself as a recognizable mode of intellectual inquiry with a certain kind of methodological position of analyzing both gender and sexuality. The recognizable nature of the intellectual endeavor encouraged Teresa de Laurentis, the coiner of the term, to abandon it just three years after its inception because it lost its radical deconstructive quality due to its recognizability.[42]

Problems for Identity

The easiest target for queer theorists in their analysis of identity interpellation is the binary structure of identity category pairs: male/female, black/white, gay/straight. The idea of a simple either/or structural system of identity that can in theory contain all persons is under immediate suspicion. But a radical alternative, in which categories of identity are not employed to delineate any recognizable set of character qualities is also an untenable solution. It is the difference between identities that allows for the categories to solidify their boundaries. So, identity functions in such a way that it depends on both repetition and commonalities and also emerges from difference.[43] Of particular interest to queer theorists is how power is distributed among persons as well as how certain identities require an abjection of other identities.[44] The process of abjection of another identity means that the pride and satisfaction in one's identity is partially (or entirely) dependent on treating another identity as repulsive and by definition oppositional and worthy of expulsion from the self. Examples of this kind of abject relationship between two oppositional identities might include: abortion doctors and pro-life activists, anti-gay demonstrators and gay activists.

Additional questions about sexual identity and power look into the potential results of a scientific discovery about the etiology of sexual orientation. Inquiries of this type expose the inherent biases and potential abuses of power that could easily arise, demonstrating the relevance of questions of power, ethics, and abjection in relation to sexual identity. For example, if a gene for sexual orientation were found, how would that piece of "scientific evidence" be wielded amongst queer-identified people? Would there be a screening process that demanded queer children be aborted? Would straight-acting genetically gay people be forced to act gay? Would sexual orientation become a medical condition established at birth? What about people who have lived their lives as queer only to discover that they don't have the gene? If queer identity were something that was "rationalized" through medical discourse, what impact would this have on our sexual subjectivities? William Turner argues that to ask these kinds of questions "entails placing the entire epistemological ethical edifice of Western culture under question. That edifice rests on the assumption that universality and rationality will typically serve the needs of justice."[45] These are exactly the kinds of investigations queer theorists are interested in undertaking because in the counter perspective it can provide us to the major cultural trends and themes we've been taught to trust and invest in. It helps us to deconstruct the edifices of Western modernity through critical examination of sexual subjectivity.

The difficulty is, of course, that queer theory cannot fall into the trap of rectifying its own edifice, which it has been argued other kinds of identity based sexual politics have done. "Queer," therefore, must maintain constant room for flux and ambiguity, so in this regard the gesture towards a queer identity becomes the gesture towards a non-identity. Annemarie Jagose argues,

> queer may be thought of as activating an identity politics so attuned to the constraining effects of naming, of delineating a foundational category which precedes and underwrites political intervention, that it may better be understood as promoting a non-identity or even anti-identity politics. If a potentially infinite coalition of sexual identities, practice, discourses, and sites might be identified as queer, what it betokens is not so much liberal pluralism as a negotiation of the very concept of identity itself.[46]

So even if we might be inclined to view queer theory as a kind of celebrated liberal pluralism, we'd be misguided to view it as such, even if this is how the term operates in contemporary sexual politics. Queer theory, as an academic endeavor, is directed at epistemological re-workings of identity itself. This anti-identity intellectual commitment is also supposed to avoid trapping sexually minoritized individuals in "idealist" liberating practices, that themselves become disciplinary and restrictive. This was Foucault's position on sexual politics: that the employed modes of resistance for sexually oppressed persons, were themselves new oppressive regimes. But this is a political observation. An epistemological observation more in line with the intellectual goals of queer theory might seek to analyze both the genealogy of resistance, its methods, and what it inadvertently includes and employs that runs counter to its explicit libratory goals. Of course even the usage of the term "queer" must lay itself bare to its epistemological roots such that its contours, meanings, possible employments, contextual significations, and political renderings are laid bare with the added understanding that no individual or group of activists or scholars "can unilaterally control the meaning of the term."[47] At the same time, the ambiguous nature of the term frees it to be employed in numerous discussions and locations. And through its negativity creates a "utopic" possibility for its future realization where a full realization remains "impossible."[48]

Queer Theory and Ethics: An Impossible Relationship?

Since the early 1990's, academics who have self-identified as "queer theorists" have shown little interest in ethics. Queer theory has been primarily rooted in epistemology (i.e., asking questions about what constitutes knowledge), with a methodological emphasis on deconstruction. This disregard of ethics may have had both conscious and unconscious political motivations. Remember that the construction of heterosexuality was the construction of an identity of desire that would function as ethically normative. Homosexuals as a category of persons were created as moral degenerates; and their sexual behavior began to dictate much larger concerns about their character as a whole. Queers were not be trusted with children, in positions of public trust, or as religious leaders. And the knowledge that someone was gay might cast such doubt over their entire person, that removal from jobs and other social roles was considered appropriate. Sometimes it still is. So, it is no wonder that a group of theorists who were looking to deconstruct and demonstrate the contingent nature of sexual identity would be skeptical of the discourses and methodologies of ethics across the board. But the avoidance of ethical questions has also had political implications.

In the attempt of queer theorists to circumvent the moralizing of sexuality they have also managed to create an epistemologically-based system of theory that cannot handle any moral questions about passing, for example, or forms of abuse based on sexual identity.

A basic question should arise: is it possible to build an ethic into queer theory? Or alternatively, can we ground an ethic in an identity that queer theory has taught us to be thoroughly socially constructed and deeply problematic? My answer to the first question is no. My answer to the second question is yes and is something that we must do under our modern system of liberalism.

William Turner has argued that queer theory has a paradoxical relationship with liberalism. "Paradoxically," he writes, "queer theory both depends on and critiques the liberalism of the twentieth-century United States."[49] Liberalism tells us that we are all created equal, but the cultural discourses that we deal with on a daily basis clearly demonstrate that many of us are in fact not equal: we are degenerate, we are somehow not fully developed and morally warped subjects. But the very standpoint of judgment from which queer theory begins is that queers are equal; or at least fully formed subjects. Queer theory deconstructs the discourses of degeneracy, while queers under liberalism tell a story about striving to achieve political equality and liberty, the things guaranteed to us by our system of government.[50] At the same time, more than 200 years of history have demonstrated that our system thrives with certain individuals constituting an underclass (socio-economically, or morally).[51] Some have argued that a stable identity always requires an other-ing or abjection of some other kind of identity. And the justification for the abjecting becomes that the other deserves it, through the violation of "universal moral rules." If this is the case, any social system will always involve the exaltation of one identity at the expense of another more lowly one.[52]

Foucault expressed significant doubts about "the political eschatology of liberalism."[53] He argued that any time we adopt any kind of sexual identity we "participate in our own regulation and domination. Claiming our suppressed identities and seeking liberation for ourselves becomes a partial trap in which we merely accept the fate offered by a social organization that that wants to hold all its members in its grip."[54] We are damned to entrapment in a system of regulation and domination if we do; and we are damned to isolation and significant ambiguity about identity if we don't. This line of thinking, taken to it's logical extreme, means that "coming out simply becomes a form of surrender, and all the gains gays and lesbians have made since . . . the 1950's amount to the ever-tightening net of social control."[55] The idea is that no amount of fighting under a liberalist government, while utilizing sexual identity markers like 'lesbian' or 'gay,' will ever get us to the place where we will be free to express ourselves sexually and affectionately without the moralizing effects of the history of sexual identity.

Foucault focuses, as do many queer theorists, on questions of power and discourse regimes. Foucault thinks that the best we can do is to live within our society of power, keeping an "attitude of perpetual suspicion and critique."[56] Well this is exactly what the queer theorists do: they monitor and expose the systems of power and present them under a microscope of critique and suspicion. But what they continue to overlook is the continued psychological and social organizing force of the regimes of sexual identity and moralization. And if our concern is with the moral judgments, shouldn't the sphere of ethics be exactly the location in which we center our efforts in order to combat the discursive oppressors?

The place to start, it seems to me, is to accept the social reality, even if socially constructed, nature of sexual identity.[57] And rather than continuously looking backward to find the contingent roots of our modern restrictive regimes of discourse, we should accept our current social location as it is, enhance what is already there, productively and creatively expand the discourses, and build an ethic of gayness on top of it all. Turner argues that the primary location in which to find our role in all of this is to

> acknowledge that on a daily basis we subject each other, and our students, clients, and patients (especially insofar as we are institutionally and discursively

authorized professionals—teachers, professors, social workers, mental health professionals, physicians, lawyers, ministers, priests) to the normalizing discipline of gender and sexuality . . . and that we should pay attention to those disciplinary practices to make them consistent with our stated political preferences.[58]

I would strongly add to his assertion that our locus of intervention with others should not be only our stated political preferences, but must also be in alignment with our ethics. It is all the more important that we think critically about, create, and re-work our system of ethics, especially given the history of homosexuality as a disease of moral degeneracy. Before arguing for what I think should be the stated and overt aspects of a gay ethic, I'd like to talk more about how to employ style, and particularly gay style as a theory of identity, as the foundation of our ethic.

Notes

1. Carolyn Dean, "The 'Open Secret,' Affect, and the History of Sexuality," in *Sexuality at the Fin de Siecle,* Edited by Cryle and Forth. (Newark: University of Delaware Press, 2008), 156.

2. Anne Fausto-Sterling, "Dueling Dualisms," in *Gender, Sex, and Sexuality,* edited by Abby Ferber et al (New York: Oxford University Press, 2009), 13.

3. Dean, "The 'Open Secret,' Affect, and the History of Sexuality," 156.

4. Dean, "The 'Open Secret,' Affect, and the History of Sexuality," 160-1.

5. Jonathon Katz, *The Invention of Heterosexuality* (New York: Dutton, 1995), 22; Fausto-Sterling, "Dueling Dualisms," 13.

6. Dean, "The 'Open Secret,' Affect, and the History of Sexuality," 164.

7. William Wilkerson, *Ambiguity and Sexuality: A Theory of Sexual Identity* (New York: Palgrave Macmillan, 2007), 149.

8. Fausto-Sterling, "Dueling Dualisms," 13.

9. Lisa Walker, *Looking Like What You Are: Sexual Style, Race, and Lesbian Identity,* 107.

10. Simone de Beauvoir, *The Second Sex,* translated by H.M. Parshley (New York: Vintage, 1989), 407.

11. Beauvoir, *The Second Sex,* 409.

12. Beauvoir, *The Second Sex,* 407; 422.

13. Beauvoir, *The Second Sex,* 421.

14. Beauvoir, *The Second Sex,* 411.

15. Adrienne Rich, "Compulsory Heterosexuality and Lesbian Existence," *Signs: Journal of Women in Culture and Society* 5, no. 4 (1980), 636.

16. Daniel Buccino, "Homosexuality and Psychosis in the Clinic," in *Homosexuality and Psychoanalysis,* edited by Tim Dean and Christopher Lane (Chicago: University of Chicago Press, 2000), 278.

17. Judith Roof, "The Community of Dolphins vs. The Safe Sea of Women: Lesbian Sexuality and Psychosis," in *Homosexuality and Psychoanalysis,* 240-41.

18. Joanna Ryan, "Can Psychoanalysis Understand Homophobia," in *Homosexuality and Psychoanalysis,* 310.

19. David Halperin, *What Do Gay Men Want?: An Essay on Sex, Risk, and Subjectivity* (Ann Arbor: The University of Michigan Press, 2007), 2.
20. Halperin, *What Do Gay Men Want?*, 2.
21. Halperin, *What Do Gay Men Want?*, 2. This list of social consequences of gayness is Halperin's.
22. Halperin, *What Do Gay Men Want?*, 64.
23. Halperin, *What Do Gay Men Want?*, 69. emphasis added. This paradox of shame will be picked up again as a theme in section 5.0.
24. Halperin, *What Do Gay Men Want*, 70.
25. Halperin, *What Do Gay Men Want*, 76.
26. Halperin describes this process: "Fear turns into desire. Humiliation turns into defiance. Abjection discloses a secret grace that saves him from contempt." *What Do Gay Men Want?*, 83. Halperin continues on later to associate this process of abjection with sexual practice: "After all," he writes, "the genius of gay sex—and not only *gay* sex—lies precisely in its ability to transmute otherwise unpleasant experiences of social degradation into experiences of pleasure. That indeed in one of the good things about sex, one of the things sex is good for, and one of the things people cherish about it." *What Do Gay Men Want?*, 86.
27. Halperin, *What Do Gay Men Want?*, 95.
28. Michael Warner, "Unsafe: Why Gay Men are Having Sex," reprinted in Halperin, *What Do Gay Men Want?*, 103.
29. Michael Warner, *The Trouble with Normal: Sex, Politics, and the Ethics of Queer Life* (Cambridge: Harvard University Press, 1999), 35.
30. Margaret Nichols, "Therapy with Bisexual Women: Working on the Edge of Emerging Cultural and Personal Identities," in *Women in Context: Toward a Feminist Reconstruction of Psychotherapy,* edited by M.P. Mirkin (New York: Guilford Press, 1994), 150.
31. Nichols, "Therapy with Bisexual Women," 152.
32. Fausto-Sterling, "Dueling Dualisms," 11.
33. Alan Dowds, *The Velvet Rage* (Cambridge MA: Perseus Books Group), 2005.
34. Fausto-Sterling, "Dueling Dualisms," 11.
35. Fausto-Sterling, "Dueling Dualisms," 5.
36. Fausto-Sterling, "Dueling Dualisms," 133.
37. Fausto-Sterling, "Dueling Dualisms," 30.
38. Fausto-Sterling, "Dueling Dualisms," 5.
39. Annemarie Jagose, "Queer Theory," *Australian Humanities Review*, December 1996, 3.
40. William B. Turner, *A Genealogy of Queer Theory* (Philadelphia: Temple University Press), 108.
41. Turner, *A Genealogy of Queer Theory*, 120.
42. Jagose, "Queer Theory," 2.
43. Turner, *A Genealogy of Queer Theory*, 32.
44. Turner, *A Genealogy of Queer Theory*, 199.
45. Turner, *A Genealogy of Queer Theory*, 184.
46. Jagose, "Queer Theory," 3.
47. Turner, *A Genealogy of Queer Theory*, 123.
48. Jagose, "Queer Theory," 4.
49. Jagose, "Queer Theory," 17.
50. Jagose, "Queer Theory," 196.
51. Jagose, "Queer Theory," 181.

52. Jagose, "Queer Theory," 185.
53. Jagose, "Queer Theory," 181.
54. William Wilkerson, *Ambiguity and Sexuality: A Theory of Sexual Identity* (New York: Palgrave Macmillan 2007), 158.
55. Wilkerson, *Ambiguity and Sexuality*, 162.
56. Wilkerson, *Ambiguity and Sexuality*, 176.
57. I share this insight with William Wilkerson who does a nice job of emphasizing the political reality of sexual identity while making ample room for the insights of postmodernity and queer theory. Wilkerson, *Ambiguity and Sexuality*, 151.
58. Turner, *A Genealogy of Queer Theory*, 190.

Chapter 4
Those Shoes Look Pretty Gay, Or at Least Bi-Curious: *Style and Sexual Identity Passing*

In this chapter I argue for a modified theory of identity—that can capture the complexities of passing—using Maurice Merleau-Ponty's conception of "style" as my foundation. This notion of style is a flexible model of identity that can handle the performance of a passing identity, requires an authentic underlying identity, and can demonstrate a relationship between the two. The hope for "style" is that it intuitively and satisfyingly captures both elements of identity for an individual who is passing, as well as captures something about identity for those of us who are not passing—or who find that they unwittingly pass in certain spaces and at certain times. This constructive theoretical chapter begins with an exploration of the conceptual contours of style. I then compare the notion of style with Butler's performativity and demonstrate style's greater flexibility in relationship to passing and ethics. I conclude with an argument of how sexual identity can be conceived of as a kind of style.

The Concept of Self through Style

The term "style" is one we most readily associate with evaluations of art works, including literature, music, architecture; and in our more common parlance it is a term we associate with personal fashion.[1] The most ordinary and basic definition of the term understands style as dependent upon a distinction of form and matter, where style is characteristic of the former, not the latter.[2] Also known as the distinction between subject and style, style is the how and subject is the what. In the most problematic version of this definition, the substance of the subject is seen as the important or real half of the dichotomy and style is the superficial or dismissed half. This definition of style is inadequate.

Susan Sontag has argued that in a work of art, style is the signature of an artist's will,[3] and that it embodies an "epistemological decision" meaning that the style of a work of art establishes the way the artist wishes to control "how and what we perceive."[4] This kind of willful expression and epistemological decision is the background I want in place for set of arguments and comments I want to make about style. I want to consider what style looks like conceptually if we remove it from the world of art, and think about it as a form of expression, and as part of our very being-in-the-world. The philosopher who I think is most insightful on this is Maurice Merleau-Ponty.

Merleau-Ponty argues that style is a lived and engaged phenomenon. It is usually unrecognizable to the person to whom it belongs in the moment of its expression. It is only recognizable in retrospect and by others. For the person living within style, the expression is implicit: it's inseparable from the way that person sees the world and gestures within it. But this doesn't mean that style is natural, intuitive, or unconscious. Quite the opposite, it is both something that takes considerable time to find but will always have the capacity to develop and evolve. So Merleau-Ponty thinks of style as an "expressive gesture." It is "an extension of the body's basic capacities to intentionally intertwine with the world." All styles, for Merleau-Ponty, represent options because there is no single way that any single person can present him or herself or intertwine with the world around. And this also means that no style can claim itself as having a privileged access to the world as it "really is.'[5]

For Merleau-Ponty, style is "the affective...consequence of being an embodied point of view. Style permeates perception and its objects as the field of lived significance that arises from their intertwining."[6] And when we are experiencing style in something else, style is the thing that requires us to make a perceptual and motor adjustment. We have to adjust our anticipations and needs to the thing in question, especially if that thing is a person, or an object that is for our use. Basically, for Merleau-Ponty, style establishes the parameters of possibility for an object as well as functions as the perceptual aperture through which we are able to identify an object.

Through the concept of style, Merleau-Ponty builds a direct analogy between lived bodies and works of art. He writes, "the lived body is unified by its style in a way analogous to the unification that style effects in paintings." Both the work of art and the body have a coherence of style because both are an "expressive vehicle of a point of view."[7] Importantly, style on a lived body is the correlate of that body having a history, and interestingly style makes other lived bodies accessible through perception. The written history on the lived body of another becomes the way that we can be assured of their consciousness and their trajectory through a set of historical facts and social inhabitation. Much of Western philosophy has concerned itself in asking questions about what has been classically known as "the problem of other minds" or whether or not other people have a consciousness of their own and how we might have access to it. Merleau-Ponty's concept of style asserts that we don't have to go reaching into the far recesses of another's reflections and rationality. Style itself gives us access to the Other's inner world. He writes, "the Other exists, not behind the flow of h[er] activities and gestures, but through them."[8] Style is not a mask, but instead an actual form of existence.

The idea of associating style (corporeal, literary, or narrative) with an identity attempting to find expression under significant oppression is not new. In his introductory essay "Black Orpheus," John Paul Sartre writes about *Negritude*. Negritude refers to the stylized poetic expression by post-colonial (French) black men who are writing the knowledge of their collective souls. Negritude is a "certain quality common"[9] in the attitudes, thoughts, and behaviors of black men dispersed by their oppressors. Sartre speaks in the motifs of a liberation theologian writing "the apostle of the black soul, [will be] the herald who will tear this negritude from himself to offer it to the world."[10] Negritude requires reflection, self-scouring, self-penetration, deep emotional and spiritual work. It can't simply exist on the surface, it has been driven deep by the white hegemony that has colonized more than just the land of black people, but also their minds. Sartre quotes Leopold Senghor as highlighting the style as "the emotional fervor that gives life to the words, which converts the words in speech."[11] This is the musical rhythm of the poetry, its shape, energy, movement and meter. This also does not refer to the technique of the writing, but something much more existential. Sartre draws an analogy with white poetry in the following way:

> Of technique, the white knows all. But this merely scratches the surface of things, it is unaware of the substance, of the life within. Negritude, to the contrary, is a comprehension through sympathy. The secret of the black is that the sources of his existence and the roots of Being are identical.[12]

So it can be seen that the *style* of negritude as represented in the poetics is somewhere between the emotive and spiritual corporeal truths of the ontology of black men and the marked and measured literary meters and tropes of the poetry. Perhaps it resides in the expressive interchange of the two. Negritude as style has a hopeful element to it; it entails a kind of surpassing. Sartre argues "it represents the surpassing of a fixed situation by a free conscience."[13] Again here we can see the motif of liberation theology. Negritude, and its expression can lift one out of fixed oppression; it can provide articulation, connection and escape. Negritude retains the authentic life-giving spirit of a people brutalized under the authority of others, it is style in an essential and ethical quality that maintains strength in identity as community.

Style as Corporeal

Stylized corporeality is constitutive of all subjects. Each of us have an embodied mode, that is socially infused to meet expectations of appearance and social status. Existentialist philosophers and phenomenologists (namely de Beauvoir, Merleau-Ponty, Husserl, and Sartre), have thought about corporeality as a centralizing feature (or situation) for human experience. It is an organizing principle, around which the experience of reality is filtered. Our corporeality is the thing that allows us to interface with and explore the world; and it is a necessary feature of our subjectivity, not something added to or developed in opposition to it. Viewed through the lens of style, it is how we mold and shape our physicality (hair, body type, clothes, make up, skin tone and texture, walk, stance, posture, facial expression) to match up with the image of reception that we wish others to have and maintain in reference to us. But it is also the necessary underpinning for stylistic choices that if ignored can have disastrous political and philosophical consequences.

Phenomenologists have been dedicated to exploring the outcome of their insight that it is only as embodied beings that we can relate to and engage the world. They insist that there can be no separation: "our access to, awareness of, and possibilities for world engagement cannot be considered absent considerations of the body."[14] This means that the body is crucial to every lived experience the human subject has, or will have.[15] This is particularly important for questions of perception. All of our perceptual experiences are first and foremost worldly, embedded in an embodied perspective. Whether conscious of it or not, our perceptions of objects and experiences are grounded in proprioceptive and kinaesthetic awareness. This means that we cannot separate out our perceptual apparatus (our embodied selves) from our perceptions. But this is a good thing. We should not want to be able to do that (for political and philosophical reasons that will be discussed below). This embodied approach to the world, of course, also has its limitations. The often unconscious knowledge of our bodies often means that there are many aspects of our perception that go unnoticed, or uncatalogued.[16] It is also worth calling attention to the fact that individuals can have types of body impairment that can go unnoticed for a significant period of time: a hearing or vision loss, for example.

Our experience of our bodies, as well, cannot be separated from our world engagement. We get to know our bodies through action and experience, through interactions with other bodies and experiences. Gallagher writes "we do not first become aware of the body and subsequently use it to investigate the world [;]

the world is given to us as bodily investigated, and the body is revealed to us in our exploration of the world."[17] As we get to know our bodies through our engagement with the world we begin to develop a tacit awareness of our abilities and our bodies begin to feel like a site of potentiality for mobility, volition, and agency; what Gallagher calls an "I do" and "I can." It is also in our embodiment that we are confronted with the limitations of our agency. If our bodies are moved against our will, say in an (un)intentional shove in a crowded hallway we immediately recognize the loss of agency that we otherwise tacitly feel as we walk freely or move about the world in accordance with our own wills.[18] All of this is to establish a philosophical perspective that my argument about style must be in accordance with; namely, that our corporeality is the centralizing feature of our socio-political and otherwise lived experience and also to demonstrate that the body and the world are entwined with each other. It is not the case that the external world makes imprints on an otherwise passive body. This was one of Merleau-Ponty's key insights.[19] Bodies are subject to power dynamics, and because they are subject to them, they are also capable of perpetuating them. Cahill argues bodies "are deeply enmeshed in social and political forces, [and a]s such they serve as concrete reminders that such familiar philosophical dichotomies as self/society and mind/body are not as hard and fast as most of Western philosophy would have us believe."[20] The centralization of embodiment in our philosophical perspective can have positive implications in addition to its binary deconstructive capabilities. Centralizing the body means the bodily differences are not just viewed as secondary features or accidents, but rather as primary organizing principles of lived experience. This can make a huge difference when we begin to think of politics arising out of the body, as in questions surrounding sexed bodies and gender politics.

Simone de Beauvior particularly honed in on the philosophical and political implication of sexed bodies in her book *The Second Sex*. Primarily, Beauvoir argued that women's equality could only be had while simultaneously recognizing and insisting on the reality of sexual difference.[21] This meant that she was suspicious of both the patriarchal insistence that women should not be considered equal because of their bodies, as well as the insistence on something akin to Plato's proto-feminist argument that women should be freed up from their bodily and reproductive responsibilities so that full equality can be attained.[22] Lived female experience, instead, must be understood as embodied in a particular way that is impacted and influenced by ordinary everyday attitudes and expectations.[23] This recognition of lived female experience also has some corollaries for the politics established by certain philosophical perspectives.

Continental feminists have been quick to point out that the tendency of modern philosophy to marginalize the body is also a tendency to marginalize or simply ignore women. The argument becomes that with the forsaking of bodies that are gendered/sexed, "modern thought successfully wrote women out of its project."[24] But much more importantly, especially in terms of style, the importance of a lived gendered and sexed body is not in its biological differences, but instead in a body that is a "dynamic, fluid, contentious entity, constantly affected by and affecting its own environment. Bodies, from the philosophical perspective, are deeply social and political organisms, marked inherently by history, geography, and a host of other factors."[25] This means that the body is always taking up influence from its surroundings in a particular way. In our modern culture, for female-bodied persons, there is a significant pressure to undertake sometimes costly and painful beautification techniques. While the range of accepted feminine style might be broad, the constant comparisons to a female ideal cannot be overlooked. The continuum of feminine style always has a similar reference point, and each individual woman will find herself along that continuum, although she may well find herself at different points at different times or stages in her life.[26]

The key philosophical point to be taken from this discussion is not so much of how style inheres on bodies, (it does so through a variety of practice habituated so as to have an overall affect of a recognizable identity, whether the element of bodily style has to do with the external superficial affixings to the body: clothing, hairstyle, accessories, or something more central to the body: a walk, posture, gesture; or something biologically given to the body: sex features, skin color, skin texture, etc.) The important philosophical observation from this discussion is that bodies must be viewed as central features of our lived experience, this is what Merleau-Ponty calls a "perpetual faith' in our "inherence in the world:"[27] a guarantee that our perceptual embodied experience, the sense data upon which we rely to navigate our daily lives, is also constitutive of our identity. This kind of model of subjectivity is radically different than the kind of cogito-esque skeptical moves of modernity that seek to find a guarantor of identity and subjectivity removed from the world or through doubting the evidence of our sense embedded in the world.

Style as Narrative

I have already argued that identities—whether authentic or passing—are constructed in part through narratives: meaning-making stories or texts that produce coherence to a series of events to give an overarching impression. Those narratives are significantly influenced by the social forces of power that provide the institutional frameworks, options, and linguistic choices to make and provide meaning. In this section I will talk about the elements of style in narrative, the (historical) connection of style to human character, the role textual style plays in furthering knowledge and rationality (my example will be, appropriately, philosophy), what style is in the context of texts and constructed stories, and finally what style as narrative says directly about identity.

Narrative, Style, and Character

The general colloquial understanding of writing is that certain forms are designed to reveal the character of its author and other forms are meant to hide/to have no relevance to its author's character. Examples of the first type include memoirs, personal essays, and letters to the editors. Examples of the latter include things like software manuals, scientific papers, encyclopedia entries. In some types of textual expression we anticipate that character will be readily at hand. In fiction, in fact, we anticipate that the entire breadth and depth of a character will be retrievable from the text. The term "character," is itself a part of the history of writing. According to Berel Lang, it originally referred "in Greek to a tool for marking or engraving and then subsequently to the 'characters' of writing—the letters that were engraved; then moving to the hand, the person, and finally to the 'character' of the writer."[28] We might easily find, however, that as the etymology of the word suggests character can be found in all types of writing (or other narratives more broadly construed) if we are willing to concede that elements of character: such as precision, orderliness, empirically minded are exactly the characteristics displayed in things like technical or scientific writing that are often true of technical or scientific writers. Similarly the Latin root of style or "stilus" has a similar history. It originally referred to the carving instrument used to make inscriptions in wax and developed in an understanding of the way in which those inscriptions were made in order to eventually refer to the predictable production of inscription by a particular person.[29]

Writing, its texture, chosen elements, structure, voice, namely its style suggest aspects of character that we employ to make sense of the human world around us. Particular ways in which we talk about style in texts draws significant attention to the character of the author of those texts. Seymour Chatman, for example, defines "style" as "the trace the artists way of working leaves in his artifact... An artist is said to have a style when his *characteristic* manner is evident in his works."[30] He goes on to say that the characteristic elements arise through the process of working but that as consumers of the artifact we are only concerned with those work habits and patterns for as far as they are evident in the artifact itself. Charles Altieri defines style in a more abstract way. He argues that style is

> the making visible of the conditions allowing us our investments in the 'now' and the 'this.' Whether we imagine those conditions as fundamentally matters of how we engage the world or how we dispose ourselves towards other agents in those engagements. Style maps a will onto a world.[31]

When we think of style in this way, the mere selection of a writing topic can represent a characteristic focus of will, authorial valuation, and life energy. In this regard it is easier to say that someone who chooses to write technical manual after technical manual is expressing a characteristic trait in the repetitive focus of will. Also in this way the form and style distinction begins to dissolve, and it can be seen that the very selection of form demonstrates a characteristic preference. Van Eck et al argues that form is not an "external and arbitrary mould we use for a given content, but [is] the way we discover and construct that content for ourselves and our readers."[32] Van Eck is very concerned about the forms as styles of philosophers and what the form or styles of our intellectual work say about our individual characteristics as philosophers. He argues that the place of style is where philosophical content meets the character of a philosopher. The association of style and characteristics, of course, is not solely unique to writing and narrative. We judge the characters of individuals, all the time, based on their styles. Someone who is meticulously dressed we judge as neat, organized, orderly, and caring about his/her appearance. Someone with unkempt hair, tattered tie-died shirts, poorly fitting jeans and rope sandals we might judge unfavorably (or favorably given our values) as a free-spirited artist, hippie, or chronic marijuana user. The association of personal style with judgment of character is ubiquitous, and the same association of character judgment and style can be found in narrative texts as well.

What Is Narrative Style?

The arguments about the nature of narrative style are particularly useful when we think about identity as founded on and created through narratives. Its defining features are slightly different from the defining features of style as described by aestheticians and art historians who primarily focus on style in visual representations, mimetic or not. Historically, scholars have a tendency to conceive of narrative style in one of two ways. On they one hand, style is seen as something that is simply added on to the text (this definition of style is most readily associated with the sophists) or, on the other hand it is seen as "organically connected to thought through nature, purpose, logic, arrangement, and other features" (this is attributed to Aristotle).[33] Currently, the idea that style is inseparable from the content or meaning of something is known as "aesthetic monism." Under this model of style, because form is intrinsically and organically tied to meaning, any change in form or style also necessitates a change in meaning.

This has led to arguments along the lines of this: because a particular style is the guarantor of a particular meaning, and any change in the former necessitates a change in the latter, then style is essentially meaning.[34] An alternative model of style asserts that "Style is the Man." Known as "psychological monism," this model argues that style is essentially the sum total of an individual's personality.[35] And so in the context of narrative, no two writers will write in the same style, nor write with comparable meaning. My view of style is a mix of aesthetic and psychological monism. It is an organic element in the psychology of humankind. But also that these organic and necessary styles can be malleable in a way similar to the changes in individuals as produced by the influences of social psychology, or the acquisition of language, language quirks, dialects, or accents based on the shared identity and therefore influence of a region.

Another important historical element of narrative style is the historically debated and applied virtues of style. I've already mentioned the Aristotelian virtues of clarity, propriety, correctness, and appropriate use of metaphor. Also worth mentioning are the virtues established by the Roman orator, Quintilian, who argued for both perspicuity and the enhancing of the force of words through augmentation, comparison, reasoning, and accumulation.[36] I am not particularly interested in the debatable contours of these virtues of narrative, but I am interested in highlighting the fact that there has been a historical connection between habituation of behaviors in accordance with certain values to produce a socially preferred model of style. This historical observation will be important to my fifth chapter as well as the section in chapter 3, "Style and Ethics."

The defining features of narrative style includes something structural rather than agglomerate, self-regulating, independently semiotic, in a recognizable constant form/recurrence of pattern, and as a system of signs. The systematic nature of style is a theme many of the writers about narrative style touch on again and again.[37] The idea of style as a structure means that it is a recognizable whole that has built into it a self-regulating ability to establish its borders and symbolically exclude elements that are outside of it. This is primarily done through recurrence and repetition of certain features that become the predictable constant form or sometimes elements/qualities/expression of a group or individual.[38] This structure must be meaning bearing in its own right, or what Seymour Chatman calls "independently semiotic."[39] And as an independent semiotic system of signs, style can be understood as "the grounds of signifying upon which more and more of our social, cultural world is organized."[40] This final point is particularly important for thinking about style in the socio-political sphere.

Also present in the idea of style, as a signifying system that can provide the ground for social and cultural organization, is the groundwork for the concept style to be the support system for *a* style. *A* style is dependent upon a homology, or a formal similarity among components or elements of a style that creates a unity.[41] A particular homology becomes "a formal resemblance across different texts, actions, objects, and other orders of experience."[42] While most of this chapter is talking about style in general, the next chapter will focus on creating a particular style. The conceptual ability to talk about *a* style as rooted in the concept of style is key to my argument. A style that can be consciously cultivated to combat sexual identity passing, or at least provide corporeal narrative and a socially visible version of queer sexual identity in contemporary culture.

Narrative, Style and Identity
The nature of identity is of course under consideration here. And parts of the contours of identity are what this chapter is trying to establish. There are a few things we can consider firm: identity is in part constructed through narrative: the stories we weave about ourselves and the way we construct those narratives for others. This means that because of narrative, identity can be understood analogously to texts. Therefore, the considerations we make about style in the written word should also be compared to how style operates in identity, with the assumption that the former may provide us insight into the latter. Barry Brummett

argues that identity is "inherently symbolic and imaginary." He stakes his claim on the observation that identities are both representational "to ourselves and others" as well as unstable. Although he is quick to instate identities as having a 'sum total of self' type of importance.[43] In our technology-based postmodern world, the symbolic and imaginary aspects of identity take on a more salient importance. He notes that this both has an impact on our sense of shared community and creates room for politics. Internet social networking sites and the mass production of identity grounding and producing media means that developing a rich sense of identity can take the place of actual social contacts. In other words, "a sense of identity can substitute for actual connection" with a real community.[44] So the role of identity takes on even greater importance.

But the postmodern conditions of identity that amplify the performed elements of identity, as well as its technologically pluralized instability, are also the same conditions that allow for a politics of identity for "only if something can be struggled over and changed will politics and rhetoric connect to it."[45] Brummett also argues that we are more apt to consider identity unstable if we think of it as performed rather than natural.[46] This, too, is a location for intervention by the concept of style. Style still allows for the flexible nature of identity under the pressure of technology, for the socially constructed elements, and at the same time allows space to claim identity as having a natural element. This should strengthen both our trust in shared identities as well as our politics founded upon that trust.

Identity and style begin to intertwine when it can be seen that there is a direct line of connection between aesthetic preferences and representational expressions of self: "*I like that* merges into *I'm like that.*"[47] Markers of self—through aesthetic self-presentation, or choice in leisurely activities—or online profile styling extends beyond expressing likes and begins to transcend into manners of being and approaches to the world. At times this immediately involves products, commodification, and consumption; at other times it involves linguistic gestures and intellectual commitments. The initial enticement to identity commitments can be traced in the movement of aesthetic pleasure to self-association. The inherent communication involved in appropriated style also contains movement of identity as well as movement of power. Brummett argues,

> style is a complex system of actions, objects, and behaviors that is used to form messages that announce who we are, who we want to be, and who we want to be considered akin to. It is therefore also a system of communication with rhetorical influence on others. And as such, style is a means by which power and advantage are negotiated, distributed, and struggled over in society.

The complex interweaving of power and identity in technologically mass-produced styles is worth considerable attention.[48] It is significant to note that our choices regarding style are choices about identity. At times these stylistic concerns are about actions, objects, and behaviors. At other times they are about narrative: the choices we make about how to discuss our lives and present ourselves through language and texts whether consciously or unconsciously, overtly or covertly.

Narrative, along with discourse more broadly, both what is said and how it is said, establish differentiation between types of individuals. At times discourse is "invoked to *explain* the pattern of differentiation in people's behavior; where as it might be more enlightening to say that discourse *constructs* the differentiation, makes it visible *as* differentiation."[49] In the instance of gender, it is argued that men employ a style of discourse that is 'competitive,' used to gain status and exchange factual information; women employ a style of discourse that is 'cooperative,' meant to forge intimacy, connection, and build rapport.[50] Cameron argues that analysts of discourse bring gender biases into their analyses, thereby encouraging certain interpretations over others. She also argues that the very act of engaging in identity-based discourse will produce some of the effects of identity. Speech is a "repeated stylization of the body," she writes. We can see that identity based speech is habitualized communication in an alignment with ideals of identity self-presentation. The case of masculine and feminine styles of speech, social actors are attempting to constitute themselves as proper men and women through the appropriated styles of speech.[51] The understanding of the style of speech as constituting the speaking agent—as opposed to the agent constituting the speech—is clearly in alignment with the kind of subjectivizing emphasis that post-modernity calls into clarity.[52] And this postmodern approach to style and subjectivity is necessary for us to have something like identity politics. For only if identity is subject to habituation and change through mechanisms like style, can we see that identity can be under the influence of political power and calls to action, allegiance, and opposition.[53] This capacity for the socio-political malleability of identity through style demonstrates the inherent sociality of style, which is the next key aspect of style to discuss.

Style as Social

Brummett argues that "public displays of styles are like magnets moving through the world, attracting whoever resonates with the style, attracting those whose own styles seem consonant with the one displayed."[54] In other words, style has inherent social properties that help to organize communities of like-styled individuals, and these like-styled groups might find simultaneously that their like-style is also indicative of like-politics, like-religious ideology, or like (racial, sexual, cultural, or gender) identity. Style, too, can also be developed or employed around what Brummett refers to as an "imaginary community." Rather than style organically attracting like-minded folks, individuals can tailor a social text around a style intended for a community. The discursive production, then, happens in the context of imagining the needs and reception of a particular community. This is particularly true of communities that organize around texts. Brummett cites Episcopalians as one example, and online social groups as another.[55] He argues about the cohesive nature of texts for these imaginary communities through the mechanism of style. He writes, "texts created in the name of the imaginary community have great cohesive power. They exert a strong pull to display style of one sort or another. This is one reason why people of stigmatized groups display risky styles, for to imagine a community of which one is a part is to acknowledge and to feel the symbolic demands of that community, regardless of cost."[56] The symbolic demand of stylized adherence to a community and the "constraints that people feel to perform or not perform" demonstrates for Brummett, "how fundamental is style to social existence."[57] I've already argued that style is ontological—a very part of our human being.[58] The social influence, development, and constraint on style also demonstrates style's inherent necessary location in sociality.

Aesthetics and style have presumably always played an important role in human communities. Certain communities develop what Brummett calls aesthetic engrossment: "the absorption of public attention in the aesthetic dimensions of texts, more than in underlying structural conditions."[59] Under conditions of communal coherence to a particular aesthetic engrossment in a set of texts, those texts become the basis and location of return for the formation of both the community and individual subjects. This is not to say that these aesthetic preoccupations or community structuring are intentional or even conscious. Most of this kind of community-based style is tacit rather than consciously or self-consciously employed. This does not preclude the possibility of conscious aesthetic investments and developments, nor would it be an accurate description of individuals that we do not consciously employ our thought processes in making decisions about our self-(re)presentations and these relationship of those (re)presentation to our membership in a particular community. For example, most of us employ basic reasoning about our day and the community/ies we will engage when choosing a style of dress in the morning (professional, social, familial, causal, event-based such as a Cubs game, etc.) Some of the nuances of those styles might remain significantly tacit.

Much of my discussion about style has taken the perspective of the individual's entrance and adherence to community, and the stylistic workings of a community to maintain membership allegiance through style. At the same time, style also organizes smaller communities within a larger regional or global perspective, meaning that we organize those around us into communities based on their styles. In other words, "style organizes the social through aesthetic perceptions and categories, such as, clothing, the look and feel of the urban environment, geographic associations, race, and culture."[60] We read onto others their social allegiances and affinities through their self-(re)presentations. Class distinctions are, of course, also deeply represented in the symbolic associations of style: brand names, designers, certain class values. And there can even be legal implications for impersonating the style of particular professions that are marked by styles (uniforms, etc.): police officers, physicians, military, postal employees, etc.[61]

The Role of Pop Culture

Popular culture is a particular kind of social-based aesthetic engrossment and obsession. It consumes large quantities of financial resources and human energies to maintain and promote. It is most notably about the dissemination of identities established and made coherent through style. Pop culture also encourages a hyper-consumption around identity. It is not enough to buy a single product that manifests a commitment to a certain kind of identity. One must be surrounded by products, images, clothing, music, food, and media that reinforces that identity. Communities develop under these hyper-consumptive demands, and placement within these communities can be thoroughly dependent on having the latest and greatest product X that is the current communal object of obsession. Brummett argues that the particular kind of aesthetic obsession that is the product of popular culture can only occur after all of a communities basic needs are met: food, shelter, clothing, basic human rights. Once these needs are met, significant energy can be expended on style, and will be spent on style.[62] He also argues that the rhetoric of popular culture is so centralized on style that popular culture's rhetoric is essentially one of style. One could also say that thinking about style is essentially a way to think about popular culture and for this reason Brummett thinks that there is a lot of exchange between the concepts, or that they are "highly porous" with one another.[63] One of the brilliant aspects of style, as it can be employed in identity politics, is its ability to be historicized right along side the movements of culture, politics, and legal structures.

Style over Performativity

In this section I will argue that the concept of style I have been outlining should supplant the concept of performativity as the major descriptor of sexual identity production in the modern academic climate. This is not to say that I think performativity has been misguided or specifically ill conceived, or that we should ignore the brilliant insights Judith Butler has made in her earlier work on performativity or more recent work. Performativity has done significant intellectual work and has revolutionized the way in which we think about identity. I do not wish to minimize this in any way or to do away with those advances. Butler's more recent work is imperative for my project. My disagreement with Butler is not with the work she produced in her later works beginning around 2004 regarding the ethics of identity (although I don't think she would use this phrase); rather, I take significant issue with 1) performativity as a model of identity that can accurately or even adequately explain the processes of identity formation especially the double identity inherent in passing, and 2) the ability of performativity to ground a system of power inversion ethics. It is my contention that style, in the contours I've outlined in this chapter, can accomplish both 1 and 2.

Style and Passing

My largest criticism of performativity is in the way it thinks of stylized corporeality as the end sum of identity and thereby overlooks stylized corporeality as it functions in passing. Performativity captures questions of stylized corporeality in terms of repetitions of pre-established norms. The pre-established element of performativity is one of its greatest criticisms by scholars more generally. Vikki Bell argues, that if under performativity,

> everything is pre-given in the realm of the possible, the argument runs, the passage of realization is not a creation; it is what amounts to a sort of *preformism*... That is, performativity is *preform*ativity wherever analysis claims to describe the idea(l)—form that the subject is said to imitate or instantiate.[64]

This means that there can be no creative form of self-production. In ordinary life there can be no break from a pre-given mould, and there is also a strong sense in which we are pre-interpellated into the only pre-given mould we are allowed to employ. This means that passing is not something that occurs naturally, unless we think of all identity manifestations as performance with no difference between the person who considers themselves as passing and the person who does not consider themselves as passing.

It may be true to say, however, as an insight given to us by Butler's performativity, that someone who is heterosexual is performing heterosexuality just as much as the queer person who is performing heterosexuality. But the difference is in the psychic comfort and internal experience of that performance. This difference isn't something that Butler's theory can capture.

Performativity overlooks the body as a central organizing feature of lived experience. The body can't be overlooked when it comes to questions of stylized corporeality. Take drag performance into consideration. You will remember that Butler explores the phenomenon of drag as something that exposes the inherent mimicry in the production of gender. She does not claim that gender identity is a kind of drag performance; the kind of theatrical intentionality in drag is not found in an agent who is participating in the cultural constructs of natural gender expression.

Drag most readily demonstrates the stylized corporeal definitional component of passing. In drag shows the appropriated embodiment of a gender, which is not one's own, is the explicitly stated motivation for the event. As Halberstam explains, the concept of passing becomes the litmus test for judging the winners of these competitions:

> In the drag king contests, the winner would very often be a biological female who was convincing in her masculinity (sometimes convincing meant she could easily pass as male).[65]

That which is a convincing gendered stylized corporeality is established by/through the concept of successful passing.

But gender performance as stylized corporeality should not be thought of only in terms of theatrics. In New York City, Dianne Torr, a performance artist, conducts worldly drag shows for novice clients. As Danny Drag King, she runs a workshop where women perform masculinity and test their abilities on the streets of New York. The workshop is centered on stylized corporeality. Danny/Dianne

> instructs her students in the manly arts of taking up space, dominating conversations, nose picking, and penis wearing, and she gives them general rudeness skills. Torr's students become men for the day by binding and jockey stuffing, and then she shows them how to apply facial hair and create a credible male look.[66]

Passing as a phenomenon cannot be accomplished without a biological situation in which it can adhere. Stylized corporeality, you will remember, is an ontological mode, it is something that all subjects share whether or not they are employing a style for purposes of passing, or for engaging an identity marker that all of society has deemed appropriate for the body and the social particularities in which the individual is born.

The biological body, then, is an inescapable component of the passing phenomenon. Simone de Beauvoir argues, in *The Second Sex*, that "... the body is not a *thing*, it is a situation ... it is the instrument of our grasp upon the world, a limiting factor for our projects."[67] This definition of body as a limiting situation is clearly illuminated in situations of gender performance and passing. Think of a woman attempting to pass for a man in Torr's workshop. Of primary concern are the secondary sex features that are associated with the female body. The soon-to-be passing agent must bind her breasts, (re)style her hair, minimize the curve of her hips. This must be accomplished before she can take on the stylized performance of masculinity, before she can concern herself creating a bulge in the image of the phallus, before she can sketch in lines of facial hair, before she can readjust the length and breadth of her gait. The biological must precede the corporeal (re)stylization. Performativity overlooks the role of biological bodies.

Another central concern of passing that performativity cannot capture is the element of temporal ambiguity in situations of passing that are dependent on stylized corporeality, where at times an individual is read as something other than what s/he is (a case of successful passing) and at other times is read as a deviation of what s/he is. If a female gender deviant, for example, can be "read as" butch (or anything else other than male), what traps her in the liminal space of deviance is the receptive gaze upon her gender performance. She remains identifiable *as* a gender deviant female, which restricts her to "keeping the middle," occupying the transitional space between male and female. But given the legibility of her "true" gender, she cannot be classified alongside women who are passing for male.

Traditional definitions of the concept of "passing" (not as a referent to a phenomenon, but simply as a functioning adverb within the English language) contain residue of temporal ambiguity. The *Oxford English Dictionary* defines passing (not in relation to identity) as "that which passes away or elapses; of time or things measure by time: transient, transitory, temporary, fleeting; ephemeral, vanishing." It's important for a properly complex notion of passing (as related to identity) to maintain the temporal residue that can be found in the non-identity uses of the term. Performativity won't do much for us if we think of passing and an inability to pass as happening in the same day, or even in the same moment depending on the uptake and stance of the receptive gazes. Style can capture this ambiguity through the recognition that style is always dependent on the gazes of others, and that given the social aspects of style it is easy to expect that some social environments will read a particular style in one way, while a different social environment will read it in another way. Or even that diverse individuals from diverse social environments will find themselves in the same location reading a third party in two different ways based solely on that person's corporeal style.

The final concern I would like to raise that evidences the difficulty of performativity is with cases of gender identity expression where someone's self-presentation encourages others to read him/her as straight (for example) when s/he is lesbian or gay identified (the corollary to the example). Take as an excellent example, the feminine lesbian. Literary scholar, Lisa Walker, wrote a monograph about questions of style and identity that have arisen from her own experiences and identity concerns related to being a feminine lesbian. Femmes (as they are colloquially called) are often read as straight, usually by the general population, giving them the "convenient"[68] option of passing, and sparing the all-too-often "verbally abusive and physically threatening homophobia"[69] that butch women must endure. Femme women, must of course, also put up with unwanted sexual advances from men, and if they take pride in their identity as a queer woman may very well experience frustration from the enforced passing. Feminine lesbians are also often received with suspicion from the larger lesbian community, who sometimes experiences femmes as potential traitors, who given their natural access to heterosexual privilege could decide that they like the social comforts and protections it can afford them, leaving or denying their lesbian community or lover.[70]

Early sexologists (late 1800's) were unable to consider a feminine woman as a type of female homosexual. They theorized that the only true type of female "invert" was the male-identified woman. Her sexual desires were seen as a product of her female masculinity. It was her urge towards cross-dressing that made her an invert, not her sexual behavior. Based on this understanding, a feminine woman could not be an invert. It was a "deductive impossibility." Instead sexologists, like Krafft-Ebing, thought that all same-sex behavior in "womanly" women was a product of their lover's masculine self-presentation, so as to retain the status of her heterosexuality. The feminine lesbian was said to desire the masculinity in her cross-dressing mannish lover, not any aspect of her femininity.[71]

Performativity might have something to add here in terms of an explication and analysis of what is happening under the case of the feminine lesbian. But it is readily clear to me that the concept of style can do much more work in explaining the social components, the receptive gaze, the production of self, and what may even be the problematic continuation of a feminine style for a queer woman who wants to stand boldly and visibly for her community. If style can do such a superior job of analyzing this kind of case, why should we want to undertake the intellectual work of making performativity do explanatory work for us, when that would be a laborious endeavor?

Style and Ethics

At least three significant philosophers have argued for a necessary relationship between style and ethics: Charles Taylor, Friedrich Nietzsche, and Charles Altieri. In this section I will discuss some of the insights they have to offer, as well as additional insights from a few other academics on the relationship between style and ethics. These insights are central to the motivation behind the kind of ethic I will argue for in chapters 5 and 6.

In *Sources of the Self* Charles Taylor identifies two key components to personal identity that situate and direct the energies of an individual: an orientation to "the good" and a life narrative that articulates that orientation. The sense of self-knowledge and its dependence upon one's conception of the good is a clear relationship for Taylor. He argues,

> to know who you are is to be oriented in moral space, a space in which questions arise about what is good or bad, what is worth doing and what not, what has meaning and importance for you and what is trivial and secondary.[72]

Some sort of operative or tacit definition of the moral is the psychological touchstone for organizing life activities and decisions. It is interesting that he describes this in spatial terms. In this *space* questions "arise" which provide orientation for movement towards a particular goal. The use of the word "space" may be a simple rhetorical short-hand referring to a kind of focused mental space. But it is also worth noting that this moral space provides physical and metaphorical movement through the landscape of one's life.

Taylor connects this orientation to the good to the concept of a narrative. He writes,

> ... in order to make minimal sense of our lives, in order to have an identity, we need an orientation to the good, which means some sense of qualitative discrimination, of the incomparably higher. Now we see that this sense of the good has to be woven into my understanding of my life as an unfolding story.

But this is to state another basic condition of making sense of ourselves, that we grasp our lives in *narrative*.[73]

In the story of our lives the role of the protagonist is played by *the good*.[74] And the mere fact that the good can function as a protagonist means that there has to be a storyboard or framework for that protagonist to operate within. Perhaps it would make more sense to declare ourselves the protagonist of our own story, with the good as the author,[75] or perhaps the good as that which provides the contours and style of our individual narrative. However, we are to conceive of it, this transitional and interdependent relationship between personal identity ⇒ the good ⇒ narrative is foundational, for Taylor, to any analysis of the self. Because the style of the narrative is that which situates the good into personal identity, style is inherently bound with ethics.

The most interesting way that I could conceive of grappling with "the good" and its relationship to our identities and our narratives is through its potential of the good as a stylizing force. In this regard, I mean the good is something which provides the basic recognizable character of a life, although not necessarily the basic recognizable attributes of an individual. It is that which provides the story line, the plot, the arch of the trajectory/ies of the individual's directive aim towards the good. It is the stumbles and the quirks, and the metaphorical turns of phrase that either delight or repel its onlookers.

If Taylor is correct, and "the good" can be found within the style of any life narrative, then a few things result. First, we have a ubiquitous structure in which the good must operate for all individuals. Second, it must always produce some basic structural life components. Third, it allows for an individualized contingency, so that the good can manifest in unique and individualized ways without needing to be radically individualized. Taylor's discussion of the good is one way to think about how style can allow for the intersection of morality and identity.

Friedrich Nietzsche argued for a direct relationship between style and value; he used aesthetic concepts in general, like style, to explain the construction of values. In *Birth of Tragedy*, for example, he argues that we can only justify life and order as aesthetic phenomena.[76] Kemal argues that Nietzsche uses aesthetics as redemptive and constructive of values because style is "serious and significant because there we make ourselves, display our personalities, our mode of living, our sensitivity to the requirements of a good life, and give as beautiful an order as possible to the material of our lives."[77] This is the way that Kemal makes sense of the use of style for Nietzsche, which also has a nice resonance with the role of style in Taylor's assessment of the holding place of the good within our personal narratives. Nietzsche seemed to be much more concerned with the role of creativity in the production of one's system of values; so the emphasis for Nietzsche is on the production of original codes of conduct rather than blindly following the rules set up prior to the subject and his/her situation. Any model of creativity, it is understood, will involve elements of style.

Charles Altieri is another philosopher who clearly sees the connection between style and ethics. "Personal style," he argues, "is a dimension of purposiveness... [it] has its greatest resonance when we come to appreciate the rendering of intentionality as a deliberative communicative act." The role of agency and intentionality within style is of clear importance to Altieri, it is the locus within style for its moral capabilities. He continues on to assert that the moral aspect of style is seen "when we imagine an agent treating how he or she self-reflexively carries out some task as part of what constitutes the action." The moral here gets equated with "the how" not "the what" or even "the why." And given the importance of style, its fluidity, and its resistance to traditional analysis, he thinks the concept of style poses serious concerns for philosophy and philosophical inquiry because style simply can't be subsumed under models of desire, judgment or subjectivity.[78] Altieri also thinks that by acknowledging the role and importance of style within our daily lives and decisions we can become more self-conscious and responsible about our expressive energies and mode(s) of comportment.

Aesthetics—and style—in particular can also establish the parameters of the good: a good decision, a good purchase, a good piece of writing, a good film, etc. In ordinary conversation we use style as a rationale for our behavior or our desires: "I wanted to go to her dinner party because they are always such stylish events."[79] And style can also be the source or topic of moralization: bad writing or a bad neighborhood because it looks run down.

Sometimes, too, we want style to be the handmaiden of ethics. The crux of an ethical moment in which we want our loved one to tell us the truth may be entirely directed at receiving the sought after truth, perhaps even if we are willing to disregard how it is told. But under ordinary circumstance, and perhaps even under desperate pursuit of the truth, the way a difficult truth is told is of importance; we want painful truths told gingerly, or with appropriate tact and sensitivity. We want to be able to hand our truths to others in the same way.

Lang argues that in the process of moral education we are appropriately first taught the *how* of human action: how to treat others with kindness, respect, and to communicate genuinely and honestly. And then after these techniques of interactions are mastered we can handle any content or situation that might come along. He argues this through an analogy with learning the techniques of good writing, which once fully formed can handle any content or subject aptly and with the same good skill.[80]

The relationship between style and ethics that I would like to put forward contains all of these elements. We want to anticipate that our life narrative and the styles through which we tell them will contain our values and our sense of personal development in alignment with those values. We want our system of ethics to be creative and to involve production, not just obedience. We want our personal style to be deliberate, conscious, and developed with enough elasticity that it can contain, structure, and shape any situation or ethical encounter. The employment of this relationship between style and ethics will be of central importance in chapter 5 in building a creative sense of queer ethics based on the style of individuals and of a community.

Style as Sexual Identity

Historically gay style has been associated with what is known as "camp." Camp is a kind of aesthetic sensibility that is known for being ostentatious, affected, effeminate and frivolous. Susan Sontag has described it as a "badge of identity,"[81] as a way of viewing "the world as an aesthetic phenomenon,"[82] and concerned not with beauty but with *stylization*.[83] She has also described it is a "solvent of morality" insofar as it "neutralizes moral indignation [and] sponsors playfulness."[84] It has also been argued that the value for homosexuals in employing camp is that it defines social roles, and particularly sex roles as superficial.[85]

Camp began to be a popular aesthetic as early as 1909. And it is interesting that queers immediately attached themselves to this type of aesthetic given its tendency to protect interiors and content by focusing in on superficiality and appearance. A style of queerness, as the form of superficiality and appearance, made a resurgence for gay people in the latter part of the 20th century. It began to be clear that there was a certain "look" that could establish one as gay, rather than sexual behavior establishing individuals as such. Commodities, in certain arrangements, began to signify sexual meanings.[86]

When I present the idea of creating a style that is gay/queer, I do not wish to evoke the kind of superficiality that is central to the concept of camp or to suggest that it must engage either the theatrical ostentation of camp or the commodification of more recent years. I wish to evoke the deeper sense of style as outlined earlier in this chapter, one that involves ontology, is developed through habituation, and seeks to balance the individual and the social.

The elements that would need to be included in a style that signified sexual identity for the purposes of building an ethic are minimally: narrative, some aspect of corporeal style without leaving us dependent on the visible, and a respected intact notion of subjectivity.

The narrative aspect of style should include: narrative discourse, narrative story, media, and narrative imitation filtered through a gay perspective.[87] Narrative discourse entails the way in which a narrative is constructed and transmitted, how the narrator fits into the discourse, and the timeframes used within the discourse (present, future, flashback, etc.). Narrative story includes events, characters, and settings. Media is a wide array of consumable story telling products including films, television shows, books, magazines, advertisements, theatre, dance, and music. And the imitative approach to narratives means that all the fairy tales, basic mythologies, and social scripts can be told in a gay way as easily as they can be told in a straight way.

Visibility produces a complicated paradox. Style should be something that is both recognizable by sight, and something that should not be defined solely by sight. We are a visually-based culture. Our organization of people and subjects by visual perception is the most predominant form of social organization that we have. A constructed gay style should have elements of visibility to it, but we should be careful not to allow them to dominate. Two issues result from allowing visibility to remain dominant: erasure of individuals from the community who do not fit the expected visual standards (such as femme lesbians, or butch gay men),[88] and a certain instability that's inherent to visibility. Brummett argues,

> an aestheticized, stylized world based in images is likely to be inherently unstable. ... Such a world is also inherently malleable, and, thus, rhetorical to its core, for what can be changed through the manipulation of signs, and images must be maintained through the manipulation of signs and images.[89]

If we rely too heavily on the visual, then we are relying too heavily on a foundation of style that can be easily manipulated, mimicked, marketed, and changed.

Respected subjectivity means that individuals are encouraged to establish themselves within the framework of style, not the other way around. However, agreeing with Louis Althusser (1971) that our subjectivities begin to develop as a result of being interpellated by ideology beginning with the moment that we recognize ourselves within an already established discourse, it is clear that we will find ourselves in the midst of a discourse and style of sexual identity that precedes our presence. It is important that gay style is malleable and hospitable enough to respect the location we define for ourselves within it.[90] The lack of this kind of malleability and respect for subjectivity has been cited as one of the central and key problems of the current model and rhetoric of gay and lesbian identity, particularly in its uncompromising elements of coming-out, shame, and gender dystopia.[91]

Any developed queer style must also recognize the role and context of heteronormativity. Even though heterosexual identity was constructed as a style all its own, it has managed to encode itself as the natural—and therefore "silent uninterrogated"—identity. Its normative contours are that which allow for the transgression of queer sexuality.[92] Any queer style must also combat the paradox inherent in heteronormativity that assumes itself as default creating a situation in which to "'come out' discursively and linguistically presupposes straight as standard, and homosexuality as hidden needing to be explicitly revealed... [while] staying in the closet has the same effect."[93] As the narrative style of the gay community currently stands, being stealth within heteronormativity and being in the closet are the same thing. A positively infused and intoned gay style should be able to establish a different neutral location.

It is important in constructing a new gay style that we are wary of allowing the importation of the medical and pathologizing discourse regimes, and social models of inferiority and rejection, into the new style. At the current time, coming-out narratives are speckled with the shame and self-reproach that is indicative of the invention of homosexuality. Linguistic analysis of coming-out narratives by Morrish and Sauntson clearly reflect that individuals are developing a social identity rather than reflecting on sexual desire.[94] In fact very few narratives included any reflection on sexual desire at all. It is in these discursive rhetorical gestures that we can see the role of a broader social style and identity taking hold of an individual's subjectivity at one of the earliest stages of his/her entrance into that community. Morrish and Sauntson undertook an extensive linguistic analysis of coming-out narratives, focusing on "appraisal" which refers to the "semantic resources used to negotiate emotions, judgments, and valuations, alongside resources for amplifying and engaging with these evaluations.[95] Within this appraisal system, they focused on affect—"the linguistic resources deployed for construing the individual's responses"; judgment—"the linguistic resources deployed for construing moral or social evaluation of behavior"; and appreciation—"the linguistic resources for the 'aesthetic' qualities of processes and natural phenomena."[96] What they discovered within coming-out narratives should be of little surprise to individuals within the modern gay community. Judgment particularly centered on questions of normality and truthtelling. Narratives had a tendency to touch on the themes of family, religion, education, media, and the internet. Negative attitudes in both judgment and affect were associated with secondary education, religion, rural areas, and family. University education, gay media, urban areas, and the internet all allowed for more positive judgment and affect where different socio-cultural norms could be explored and negotiated. Gay-centered media or even media that featured gay characters significantly increased the sense of normality in the narratives. It is clear that the old "style" of sexuality that was created in the late 1800's and thrived through the 1950's is alive and well in the psyche and social development of many young gay people. These scripts are consumed scripts, and with a focused re-working of what it means to be gay, over a period of time, these narratives could (and should) be overwhelmingly positive.

Other things to beware of before re-working the concept of gay style are the ways in which style has been used against certain members of the gay community. Feminine lesbians, in particular, have complained that their "straight style" has been the cause of judgment and minoritization within the gay community and has sometimes been said to be indicative of a feminine woman's desire to pass for straight (with pejorative judgment).[97] It has, of course, been the case from the earliest of sexology studies on homosexual persons that inverted gender identity is indicative of queer sexuality and that ordinary gender identity suggests heterosexual identity. However, in a contemporary construction of a gay style, I am aware that I cannot uncritically import the assumption of gender queerness into our style. It should be the case that one could consciously and politically engage in gay style while participating in other separate cultural norms of gender expression. Sexual style cannot be gender style.

Gay Style and Passing

Before I articulate a constructive model of gay style—the particular elements with which my reader may agree or disagree, and are certainly culturally bound in the current political stream of LGBT/Q politics—I want to suggest the theoretical ability of any notion of gay style to capture elements of sexual identity passing.

Merleau-Ponty thinks of personal style as a mixture of the anonymous and the personal, the inherited and the created. Style is never completely given or completely chosen. And style is not something that we can separate from the objects that it discloses. Style cannot be "extracted and investigated on its own," but the interplay of the social and the embodied reaction to the conditions of existence is the only way we can make sense of passing as something other than simply a false veneer or a masquerade, something that is inconsequential, removable, or otherwise not a threat to our political or spiritual selves.

A gay style will include corporeal and narrative elements in it that are both personal and about anonymous collectivity, it can involve elements that are historical and elements that are constructive, it will be something that is neither completely chosen nor something that is completely given. And gay style—like camp—must be something we are capable of naming and exploring as a social and embodied phenomenon that is a reaction to very particular social conditions. And at the same time we need a concept that penetrates beyond the superficial manifestation of behaviors (yet can also explain a superficial manifestation of behaviors). Style can do this—and a distinction between heterosexual and gay style can demonstrate how some LGB/Q individuals are able to pass as straight.

However, the decision to pass can also not be simply rendered as an unimportant and superficial decision. The connection between passing for heterosexual and its implications for LGBT/Q political agendas, subjectivities, and morality must also be something that a theory of identity can establish.

The depth of style and therefore of passing, its inextricable nature from the subject on which it inheres, and the outward representation of consciousness that it manifests means that choosing to pass cannot be a flippant decision in which no greater or deeper damage is done to the self. The concept of style testifies that individual LGBT/Q people can extract meaning and significance from the world and make it one's own. It also suggests that politically aware LGBT/Q people ought to choose our styles carefully. Style as a historical phenomenon also testifies to the history of meaning-making that human beings as a species undertake. And so style also adds gravity to decisions to pass by recognizing that to pass is to implant in the self the history of the tradition of heterosexuality.

Notes

1. For example, Tim Gunn's television series "Guide to Style," and companion book *A Guide to Quality, Taste, and Style* (New York City: Abrams, 2007).
2. Nelson Goodman, Susan Sontag, and Leonard Meyer all define it as such.
3. Susan Sontag, "Notes on Camp" in *Against Interpretation,* (New York: Doubleday, 1966), 32.
4. Sontag, "Notes on Camp," 35.
5. Linda Singer, "Merleau-Ponty on the Concept of Style," *Man and World* (1981), 236-9.
6. Singer, "Merleau-Ponty," 240.
7. Singer, "Merleau-Ponty," 240-1.
8. Singer, "Merleau-Ponty," 242.
9. Jean-Paul Sartre, *Black Orpheus.* Translated by S.W. Allen. (Paris: Gallimard, 1949), 17.
10. Sartre, *Black Orpheus,* 17.
11. Sartre, *Black Orpheus,* 41.
12. Sartre, *Black Orpheus,* 44.
13. Sartre, *Black Orpheus,* 63.
14. Debra Bergoffen, "Simone de Beauvoir," *The Stanford Encyclopedia of Philosophy* (Summer 2009 Edition), edited by Edward N. Zalta. http://plato.stanford.edu/archives/sum2009/entries/beauvior/
15. Ann J. Cahill, "Continental Feminism." *The Stanford Encyclopedia of Philosophy* (Fall 2008 Edition), edited by Edward N. Zalta. http://plato.stanford.edu/archives/fall2008/entries/femapproach-continental/
16. Shaun Gallagher and Dan Zahavi, "Phenomenological Approaches to Self-Consciousness," *The Stanford Encyclopedia of Philosophy* (Spring 2009 Edition), edited by Edward N. Zalta.http://plato.stanford.edu/archives/spr2009/entries/self-consciousness-phenomenological/
17. Gallagher, "Phenomenological Approaches to Self-Consciousness."
18. Gallagher, "Phenomenological Approaches to Self-Consciousness."
19. Bernard Flynn, "Maurice Merleau-Ponty," *The Stanford Encyclopedia of Philosophy* (Fall 2008 Edition), edited by Edward N. Zalta. http://plato.stanford.edu/archives/fall2008/entries/merleau-ponty/
20. Cahill, "Contintenal Feminism"
21. Bergoffen, "Simone de Beauvoir"
22. Bergoffen, "Simone de Beauvoir"
23. Bergoffen, "Simone de Beauvoir"
24. Cahill, "Continental Feminism"
25. Cahill, "Continental Feminism"
26. Cahill, "Continental Feminism"
27. Flynn, "Maurice Merleau-Ponty,"
28. Berel Lang, *Writing and the Moral Self* (New York: Routledge, 1991), 12.
29. Barry Brummett *A Rhetoric of Style* (Carbondale: Southern Illinois University Press, 2008), 1; Lang, *Writing and the Moral Self,* 12.
30. Seymour Chatman, "The Styles of Narrative Codes," in *The Concept of Style,* ed. Berel Lang (Philadelphia: University of Philadlephia Press, 1979), 169. emphasis added.

31. Charles Altieri, "Personal Style as Articulate Intentionality," in *The Question of Style in Philosophy and the Arts*. eds. Caroline Van Eck, James McAllister and Rene e van de Vall (Cambridge: Cambridge University Press, 1995), 213.

32. Caroline Van Eck, James McAllister, and Rene e van de Vall eds. "Introduction" in *The Question of Style in Philosophy and the Arts* (Cambridge: Cambridge University Press, 1995), 3.

33. Paul Butler, *Out of Style: Reanimating Stylistic Study in Composition and Rhetoric* (Logan, Utah: Utah State University Press, 2008), 25.

34. Monroe Beardsley, "Verbal Style and Illocutionary Action," in *The Concept of Style*. ed. Berel Lang (Philadelphia: University of Philadelphia Press, 1979), 162.

35. Butler, *Out of Style,* 47.

36. Butler, *Out of Style,* 42.

37. Examples include Seymour Chatman, Monroe Beardsley, Barry Brummett.

38. Beardsley, "Verbal Style an Illocutionary Action," 151.

39. Chatman, "The Styles of Narrative Codes," 173.

40. Brummett, *A Rhetoric of Style,* 3.

41. Brummett, *A Rhetoric of Style,* 36.

42. Brummett, *A Rhetoric of Style,* 131.

43. Brummett, *A Rhetoric of Style,* 83.

44. Brummett, *A Rhetoric of Style,* 85.

45. Brummett, *A Rhetoric of Style,* 85.

46. Brummett, *A Rhetoric of Style*, 86.

47. Virginia Postrel quoted in Barry Brummett *A Rhetoric of Style,* 88.

48. Diasporic study of a cultural stylistic movement would be a clear and in depth example of such a study.

49. Deborah Cameron, "Performing Gender Identity: Young Men's Talk and the Construction of Heterosexual Masculinity," in *The Discourse Reader* (2nd Edition), eds. Adam Jaworksi and Nikolas Coupland (London: Routledge, 1999), 420. This particular author establishes this argument in the context of gender identity, but the same structure could be used to argue for other kinds of identity.

50. Cameron, "Performing Gender Identity," 425.

51. Cameron, "Performing Gender Identity," 421.

52. This focal point on style by social linguists can also be seen in the trend of artistic theory and literary criticism to focus on style. Van Eck et al. argues that style has become the focus in my artistic endeavors since around the time of 1800 which she marks as the time of a "loss of belief in the absolute standards of reason, nature, and antiquity." Van Eck et al., *The Question of Style,* 11.

53. Brummett, *A Rhetoric of Style,* 95.

54. Brummett, *A Rhetoric of Style,* 120.

55. Academic communities, such as a group of analytic ethicists, seem to me to be another clear-cut example of such a phenomenon.

56. Brummett, *A Rhetoric of Style*, 123.

57. Brummett, *A Rhetoric of Style,* 3.

58. Virginia Postrel argues that aesthetics is the fundamental human element, but defines it as a need rather than an ontological feature and moves from this assertion to an argument that "if aesthetics is intimately connected to style, then the manipulation of style in life is likewise a central human need." Brummett, *A Rhetoric of Style,* 18.

59. Brummett, *A Rhetoric of Style,* 148.

60. Brummett, *A Rhetoric of Style,* 23.

61. Under feudal systems, clothing styles were legally assigned to different classes, so as to guarantee a readable aesthetic marker. Brummett, *A Rhetoric of Style*, 9.

62. Brummett, *A Rhetoric of Style*, 47.

63. Brummett, *A Rhetoric of Style*, xiii.

64. Vikki Bell, *Culture and Performance: The Challenge of Ethics, Politics, and Feminist Theory*, (New York: Berg, 2007), 106.

65. Judith Halberstam, *Female Masculinity*, (Durham: Duke University Press, 1998), 246.

66. Halberstam, *Female Masculinity*, 251.

67. Simone de Beauvoir, *The Second Sex*, Translated by H.M. Parshley. (New York: Vintage, 1989), 34.

68. Lisa Walker, *Looking Like What You Are: Sexual Style, Race, and Lesbian Identity*, (New York: New York University Press, 2001), xv. This is Walker's descriptive term, although it becomes readily apparent that passing is both personally, politically, and intellectually problematic for her. While under certain circumstances a quick decision to pass in a hostile or homophobic situation, may prove convenient as a regular and unavoidable occurrence it leaves something to be desired.

69. Walker, *Looking Like What You Are*, xv.

70. Walker, *Looking Like What You Are*, xv-xvi.

71. Walker, *Looking Like What You Are*, 4.

72. Charles Taylor, *Sources of the Self: the Making of Modern Identity* (Cambridge: Harvard University Press, 1992), 28.

73. Taylor, *Sources of the Self*, 47.

74. A healthy amount of philosophical skepticism arises for me on this point. Certainly it rings true for me, but I am writing a book on a practical issue within the field of ethics. It is not a stretch to say that my life is organized very literally and practically by an orientation to the "good". I suspect there are certain professions, as well, for who this wouldn't seem to be far from the literal mark of daily activity: workers for social justice and global peace, clergy. But I am wondering it if holds true for humanity as a whole, and not just for the obvious counter-examples: career criminals, sociopaths, etc., but also the ordinary expanse of the population.

75. Or author-function.

76. Salim Kemal, "Style and Community," in *The Question of Style in Philosophy and The Arts*. eds. Caroline Van Eck, James McAllister, and Rene e van de Vall. (Cambridge: Cambridge University Press, 1995), 124.

77. Kemal, "Style and Community," 124.

78. Altieri, "Personal Style as Articulate Intentionality," 202.

79. Brummett, *A Rhetoric of Style*, 127.

80. Lang, *Writing and the Moral Self*, 12.

81. Sontag, "Notes on Camp," 275.

82. Sontag, "Notes on Camp," 277.

83. Sontag, "Notes on Camp," 277.

84. Sontag, "Notes on Camp," 290.

85. Brummett quoting an argument by Jack Bubuscio. Brummett, *A Rhetoric of Style*, 7.

86. Brummett, *A Rhetoric of Style*, 8 and 13.

87. Chatman, "The Styles of Narrative Codes," 174.

88. Walker, *Looking Like What You Are*, 210.

89. Brummett, *A Rhetoric of Style*, 22.

90. Liz Morrish and Helen Sauntson, *New Perspectives on Language and Sexual Identity* (New York: Palgrave Macmillan, 2007), 87.

91. Morrish and Sauntson, *New Perspectives on Language and Sexual Identity*, 93.

92. Eve Sedgwick has argued that the silent uninterrogated nature of heterosexuality means that it does not "count as sexuality at all, to the point where it is in effect the opposite of sex." Quoted in Morrish and Sauntson, *New Perspectives on Language and Sexual Identity*, 92.

93. Maher and Pusch (1995: 27), cited in Morrish and Sauntson, *New Perspectives on Language and Sexual Identity*, 98.

94. Morrish and Sauntson, *New Perspectives on Language and Sexual Identity*, 53.

95. Morrish and Sauntson, *New Perspectives on Language and Sexual Identity*, 54.

96. Morrish and Sauntson, *New Perspectives on Language and Sexual Identity*, 57.

97. Walker, *Looking Like What You Are*, 202.

Chapter 5
Political Perversity:
Queer Sexuality and the Moral Majority

I want to begin this chapter with an eschatological image. Let's call it "queertopia." In queertopia sexual orientations are understood to be nuanced and particular. They are inborn characteristics that begin to evidence themselves at a young age—in the way that a special talent for music or sports shows itself in young children. The adults surrounding the children model a variety of relationships: same-sex, opposite-sex, serial monogamy with multiple genders, simultaneous amorous relationships, etc. They mirror the developing sexual identities in children, acknowledging and accepting the child's emotional attractions to different people of different genders and gender identities, helping them to see themselves and literally orient them as they enter into the adult world. There is no shame, only healthy, productive conversations that help the child explore their inner world of budding desires and associated character qualities that will help them as adults find mates and other forms of sexual companionship. Every child develops self-confidence and an ability to speak about his/her developing sense of sexuality and is taught to explore and develop ethical and moral compasses. By the time a child reaches adulthood, s/he is ready to enter the world as a responsible, self-possessed individual loved and seen by his/her community and family of origin.

This is not the world we live in. Most children, queer or heterosexual, monogamous or polyamorous, are raised in homes that propagate certain idealized images of heterosexuality. Queer children and heterosexual children are raised as heterosexual, the queer ones innocent until proven guilty. The process of queer self-identification is almost entirely the burden of the queer child, struggling to express a subjective reality that often must remain hidden until the child's life is no longer dependent on the emotional and financial support from his/her family. In adulthood, many queer people continue to manifest heterosexual identities to perpetuate the sense of safety that was so desperately needed in childhood, now needed in continuum from society at large. Passing becomes a viable choice for many, as a form of survival. Gay, lesbian, and queer activists advocate for visibility so that the arc of social justice can continue to manifest, and one day queer children will grow up in an environment closer to queertopia. We still lack an ethical model of visibility.

In this chapter, I will seek to establish a kind of style to associate with queerness. The style will be one that can be both consciously adopted and personally adhered to, that has certain ethical expectations and parameters. I will call this style "political perversity." It is meant to encompass all the identities covered under the umbrella term "queer." Integral to the idea of political perversity is the role of shame in LGBT/Q communities: the shame we feel, the shame we have internalized, and the shame we must express in our politics and our art. This context of shame, I argue, is foundational within and reinforced by a moral dilemma that frames all sexual identity: namely the liar vs. the pervert. Political perversity must be able to answer both to this moral dilemma and its consequences of shame and passing.

A note on gender: many adult (and even child) queers are recognizable by their gender deviance. Certain kinds of flaming effeminacy and tomboyish butchness are unmistakably associated with homosexuality whether or not it is an accurate association. The relationship between gender expression and sexual identity is complex and worthy of many of its own monograph length texts, but gender identity and sexual identity are two different types of identity, even if they inform one another. For the purposes of constructing political perversity as a normative model for sexual identity, I want to simplify the endeavor by not depending on gender identity as a resource.

Shame and Sexual Moralism

"*My pride takes its royal hue from the purple of my shame.*"
—Jean Genet

Of particular political, moral, and stylistic importance to the concept of political perversity, as well as the underpinnings of passing, is the experience of shame. Many top queer theorists and activist writers have emphasized the role of shame, including most notably Michael Warner, Eve Sedgwick, and Leo Bersani. Countless others have written about the psychological role and cultural history of shame. Shame, the psychological experience of it; and the social manifestations of it in queer art, literature, and politics, is central to queer identity and should be central to any moral understanding of gay and lesbian ethics.

Michael Warner

In *The Trouble with Normal: Sex, Politics, and the Ethics of Queer Life* Michael Warner spends much of a chapter delineating the way heteronormativity instills its control through ethics. He explains that it isn't ethics or morality, but rather moral*ism* that dictates "when some sexual tastes or practices (or rather an idealized version of them) are mandated for everyone."[1] Moralism, then, bridges the gap between politics and ethics. Centered on the concept of sexual shame, Warner argues that this moralism establishes a social hierarchy of those who lead what is considered an ethical sexual life, and thereby receive the benefits associated with moral superiority (increased social respect, increased sense of self-worth/ value and thereby esteem). Sexual shame, he explains, therefore becomes a political act. It's a social maneuver that establishes the moral majority as superior to the moral minority.

The politics of shame, however, extends beyond the "overt and deliberate shaming produced by moralists, it also involves silent inequalities, unintended effects of isolation, and the lack of public access."[2] The politics of shame works most effectively through its insidious pervasiveness that serves as both an undercurrent and tidal wave of moral self-evaluation, and thereby as an extension of social control. The effects of isolation and the lack of public access become the key politicizing components, rendering some voices silent in the public sphere while enhancing and empowering others. This leads Warner to conclude that having an ethics of sex isn't about having a theory about "what people's desires are or should be."

Sexual shame renders some individuals as criminals or deviants. As Warner reminds us, "they might even be impeached." More commonly, he explains, sexual shame leaves people "rendered inarticulate, or frustrated, since shame makes some pleasure tacitly inadmissible, unthinkable."[3] The isolating capacity of shame aggressively impacts some more than others. When it comes to the LGBT/Q community the encounter with the politics of shame becomes a centralizing feature. The vulnerability to shame is instilled in childhood. A cavernous space exists where a sense of connection to family should be felt. This open space leaves individuals vulnerable to political manipulation centered on ethical failing. But within that matrix of shame an inherent paradox arises. In the words of Warner,

> Gay people have been especially vulnerable to the shaming effects of isolation. Almost all children grow up in families that think of themselves and all their members as heterosexual, and for some children this produces a profound and nameless estrangement, a sense of inner secrets and hidden shame. No amount of adult "acceptance" or progress in civil rights is likely to eliminate this expe-

rience of queerness for many children and adolescents. Later in life, they will be told that they are "closeted," as though they have been telling lies. They bear a special burden of disclosure. No wonder so much of gay culture seems marked by a primal encounter with shame, from the dramas of sadomasochism to the rhetoric of gay pride, or the newer "queer" politics. Ironically, plenty of moralists will then point to this theme of shame in gay life as though it were proof of something pathological in gay people. It seldom occurs to anyone that the dominant culture and its family environment should be held accountable for creating the inequalities of access and recognition that produce this sense of shame in the first place.

Here we have the primary paradox of shame that structures the process of moral development for LGBT/Q people. For the sake of survival, secrets are kept in childhood and in adolescence. Shame and associated self-loathing develops. If the child matures and comes to terms with his/her LGBT/Q identity then the shame is reinstalled in adulthood through the psycho-socializing function of the closet.

The politicizing capacity of shame is not unique to LGBT/Q identities. Autonomy is often politically confined "through moralism, law, stigma, shame, and isolation," Warner argues. But its inherent strength in relation to LGB/Q identity is its inherence in sexuality. For "in the realm of sex, more than in any other area of human life, shame rules."[4] And if we think of human energy as always engaged with human eroticism then it can be seen how the politics of shame can be crippling at an ontological level.

Warner envisions the war against the politics of shame as the ideal battleground of the gay and lesbian movement, a movement which has spent much of its energy attempting to "articulate the politics of identity rather than become a broader movement targeting the politics of sexual shame."[5] Inherent in the movement's desire to articulate an identity politics has been a subtle undercurrent of the subject's relationship to and position between dignity and shame. This battle within the community manifests in an internal hierarchy that privileges some over others based on their perceived relationship to shame from the gaze of heterosexual outsiders and the gaze of other homosexuals.

> On top of having ordinary sexual shame, and on top of having shame for being gay the dignified homosexual also feels ashamed of every queer who flaunts his sex and his faggotry making the dignified homosexual's stigma all the more justifiable in the eyes of straights. On top of that he feels shame about his own shame, the fatedness of which he is powerless to redress.

Warner aptly points out that centered on a politics of identity, the movement has "never been able to resolve its sense that dignity and sex are incompatible."[6] He directs his primary force of counter argumentation at Andrew Sullivan and his expression of LGB/Q politics in his book *Virtually Normal* (1995) which argues that the only two political issues that queer people should politicize are military service and marriage. Arguing from an assimilationist platform, Sullivan identifies theses two as the only remaining rites of passage for queers to achieve full normalcy status.

Eve Sedgwick

In her article "Queer Performativity," Eve Sedgwick argues that shame is perhaps "the collective essence of queerness." She establishes this through a close look at the interpellating ability of the phase "shame on you" (presumably in association with other shaming type gestures, facial expressions, and sayings). Sedgwick wrote this essay through the lens of performativity to establish shame and its relationship to sexuality as a kind of corollary to gender norms and gender identity.

Remember that Butler's performativity is based in J.L. Austin's analysis of speech acts. Sedgwick argues that "shame on you" functions in much the same way as the kinds of examples that Austin cites (such as "I now pronounce you man and wife"). "Shame on you" has illocutionary force, i.e., it confers shame. It is dependent on the interpellation of a witness, and occurs within a "pronoun matrix" in which the identity of the shame inflictor is both safely removed from the receipt of shame, but integral to the shaming production.[7]

She writes that "shame on you" is the repetitive experience of the queer child. And the word "queer" becomes such a powerful political term to describe the modern LGBT/Q community because it is so "unsanitizably" reminiscent of the shaming effects and "near-inexhaustible source of transformational energy" that is the experience of stigmatized gender and sexual non-conformity in childhood.[8] The experience of being shamed, she writes, is both "peculiarly contagious and peculiarly individuating."[9] The shamed experience of a child is one marked by a feeling of the connection with another human being as broken, an inability to arouse another person's positive reaction to one's communication. She notes that many developmental psychologists think of shame as the dominant affect that defines the space in which one's individual sense of self develops.[10] Given both the natural psychological potency of shame, and the recurrent employment of shame for children who are gender non-conforming, Sedgwick's argument of the performative aspect of shame for queers begins to become clear. Queer shame becomes the location of personal identity development. The sense of shame begins to feel natural. Shame is initially an affect, but becomes central not just to one's behavior, but also to his/her identity. Shame becomes the affect that creates the shift from behaviors to identity.

The adult politics, then, of the queer community become evidenced through the transformational change of the experience of shame. Sedgwick writes, "shame and pride, shame and self-display, shame and exhibition are different interlinings of the same glove."[11] The LGBT/Q communities' pride parades and calls for visibility are driven by the experiences of shame, as well as participate in those shaming structures: they both invoke the resources of shame while attempting to re-inscribe pride and visibility upon those same experiences. "Queer performativity," therefore for Sedgwick, is "the name of a strategy for the production of meaning and being, in relation to the affect shame and to the later and related fact of stigma."[12] Sedgwick cites some common identity vernaculars for LGBT/Q communities that participate in "shame consciousness" and "shame creativity" as "butch abjection, femmitude, leather pride, SM, drag, musicality, fisting, attitude, zines, histrionicism, asceticism, Snap!, culture, diva, worship, florid religiosity, in a word, *flaming* . . . and activism."[13] Even for those of us who escaped a childhood of direct queer shaming whether for reasons of invisibility or gender conformity, participation in the queer community means a constant confrontation of "shame on you" from political and interpersonal sources, as well as a perpetual awareness that we, too, could have been interpellated by shame from the earliest of ages. And many of us who escaped direct shame managed to internalize its effects if only it could reach us.

Leo Bersani

Leo Bersani begins his book *Homos* with the bold assertion: "No one wants to be called a homosexual."[14] He continues on to assert that no one on the Christian right would ever be able to stomach such a declaration, straight activists who are sympathetic to LGBT/Q causes don't wish to be confused as homosexual, and confusingly even most of strongest LGBT/queer activists who are LGBT/Q themselves abhor the term, spending large quantities of intellectual energies to deconstruct its history and usage. In essence, the term "homosexual" is so downtrodden with social stigma and shame that not even those most ready to declare their same-sex desire are comfortable with its contours.[15] The analysis and history of queer theory in the last chapter shows these types of intellectual moves where a look at the shaping of the terms to describe sexual identity are more important than recognizing the cultural applications of such terms as they are being utilized in a politically tense and complicated environment. Bersani writes "gay men and lesbians have nearly disappeared into their sophisticated awareness of how they have been *constructed as* gay men and lesbians . . . we have erased ourselves in the process of denaturalizing the epistemic and political regimes that have constructed us."[16] But this recognition of the deconstruction of LGBT/Q identity leads Bersani to make a number of observations about how the terms homosexual, gay, queer, lesbian operate in a culture more obsessed with the nomenclature than with the personhood behind the identity.

    The newest intellectual versions of the terms that locate same-sex desire carry with them requirements of intellectual and political sophistication that we "have to earn the right to [the designation of queer] and to the dignity it now confers."[17] The designation of "homosexual" once was a form of surveillance, one which made individuals visible as pathological social deviants that were in need of treatment. Now through the intellectual re-inscription of words like "queer," those who would once have been designated "homosexual" against their will must earn entry into the queer class of persons. This is one of the major shifts in sexual identity politics to which Bersani wants most to call attention. At the same time he recognizes the intellectual project of stabilizing the identities of queerness as disciplinary: engaging and producing discourse.[18] Shame is a deep theoretical resource of that discipline. He sees this as the ultimate paradox in sexual identity politics. The term queer is purposely employed to repeat with pride a pejorative term established by heterosexuals: a term that is meant to shame, while at the same time the intellectual endeavors behind the term (queer theory) are attempting to dispense the term of its homosexual referent.[19] Clearly shame is central to the paradox both in its re-visioning of "queer" as a term of pride with ample reference to its shaming qualities, all the while seeking to remove the pathologizing and medicalized import of the word "homosexual."

Sarah Schulman

In her book, *Ties that Bind: Familial Homophobia and Its Consequences*, lesbian author Sarah Schulman writes about what she argues as a primary experience of many LGBT/Q people: the experience of "shunning" from family and other loved and trusted individuals. Shunning a LGBT/Q family member, friend, or colleague means cutting them off from emotional, financial, or professional resources; severing conversations; or disregarding/minimizing the voice, role or importance of a LGBT/Q individual. Schulman describes it as a passive process with active and assaulting results. She writes that shunning is the source of significant long-term damage done to both the relationship and the LGBT/Q individual on the receiving end. She argues that LGBT/Q people learn from their families that straight lives are to be more valued than LGBT/Q lives, and manage to repeat this treatment on their lovers. Therefore, both inside the LGBT/Q community and outside of it, LGBT/Q people are not treated as valued and valuable individuals. Her description of shunning is in line with the types of descriptions above of shaming. Similar to the arguments of Crimp and Sedgwick in regards to shame, we see that shunning creates social breakage, clearly and expectedly between the straight and LGBT/Q community. But it also creates breakage within the LGBT/Q community. Although all LGBT/Q people are the recipients of shunning, rather than finding this as a source of community bonding, it creates more breakage and repulsion. Shunning is clearly not the same thing as shaming; shunning is a passive form of shaming. But existing along the same continuum, it can be seen that with increased rights, "tolerance," and "acceptance" of LGBT/Q people and LGBT/Q lives active shaming is harder to accomplish socially, but shunning remains an easy and popular way to establish a social hierarchy that elevates straight people above queer people.

Psychological Experience

Psychologists argue that a sense of oneself as gay or lesbian, necessarily developed and centered on the experience of shame in our culture, creates negative core beliefs that produce what we colloquially refer to as "internalized homophobia." The development of core negative beliefs about the self develops in stages. First, there is the recognition that the self is different. This often occurs during childhood. Second, there is the recognition that in social groups, being different is not a good thing. When adolescence hits, the recognition of same-sex attractions or atypical gender behavior intersects with an "internalizing [of] the message 'homosexual is bad,'" and calls back the childhood developmental realization that within a group being different is bad. The resulting belief about the self becomes something like "I am bad because I am different and I am homosexual." This belief can be the cause of a range of "affective and behavioral difficulties, such as depression, social withdrawal, and avoidance of people associated with the . . . lesbian [and gay] community."[20]

Internalized homophobia "consists of two distinct forces: erotophobia (fear of or discomfort with one's own sexuality) and xenophobia (discomfort with one's strangeness)."[21] It can manifest itself in a number of ways ranging from subtle to pronounced. Some of the more subtle expressions of homophobia may include the following:

1. fear of discovery
2. discomfort with obvious "fags" and "dykes"
3. rejection/denigration of all heterosexuals
4. feeling superior to heterosexuals
5. belief that lesbians are not different from heterosexual women
6. an uneasiness with the idea of children being raised in a lesbian/gay home
7. restricting attractions to unavailable women/men, heterosexuals, or those already partnered
8. short-term relationships[22]

Regardless of the symptoms of the internalized shame and homophobia, it becomes clear that its presence is always palpable: in the history of queer identities, in the culture (both straight and LGBT/Q), and in queer subjects themselves. Morrish and Sauntson have argued that the "really astounding thing about shame is how the queer subject accepts its apparent legitimacy."[23] And this becomes the need for its remaining presence within LGBT/Q culture: as both the foundational subject, and the primary source for inversion (e.g., "gay pride"). Caron (2005) has argued that because shame is so isolating and "hyperindividualizing that its effects are so intense, but by making it collective, we undermine its power and destabilize its legitimacy."[24]

Cultural Representations of Shame

Douglas Crimp writes about the importance of shame in the queer art world in the 1960's (specifically in the videography of Andy Warhol—specifically *Screen Test #2* which is a close up of just the face of a drag queen who is repeatedly shamed by the director of the film, through sexual requests, performances, etc). Through a close look at the queer shame politics of Warhol's films, and its importance in establishing the parameters of queer identity, he argues for shame's central importance in our modern day understanding of queer identity despite the modern "supposedly shame-eradicating politics of gay pride."[25] Crimp specifically thinks that the ethical project of bringing to light the shame in the queer art of the 60's, before the political visibility project that began with Stonewall in 1969, is an ethical project.[26] Crimp advocates the aesthetics of shame as an ethico-political platform that engages and honors our queer history as one full of shame and shaming.[27] He sees this as an important counter to much of the post-Stonewall gay and lesbian politics that advocates for dignity, pride, and homogeneity with the broader heteronormative culture. He writes that contemporary gay and lesbian politics "sees shame as conventional indignity rather than the affective substrate necessary to the transformation of one's distinctiveness into a queer kind of dignity."[28] It is only through embracing and showcasing our shame that we can reach the state of authentic queer political dignity.

Heather Love equates internalized homophobia with false consciousness, and argues shame as the both "the modality in which homophobia is lived" as well its intimate effect.[29] Her literary essay "Spoiled Identity: Stephen Gordon's Loneliness and the Difficulties of Queer History" focuses on the main character, Stephen, of *The Well of Loneliness*, whom she conceives of as an exemplar of queer history. Stephen is a figure of British aristocracy who struggles with the underworld of her fellow queers and the upper world of social responsibility, grace, and perception. Stephen is repulsed and repelled by her fellow inverts, and Love argues that modern day readers are repulsed and repelled by Stephen's self-loathing.

Love writes that any endeavor in queer studies must always face the central paradox that for all the dreams of a better future, our history is one founded upon "a history of suffering, stigma, and violence."[30] She notes that the paradox of this history is found in the terms used to describe the academic endeavor "queer." She writes, "the word *queer*, like *fag* or *dyke* but unlike the more positive *gay* or *lesbian*, incorporates the history of stigma and homophobic abuse into the name of the discipline."[31] This is why I wish to employ the phrase "political perversity" in this chapter as the overarching style: because it both begins to capture part of the shame of queer identities, and recognizes the history that creates our current possible political freedoms.

Love argues that the psychological continuance of pre-stonewall forms of queer existence can be seen in post-Stonewall subjectivities through the ease with which those of us in the modern political climate can empathize with the structure of feeling that "emphasizes shame, suffering, stigma, and violence, solitude, and secretiveness."[32] Queer figures from history, she argues, are not something we conceive of as role models, but instead we allow to represent as that which we fear becoming.[33] Our history strengthens us only through models that we do not wish to mimic.

Love continues on to argue that it is clear we have yet to produce the necessary critical tools in queer studies, because we have yet to produce a vocabulary to capture the structures of feeling historically present in queer subjectivities, what she describes as the "destitutions and embarrassments of queer existence."[34] And she argues that this is an absolutely necessary supplement to the history of laws, ideologies, and practices that impacted the lives the queer community.[35] This seems to be particularly true for defining an ethic for the queer community. There is an unavoidable need to integrate the subjective experiences and structures of feeling into an ethic that can enhance our group identity and political aspirations. Love writes in reference to our modern LGBT/Q culture of pride and celebrations that, "celebration gets us only so far, for pride itself can be toxic when it is sealed off from the shame that has nurtured it."[36] Any queer political identity must seriously take into consideration and integrate the experience of shame, both culturally, in our cultural products, subjectively, and in the re-countings of our subjectivities.

It is also important to acknowledge, explore, and incorporate an understanding of the way queer shame utilizes gender shame or hides itself under the mask of gender shame. At times, queer individuals can experience their shame as a kind of failure of gender. The female gender "ought" to display femininity and sexual/emotional desire for masculinity. If someone who is female is neither feminine nor attracted to male persons, then she might experience self-reproach for the failure to be a good female. And clearly there is a cultural equation, especially in childhood, between displays of effeminacy and butchness with queerness. I think it is important to recognize these relationships and the transference of shame between gender identity and sexual identity, but it is also important to explore and learn to articulate the differences between gender identity shame and the kind of shame that is equated with queer sexuality and sexual relationships. It is also important to explore, acknowledge, and articulate the ways in which the LGBT/Q community uses gender identity to establish internal hierarchies and shaming effects against both effeminacy and butchness.[37]

Removing the complicating factor of shame that is connected to gender identity and focusing on shame that is a product of queer sexual identity, I will argue that whatever one's gender identity, a queer sexual identity immediately plunges an individual into a shame based paradox that does not allow for a morally uncompromised escape. In the next section I will argue that all queer subjects are always already morally suspect, in that s/he can only ever choose between one of two moral locations: "the liar" (in this instance, some form of the closet or passing), or "the pervert." Any queer ethic for political advancement must take seriously this paradox as its starting point.

The Moral Dilemma of Queer Sexual Identity: The Liar or The Pervert

Homosexuality is still seen by many in our culture as a deep moral and character flaw, as a kind of perversion, and as something that is worthy of deep shame. This perception is clearly changing, and will continue to be shared by fewer and fewer people. The reality remains that at least some people in every LGB/Q person's life will maintain the "homosexuality as morally bankrupt" view, and every LGB/Q person will continue to face the potential for rejection, shaming, judgment, and isolation. This puts each LGB/Q person in a moral dilemma. Do I tell the truth about my sexuality and run the risk of being viewed as a pervert by my loved ones and/or people in my social worlds—by those who will guarantee my future emotional, financial, and social well-being? Or, do I hide this aspect of who I am and feel like I am, and run the risk of being branded a liar?

Remember that Charles Taylor understands our personal narratives of identity to be about situating ourselves as the protagonist in the story of the good. This means that each of us tries to articulate and organize our lives in such a way that we are configured as seeking the good, however we might define it. Our conception of the good will be profoundly influenced by social milieu in which we have been raised. Configuring a "good" LGB/Q subjectivity into a cultural or social narrative that can only conceive of a LGB/Q subjectivity as bad means an inescapable moral paradox.

In Erving Goffman's famous 1960's book *Stigma*, about the management of spoiled identities, he specifically defines homosexuality as a blemish of character. Goffman writes,

> there are blemishes of individual character perceived as weak will, domineering or unnatural passions, treacherous and rigid beliefs, and dishonesty, these being *inferred from a known record of,* for example, mental disorder, imprisonment, addiction, alcoholism, *homosexuality,* unemployment, suicidal attempts, and radical political behavior. Finally there are the tribal stigmas of race, nation, and religion, these being stigmas that can be transmitted through lineages and equally contaminate all members of the family.[38]

For older generations this conception of homosexuality as a failure of character remains, and for some in younger generations. In any family, for example, the reception of LGB/Q identity and its situation in a narrative of the good is going to be difficult to square with the social conception of homosexuality as an unacceptable frustration of the will.

Both the burden of secrecy and the burden of honesty are also placed on the LGB/Q individual. Public morality in many social institutions invites or demands the secrecy of homosexuality, while at the same time the rhetoric of the closet is one of lying, secrecy, and hiddenness. Every LGB/Q person must go through the burden of coming out and exiting the closet. We are all presumed heterosexual until actively and assertively proven otherwise through countless coming out moments. Our honesty is compromised before we have the chance to be honest. And our dishonesty is encouraged by conservative ideologies that presume it is bad for children to know about gayness, or bad for a military troop. Richard Mohr calls this a "coerced hypocrisy," using in particular the example of a teacher who is encouraging her students in truth-telling only to be told she must lie to them about who she is.[39]

So it can be easily seen that sexual identity passing is often motivated by moral considerations, by a desperate hope to maintain one's access to a narrative of the good that can be received by all of those in one's social network or community. Rosemary Hennessy has called this "passing as a proper subject."[40]

Richard Mohr argues, in line with the Goffman quote above, that LGBT/Q people can be viewed and judged with a combination of both individual character and tribal stigmas. But they are judged in line with the stigmas, rather than in light of actual behavior, virtue, or personal character. Mohr writes, "gays are viewed first and foremost simply as morally lesser beings, like animals, children, or dirt."[41] The paradox of the liar vs. the pervert traps LGBT/Q people below a moral threshold. This moral threshold often becomes the justification for the mistreatment of LGBT/Q people as a minority. It becomes the justification for denying equal rights, employment protections, or social respect. Mohr argues that if one finds that s/he is classified as a moral inferior without the benefit of establishing his/her own character, then this becomes the definition of unjust treatment.[42] He continues, "Catholic theology, health policy, and constitutional law—does exactly this: presuppose and reinforce the moral vision that gays are lesser moral beings."[43] To claim that LGBT/Q people are morally inferior is to engage a descriptive moral framework that acknowledges the history of moral thinking that has systematically stigmatized LGBT/Q people.[44]

In contemporary sexual politics, the stigma of pervert still remains an effective way to discount the perspective of equality that most queer and LGBT activists bring to the table. Members of the conservative right utilize tactics of sexual shame to dismiss and judge queer people as "perverts," while the reverse may be true: those on the left refer to those who are afraid of sexual shame or aversive to social shaming tactics to as "prudes."[45] Either way, the politics of shame and the marker of perversion remain central to the moral experience of out and closeted queer people.

Countering Passing and Building Norms

"Passing . . . is ontologically perverted precisely because it involves substituting illusion for reality and perception for knowledge."
—Anna Camaiti Hostert[46]

It is my argument that the liar/pervert paradox is at the foundation of modern queer identity, as well as at the center of our style and our politics. It is also my argument that this—often unconscious—paradox should be fully brought to consciousness in our moral theory, political practice, and cultural self-understanding. The first thing I would like to do in this section is talk about what I think is a common and appropriate political style for our times called "political perversity" that both counters passing and engages queer theory and can be described using the concept of style that I began developing in chapter 3. I will then suggest how we can begin to build norms within that model of political perversity to start addressing and resolving the paradox of the liar/pervert. This will suggest the need for a model of normativity that can be prescriptive for the LGBT/Q community which I begin building in the next chapter with the help of Christine Korsgaard's "practical identities."

Political Perversity as a Political Style—Countering Passing

When queer people decide to make themselves visible, they begin by employing many of the rhetorical phrases and opportunities available in our culture to express their developing LGBT/Q identities. They come out of the closet using heartfelt and often pre-packaged disclosures. They may begin to consume queer visibility products.[47] They begin to engage in queer culture through its music, media, bar life, and pride festivals. They engage in relationships and learn how to transgress social norms through public displays of affection. They begin to wear the unmistakable signs of their socially deemed perversity. Often times these displays of perversity begin in fear and shame only to develop into a sense of politically efficacious courage and self-regarding acceptance and respect.

The practice of political perversity often occurs as a strategy post-coming out to gain visibility and access to lovers. Descriptively it can be seen as a non-reflective process that moves one into the current cultural climate of the LGBT/Q community. Political perversity responds to the paradox of the liar or the pervert by embracing the pervert half of the paradox and proudly combating the liar portion. The moral judgment in the paradox has not been resolved, however, but rather the seeming lack of sexual morality, based on conservative social standards, is embraced. Most queers consciously disagree, more or less, with the moral judgment on their sexuality, but its internalization and display become a very part of their social identities. This is the element of shame in queer performativity that Eve Sedgwick so astutely draws our attention towards. Visibility is achieved through the expression of self as the pervert, and with visibility the process of advocacy for rights and recognition can begin.

There is significant moral value to be found simply in the move towards visibility that occurs in political perversity. Its basic gestures are transgressive. The sexual mores of the religious right are mocked and publicly insulted. Those who embrace political perversity refuse to accept the humiliation that is supposed to keep their desires hidden. Instead they wear both their desire and their shame on their sleeve. Out of this trek towards visibility, queer theory has found its inspiration and its beginnings. It is not surprising that queer theory has no formal understanding of the role of morality in sexual identity. I argue that this is the case, because queer theory has failed to recognize the paradox of the liar or the pervert and address both aspects of the dichotomy, as well as the failed moral thinking that underpins it. Political perversity, however, has practical long-term impact on heteronormativity. Its transgressions, social disrespect, camp, and countering of out-dated and unhelpful models of sexual morality does get those within heteronormativity to question their privilege. It undermines the ubiquitous nature of heterosexuality; and it begins critical conversations, even if only at first it begets ridicule.

In practice, the conscious moral underpinnings of political perversity are minimal. Its adherents may possess strong unexamined dependencies on contemporary popular culture understandings of authenticity and individual self-actualization. But most participants in political perversity would claim an unexamined commitment to social construction models of sexual identity that would immediately raise conceptual and philosophical problems for authenticity and self-actualization if carefully examined. Because of this observation, I'd like to begin to offer a way to consciously add moral norms to political perversity. I'll begin with some possible resolutions to the foundational LGBT/Q moral paradox of the liar or the pervert.

Addressing the Liar/Pervert Paradox—Building Norms

There are a variety of ways we can address the liar/pervert paradox. We could neutralize the distinction between heterosex and homosex, arguing for the value of sexuality more broadly as a form of human discourse and a necessary good. Timothy Murphy has taken this approach. We could argue for the inherent dignity in the quest for equal rights, as Richard Mohr does. I have already made it clear in this chapter that I conceive of the role of shame as integral to the cultural and psychic experiences of being LGBT/Q, and therefore would argue that we need shame as part of our political discourse, even if we are fighting in a principled way for our rights that confers dignity upon us. We may also be able to involve shame in our public politics, as did the Ancient Greeks. I will discuss some of what Christina Tarnopolsky has to say about Socrates and the value of political shame. We could combat the ordinary moral definitions of "honesty" and align them more closely with the queer experience of truth-telling, as does James Alison. Finally, we could argue for an ethics based on an aesthetics of living that can enhance the development of a queer sexual life rather than inhibit it. This is the intellectual move that Foucault makes. I mention all five approaches to the resolution of the paradox because I think that each is a necessary element to building an adequate ethical approach both to the historical experiences of being LGBT/Q, and the truths that LGBT/Q people know about their own lives. These approaches are also necessary to build a normative model of gayness that can improve the political present and future of our people, as well as create and provide a prescriptive normative model for present and future generations.

Timothy Murphy argues for the value of what he calls, "homosex" based on the basic argument put forward by Robert Solomon for "heterosex."[48] Solomon argues for the value of heterosex as a form of meaning making, a kind of communication, and a language that bonds people together. Murphy argues that the differences between heterosex and homosex are as negligent as the differences between French and English, only in so far as they are different types of meaningful languages.[49] Solomon argues that sexual relations should be interpreted in likeness to poetry, as a constructed by "behaviors, intentions, and interpretations" that supersede the actual acts and body parts.[50] Given the analogy of homosex as language, Murphy argues that we cannot do without the role of homosex in the defining of our culture, with the pluralities and expansiveness it offers. He argues that because the broad cultural discourse of sexuality is based on heterosexuality, LGBT/Q youth must grow up without "parental and social expectation to guide them," therefore they must create their own sets of discourses, rhetoric, meanings, and self-understandings. Because of the dearth of self-esteem enhancing media, social, and cultural role models, Murphy argues that gay and lesbian youth must develop "personal skills and capacities" that help them carve out meanings and levels of communication in a world that otherwise wouldn't exist. And so he argues for the ethical value of homosex as something that "brings opportunities for strength and heroism that are unparalleled in heterosex." He continues on that gay men and lesbians "must make a language of their own in order to express themselves. They must make their own way in finding social opportunities, seeking civic benefits and protections, and creating their own symbolism, imagery, and culture."[51] Murphy ends up taking the line that homosex is just as valuable as heterosex in terms of its communication function, but that homosex is culturally and even ethically superior because it adds to the discourses surrounding sexuality in the broader culture.

Richard Mohr frames the resolution of shame and the moral paradoxes faced by queer people in terms of the inherent dignity to be found in pursuing political equalities and a public voice. The dignity is to be found in both what LGBT/Q people are fighting for politically, and the dignity cultivated in the fight. He writes, "if I am right in the belief that what is chiefly at stake in gay politics, understood broadly, is dignity, then the gay movement primarily needs to take the form of asserting rights by acting in a principled manner."[52] Mohr thinks that the development of this principle should be the key aim of queers in the public sphere rather than coalition building or any other type of grassroots organizing. He clearly thinks that by developing such a principled approach, LGBT/Q folks will be able to find a foothold of self-respect and dignity even in the face of perpetual governmental defeat.[53] He thinks that principled speech can be simply driven by an understanding that any government has the obligation to "promote the flourishing of individual styles of living" and that in order for anyone to flourish within any style of living, there must be three things present:

"dignity, self-sufficiency, and happiness."[54] So for Mohr, dignified treatment and dignity in public policy and public representation is clearly a good.

But how can we make this square away with the history of queer identity and culture as deeply embedded in shame? As having an aesthetics of shame? How do we pursue dignity and at the same time retain our history of shame, which we need both for the cultural contours of its shared identity, and in order to make recognizable trajectories into the future? Well, one way to do this is to think about shame as having an important political function that it plays all on its own. Christina Tarnopolsky considers the role of shame in contemporary LGBT/Q politics. She argues that there is a historical precedent for using shame in political discourse, which can be traced back to the elenctic encounters of Socrates' in ancient Athens. Tarnopolsky cites Socrates' elenctic encounters as the paradigm case of respectful shame, in which one uses reason and dialogue to expose and embarrass the poor reasoning of another interlocuter. The resulting discomfort on the part of the shamed party allows for a thoughtful reconsideration of a previously held position, even if that position was poorly analyzed and poorly considered. She argues that it is through the shaming function that the individual in political discourse becomes self-conscious and is thereby able to reflect upon his/her deeply held convictions or beliefs. For Socrates, the sense of shame was employed in the search for truth,[55] and in the Platonic dialogues we see again and again how he was able to employ shame effectively in this pursuit.

It should be quite clear that queers know a lot about shame, about its occurent experiences and its effect on self-esteem and human relationships. If the experience of respectful shame can be used to enhance dignity in conversations about political convictions by evidencing poor reasoning and biased conclusions, queers might find that they can engage their experiences of shame and gain dignity by employing and shaming others in a respectful way. According to Mohr, the best way to do this would be to enhance our principled rhetoric and continue to figure out conversational moves that will result in the political consequences we are hoping for.

Another way to combat the liar/pervert paradox is to argue against the first half of the paradox. One could argue that sexual identity is not a matter of truth or truth-telling. But that position would be hard to support without reifying some of the most damaging elements of heterosexism and its erasure of homosexuality and LGB/Q relationships. General public moral opinion holds that heterosexual individuals have a moral responsibility to be honest about their sexual relationships, particularly if they are in the public eye or have an influential role in the community. General public moral opinion has historically held that LGBT/Q people have the opposite moral responsibility: to be secretive or (more positively valenced) discrete about their intimate sexual relationships, especially if s/he has an influential role in the community. One could also argue that the definitions of truth-telling, honesty, and lying are different for individuals who are queer. James Alison, an openly gay Catholic priest and theologian, makes this argument. He describes truth-telling about one's sexual identity as a gift and a process of undergoing. Alison is exploring, in particular, the difficulty of sexual identity honesty inside the Catholic Church—for clergy and lay people alike—which views queers as entirely morally bankrupt, while at the same time housing hundreds of thousands of queer souls. Alison calls into question the moral respect we should feel for closeted clergy who are invested with deep trust on "important" spiritual matters while they are deceptive in regards to "things that don't really matter, like their own or other people's sexual orientation."[56] He compares this "moral idiocy" in the church with what he claims is increasingly common moral knowledge in the secular world. He writes,

> it is increasingly common for fourteen or fifteen-year-old kids to be able to 'come out' in their high schools and not only not to be attacked for it, but to earn the respect of their peers as having moral credibility for having come out. These kids, both straight and gay understand, as do most people in practice, that the earliest and most fundamental moral questions in anything to do with things gay as they actually affect gay and lesbian people have very little to do with sex and everything to do with peer group honesty, rejection, acceptance, fear, hatred, courage, solidarity and friendship.[57]

Alison sets out to describe how these two disparities, between the deception of people who are to represent a kind of moral authority, and teenagers who are getting it morally right by being honest with their peer groups, could teach us something about the nature of honesty amongst LGB/Q people under hostile moral theology.

First he describes the experience of honesty for LGB/Q people as both a challenge and a gift. He writes that every LGBT/Q person knows the difficulty of the experience of coming out of the closet. He writes, "many of us [gay folk] will have taken long detours prior to coming to some sort of honesty—journeys away from home, flights into depression, sexually compulsive behavior, or some sort of chemical dependency."[58] And he argues that the complexity and levels of loss and desperation that can accompany the honesty that LGBT/Q people must work to achieve, means that many who have landed in a place of honesty will expect of others the same rigorous honesty. He worries that honesty can become a kind of cheap weapon for those who have conquered the heights of honesty against those who are still facing its myriad challenges. So, he wants those of us who have experienced honesty as a challenge to begin to see it as a gift.[59]

Alison continues on to distinguish honesty from both sincerity and holding to the truth. People who are sincere, he argues, are not emphasizing the truth that undergirds their statements, instead they are providing a "passionate guarantee of their good faith in saying it." Sincerity has a disturbing side effect in that the sincere person will be unable to self-criticize. Alison argues that sincerity is its own guarantee and does not allow for internal exploration, and this makes the sincere person a danger to himself and others.[60] His point about sincerity is particularly important for his analysis of honest sexual identity in the context of the Catholic Church, as it is the Church's theological conviction that anyone who identifies as being gay or lesbian is expressing a "passionate identification with something which it is a mistake to believe really exists."[61] Alison argues that sincerity cannot be our definition of honesty because it is both hyper-subjective, and because it leaves us open to the kind of identity negating critiques like that of the Catholic Church. It remains clear to Alison, that given the internal exploration and critiques one can have regarding sexual identity means that we should not see it in light of subjectivity.

Alison questions those who claim strict adherence to objectivity in the declaration of truth without admitting to subjectivity. He argues that virtues such as honesty will provide rules that no one will be able to live up to, and that it is key to acknowledge subjective failing and mercy for all those who will inevitably fail (including oneself) in the attempt to attain rigorous moral standards.[62] We can never leave ourselves entirely un-implicated in what we hold to be true. Our moral convictions and commitments to "objective truths" demonstrate key commitments and subjective truths about ourselves.[63]

Viewing honesty about sexual identity as both challenge and gift, Alison positions his understanding of honesty between sincerity and objectively holding to the truth. He writes that honesty is never something one can possess. Instead, it involves "a certain being possessed, a certain undergoing."[64] Alison thinks that both sincerity and objective adhere to the truth are things that can be possessed. One can feel a certain degree of ownership over both sincerity and objectively clinging to the truth. However honesty, he writes, "is something that can never be laid claim to."[65] He clarifies,

> Honesty is perceived in someone's undergoing something in a way which tends towards truthfulness. And it is particularly related to this sense of them undergoing something. It is precisely that they are not laying hold of something, *but are working through something outside their control having happened to them.* In short, they are possessed by a truthfulness which is coming upon them. It is not the case that they are laying hold of and wielding a form of truthfulness, whether individually or collectively.[66]

Having an understanding of the truth of sexual identity not as something one can possess, but as something one undergoes, is the kind of phenomenological trajectory any person can describe through his/her coming out process. There is both the experience of choosing to be honest about who one is, but there is also the added experience that one could not choose different and/or could not choose a different social rhetoric to engage to explain either one's identity, experience, or sense of self. This kind of coming to a place of honesty is different than other kinds of truth-telling, and accurately suggests that we might have good cause for rethinking how honesty functions as a virtue inside the LGBT/Q community, or for LGBT/Q individuals inside of the heterosexual community.

Emphasizing a location between objectivity and subjectivity in which the undergoing process of honesty takes place is important both to the relationships between honesty and sexual identity, and more broadly to the role of virtue ethics. Alison writes,

The old way of talking about what was true or not true made a distinction between objective and subjective, such that truth was objective, and self-perception was subjective, and therefore inclined to be wrong. But we are gradually learning that people's subjectivity is an objective fact about them, that the pattern of desire which forms how we relate to each other is not, and can never be, simply an individual mistake. It is always the starting point from which it becomes possible to make mistakes or not.[67]

Coming to understand the subjective roles of our desires and interpersonal attractions is key to understanding the complexities of our ability to interact with others in identifiably ethical (or unethical) ways. The process of truth-telling about sexual identity, particularly in the context of a hostile theology or community demonstrates the necessary role of subjectivity in our ethics.

Another ethical approach to dealing with or eradicating the moral paradox of the liar or the pervert is to conceive a different approach to ethics all together that can celebrate the self-design of pleasures, desires, and lifestyles. This is exactly the kind of ethics that Michel Foucault began to articulate, and it has some important resonances with the philosophical concept and role of style that I began to articulate in chapter 4.

Foucault observed about modern ethics that thinking of morality as obedience to a code of rules was no longer working. He argued that the corresponding necessity to this observation necessitated a to search for an aesthetics of existence.[68] He took his cues from the ancients,[69] and thought that the primary moral question should be 'how is one to live'? The answer to the question can only be found in "the cultivation of a relation of self to self in which the self is neither given nor produced, but is continuously worked in the labor of care and skill."[70] So the parameters of this kind of ethics is that one seeks to formulate and practice new styles of existence. Ethics is to be found in the giving of style to one's existence, with the "primary tools" of "ascesis, of self-disciplining, and self-fashioning."[71] Foucault's concern was not that we try to cultivate an authentic relationship to our self; rather, his concern was that life be lived through 'creative activity' and self-stylization.[72] With this model of self-design, it is to be understood that the self is not the starting point, but rather "an end, a task, a work which, although constantly worked, is never completed."[73] Ethics becomes the process through which one molds him/herself, and this grants significant autonomy over the desired end result. Moral practice becomes the process of monitoring, testing, and improving the self in order to find self-transformation.[74]

It is important to note that Foucault began to cultivate this sense of an aesthetics of existence through his frustration with the sexual liberation movements that were taking place contemporaneously. Foucault felt that those movements were not resolving the ethical dilemmas surrounding sexual practice. So, for Foucault, cultivating an aesthetics of existence was a literal remedy to identifying with the sexual identity movements. He thought one did not need to identify as LGB/Q, but instead should cultivate an aesthetic that allowed for a certain kind of approach to bodies and pleasures.

My argument for the concept of style in chapter 3 is based on the desire to enhance a political identity with gayness, which I will more thoroughly sketch out later in this chapter. It is important to note that both Foucault and I start in the same place, making observations about the efficacy of LGBT/Q politics in resolving basic moral questions and sexual identity. Both of us are dissatisfied, and both of us employ the concept of style to articulate a different possible conclusion. The primary difference between the two of us is that Foucault negates the need for identity politics, and I affirm it. Foucault's intuition for stepping away from sexual identity politics may have been the best move at the time he was writing. The rapid advancement of sexual politics over the last 30 years means that he and I are engaging the same movement, but at almost radically different points in its development. One of Foucault's deepest satisfactions in advocating for an aesthetics of existence is its ability to give individuals access to self development in alignment with his/her "unique rootedness in the world and history."[75] An aesthetics of existence that engages queer sexual practices may have needed to step away from sexual identity politics to achieve the status of an ethic when Foucault was proposing his role for style. I submit that at the current time engaging the sexual identity politics in the name of style is a cultural, historical, and ethical possibility.

Notes

1. Michael Warner, *The Trouble with Normal: Sex, Politics, and the Ethics of Queer Life* (Cambridge: Harvard University Press, 1999), 4.
2. Warner, *The Trouble with Normal*, 7.
3. Warner, *The Trouble with Normal*, 3.
4. Warner, *The Trouble with Normal*, 16.
5. Warner, *The Trouble with Normal*, 31.
6. Warner, *The Trouble with Normal*, 40.
7. Eve Kosofsky Sedgwick, "Queer Performativity: Henry James's *The Art of the Novel,*" *GLQ* 1: 1-16, 4.
8. Sedgwick, "Queer Performativity," 4.
9. Sedgwick, "Queer Performativity," 5.
10. Sedgwick, "Queer Performativity," 5.
11. Sedgwick, "Queer Performativity," 5.
12. Sedgwick, "Queer Performativity," 11.
13. Sedgwick, "Queer Performativity," 13-14.
14. Leo Bersani, *Homos* (Cambridge: Harvard University Press, 1995), 1.
15. Bersani, *Homos*, 2.
16. Bersani, *Homos*, 4.
17. Bersani, *Homos*, 2.
18. Bersani, *Homos*, 3.
19. Bersani, *Homos*, 71.

20. Christopher Martell et al., *Cognitive-Behavioral Therapies with Lesbian, Gay, and Bisexual Clients* (New York: Guilford Press, 2004), 9.

21. L. Margolies, M. Becker, and K. Jackson-Brewer, "Internalized Homophobia: Identifying and Treating the Oppressor Within," in *Boston Lesbian Psychologies Collective, Lesbian Psychologies: Explorations and Challenges* (Urbana: University of Illinois Press, 1987), 233.

22. Margolies et al, "Internalized Homophobia," 231-2.

23. Liz Morrish and Helen Sauntson, *New Perspectives on Language and Sexual Identity* (New York: Palgrave Macmillan), 90.

24. Morrish and Sauntson, *New Perspectives on Language and Sexual Identity*, 110.

25. Douglas Crimp, "Mario Montez, For Shame," in *Regarding Sedgwick*, edited by Barber and Clark (New York: Routledge, 2002), 64.

26. Crimp, "Mario Montez, For Shame," 63.

27. Crimp, "Mario Montez, For Shame," 64.

28. Crimp, "Mario Montez, For Shame," 66-7.

29. Heather Love, "Spoiled Identity: Stephen Gordon's Loneliness and the Difficulties of Queer History," *GLQ* 7(4), 2001, 499.

30. Love, "Spoiled Identity," 491.

31. Love, "Spoiled Identity," 492.

32. Love, "Spoiled Identity," 495.

33. Love, "Spoiled Identity," 497.

34. Love, "Spoiled Identity," 498.

35. Love, "Spoiled Identity," 498.

36. Love, "Spoiled Identity," 515.

37. One good example of this kind of analysis on butch identity and its relationship to the lesbian community is Halberstam's article: "Between Butches."

38. Erving Goffman, *Stigma: Notes on the Management of Spoiled Identity* (New York: Simon and Schuster, 1963), 4. Emphasis added.

39. Richard Mohr, *Gays/Justice A Study of Ethics, Society, and Law* (New York: Columbia University Press, 1988), 160.

40. Rosemary Hennessy, *Profit and Pleasure: Sexual Identities in Late Capitalism* (New York; London: Routledge, 2000), 2.

41. Richard Mohr, "Gay Studies as Moral Vision," in *Gay Ideas* (Boston: Beacon Press, 1992), 245.

42. Mohr, "Gay Studies as Moral Vision," 248.

43. Mohr, "Gay Studies as Moral Vision," 251.

44. Mohr, *Gays/Justice*, 31.

45. Christina Tarnopolsky, "Prudes, Perverts, and Tyrants: Plato and the Contemporary Politics of Shame," *Political Theory* 32, no. 4 (August 2004), 469.

46. Anna Camaiti Hostert, *Passing: A Strategy to Dissolve Identities and Remap Differences*, translated by Christine Marciasini (Madison: N.J.: Fairleigh Dickinson University Press, 2007),13.

47. Rainbow jewelry, HRC insignia stickers, etc.

48. Solomon argues for the value of heterosex above any kind of homosex. He argues that heterosex is important because it has a gender unifying aspect to it that creates a "natural" continuum with humans and much of the rest of the reproductive animal species as well as some of the plant species. Timothy Murphy ed., "Introduction" to *Gay Ethics: Controversies in Outing, Civil Rights, and Sexual Science* (Binghamton: Haworth Press, 1994), 15.

49. Murphy, *Gay Ethics*, 9-10.

50. Murphy, *Gay Ethics*, 11.
51. Murphy, *Gay Ethics*, 17-18.
52. Mohr, *Gays/Justice*, 321.
53. Mohr, *Gays/Justice*, 329.
54. Mohr, *Gays/Justice*, 158.
55. Tarnopolsky, "Prudes, Perverts, and Tyrants," 486.
56. James Alison, *Undergoing God: Dispatches From the Scene of a Break-In* (New York; London: Darton, Longman, and Todd, 2006), 178.
57. Alison, *Undergoing God*, 178.
58. Alison, *Undergoing God*, 180.
59. Alison, *Undergoing God*, 180.
60. Alison, *Undergoing God*, 184.
61. Alison, *Undergoing God*, 180-1.
62. Alison, *Undergoing God*, 181.
63. Alison, *Undergoing God*, 182.
64. Alison, *Undergoing God*, 182.
65. Alison, *Undergoing God*, 183.
66. Alison, *Undergoing God*, 183. Emphasis added.
67. Alison, *Undergoing God*, 186.
68. Timothy O'Leary, *Foucault and the Art of Ethics* (London: Continuum, 2002), 1.
69. Foucault produced an extensive study of the moral formation practices of the Ancient Greeks. He studied four elements: what he thought to be their ethical substance (the aspect of self and behaviors that are relevant for ethical attention and judgment), the mode of subjection (the rules of conduct people submit to and the relationship they develop to the rules), ascetics (how people choose to moderate their behavior and eradicate their desires), and the telos (the type of beings people are attempting to become through their ascetic practice). James Bernauer and Michael Mahon, "The Ethics of Michel Foucault," in *The Cambridge Companion to Foucault* edited by Gary Gutting (Cambridge: Cambridge University Press, 1994), 144.
70. O'Leary, *Foucault and the Art of Ethics*, 2.
71. O'Leary, *Foucault and the Art of Ethics*, 4.
72. Bernauer and Mahon, "The Ethics of Michel Foucault," 153.
73. O'Leary, *Foucault and the Art of Ethics*, 5.
74. Bernauer and Mahon, "The Ethics of Michel Foucault," 143-4.
75. Bernauer and Mahon, "The Ethics of Michel Foucault," 152-3.

Chapter 6
Practicing to Preach:
Gayness as a Practical Identity

There are many diverse identities within LGBT/Q communities. A difficulty that activists and theorists continuosly confront in thinking about solidarity and political action for LGBT/Q issues is how to unite these separate individuals under a cohesive and collective community for action. An additional question arises in how one can create normative force behind this collective. The particular problems of the term "queer" and its ambiguity as a term that both resists identification, and a term that suggests a collective political umbrella, demonstrates a unique paradox for LGBT/Q communities. How do we both recognize the social contingency of our identities and yet demand adherence to a community of disparate people for action? If we demand that collective identity, what should be its particular commitments?

In this chapter, I employ Christine Korsgaard's notion of "practical identities" in order to argue for a normative collective that demands participation through chosen identity. I then spell out what some of the particular normative responsibilities might be within "gayness": a constructive political collective identity for LGBT/Q individuals.

Korsgaard's Practical Identity

Christine Korsgaard's practical identities can provide us with just such a moral framework. In this section I will spell out some of the major elements of her notion of practical identity, and then provide a sketch for what I think gayness as a practical identity should look like at this time in queer politics and history. I will close with a conversation about how Korsgaard thinks of responsibility, and how same-sex sexual behavior can create relationships of reciprocity that require commitment to the LGBT/Q community.

Korsgaard's book, *Sources of Normativity,* seeks a foundation for morality. Why is it that humans engage in discourse about ethics? Where do moral agents derive their moral justification? What is the ultimate source of our concerns about relations and behavior? Our moral obligations are what make us human, she argues. And those obligations are grounded in our humanity. Our obligations, she argues, arise first out of our autonomy—which is the source of our ability to obligate ourselves—and then extends our moral obligations to commit us to the humanity in others. Our humanity, therefore, is the source of our normativity. But how is it that we conceptually model that humanity? Korsgaard argues that it arises from what she calls our practical identities.

First, we should consider how Korsgaard understands "identity." The question of what constitutes identity, for Korsgaard, isn't theoretical; rather, it is a "description under which you value yourself, a description under which you find your life to be worth living and your actions to be worth undertaking."[1] Based on this definition of identity, which she conceives of as significantly and totally practical, it is understood that we engage the world and think about our place in it by thinking through the identity markers that construct meaning for us both socially and psychologically. Her examples of such identities include "woman or man, an adherent of a certain religion, a member of an ethnic group, a member of a certain profession, someone's lover or friend, and so on."[2] Korsgaard's perspective is based in a Kantian framework. Kant closely relates the concept of identity with the 'interests of reason.' According to Raymond Geuss, Kant claims that the interest of reason is "exhausted when one has given answers to the three questions: 'What can I know? What ought I to do? What may I hope?'"[3] Our considerations about identity are derived from our reasoned explorations of basic life-navigating questions, with our personal interests at the center of that consideration.

By invoking the sense that these identities are "practical," she circumvents the debates about identity as either some kind of essentialism, or as social constructionism. The practicality of the identity allows it to be ethically productive for the individual without needing an extended explanation about how it adheres in the subject. Our practical identities appropriate what Heidegger would call our handed down identities—socially provided identities that give us a core sense of value or ethical motivation. Korsgaard's definition, however, understands identities as something we both have received and create. Some of our identities, her examples would seem to suggest, are ones we have the choice to adopt, such as one's professional identity, or one's identity as someone's friend or lover. While others are more socially confining as they are not chosen, such as "woman" or "man." The idea is that once I accept or choose a practical identity, I also commit myself to a set of behaviors and obligations to others based on that identity. Professional ethics illustrates this relationship well.

Defining Qualities of Practical Identities

Even though our practical identities demonstrate themselves in the ordinary day-to-day particulars of our lives, the philosophical contours of those identities are more robust.

To begin, each of us by necessity must have a practical identity (which can involve plural commitments to different groups). While the contingency and conceptions of our practical identities will differ, it is unavoidable that we will each have to engage our practical identities to live our day-to-day lives. Our practical identities will "govern" our lives[4] and our desires.[5] This means that they provide us with reasons to act. Korsgaard argues that "we endorse or reject our impulses by determining whether they are consistent with the ways in which we identify ourselves."[6] Our practical identities help us to align our desires with our sense of selves, especially in the instances where those desires are in conflict or otherwise incompatible.

So our practical identities, and our value-based commitments to them, become law-like structures that we can reference to make decisions about our behavior. This is the reflective aspect of practical identities. Kant would employ a conception of law-like structure to guide our behavior and desires; Korsgaard extends that conception to a formal law-likeness that we can identify with. For Kant this law-like structure is the Categorical Imperative. For Korsgaard it is a part of the "reflective structure of human consciousness."[7] For both, this structure stems from the human condition. The particulars of the structure will differ, but its presence is true for all human beings.[8] We discover the particulars of the behavior guiding structure through the use of reflective reasoning. When we are able to pinpoint a reason for behavior, then we have achieved reflective success. Korsgaard describes this process as "if I decide that my desire is a reason to act, I must decide that on reflection I endorse that desire."[9] We are clearly first motivated by desire, but it becomes our reflective reasoning that allows us to engage our desires, and our endorsement of our desires will be found within the sense of normativity that is found in our practical identities. This reflection isn't a finite process. It is understood by this model that the work of reflection will always continue forward.[10]

As we continue to reflect on our practical identities, and the content of those that will provide reasons for acting on our desires, we contribute to the contours of those identities. It is also clear that those identities appear to us with socially constructed content already in place. So Korsgaard argues that our practical identities are both given by culture and by nature, and are partially constructed by our reflective endorsement. Christopher Gowans argues that this seems to suggest "that what makes practical identities strongly normative depends not simply on what is given to the agent, but on the constructive activity of the agent's will."[11] This observation about practical identities gives us a lot of room to argue for a prescriptively normative model of identity that is both socially contrived and purposefully developed.

The next aspect of practical identities that needs to be described in some detail is the way in which these law-like reflective structures of human consciousness create moral obligation. Korsgaard describes our practical identities as the source of our normativity, and continues on to argue that "your reasons express your identity, your nature; your obligations spring from what that identity forbids."[12] She thinks that the question of practical identity is settled as the source of normativity before the question of how one *should* conceive of her practical identity is addressed.[13] So we have our identity obligations first, and then we have our moral obligations once we determine what ought be our identity obligations. And those moral obligations always should be first in terms of our identity. In the next section, I will discuss Korsgaard's understanding of moral obligation as it relates to practical identity.

Morality and Identity

There are three elements of the normative force of practical identities: excellence, autonomy, and obligation. Excellence is simply the idea that we have a general obligation to ourselves to pursue and attempt to attain the greatest possible version of our selves, to be "good at being what you are."[14] Clearly there is relevance here to our practical identities. Once we've been identified with/or choose to identify with a particular identity, we have a responsibility to our self to seek the most perfect alignment with the identity that is possible. But the virtue of excellence isn't what creates the normative aspect of practical identities.

Korsgaard claims "our autonomy is the source of our obligation."[15] We must be able to make un-coerced moral decision that engage our rational and reasoning capacities. It should be apparent already that some of the practical identities we employ are not chosen through an un-coerced rational analysis of our options. Some identities are chosen this way, but when it comes to identities such as "woman" or "homosexual," social convention limits our autonomy. Therefore, in order to maintain autonomy for the model of practical identities, it must be the case that we can determine our own obligations by "considering what a person with your practical identity can will as a law."[16] There is an interesting moral observation to be made here regarding passing. Claims of autonomy would suggest that the freedom to choose *any* social identity would leave us with greater self-governance than submitting to the general identities assigned by society and filling in the obligation details. Passing is one way to choose a new identity that is in alignment with one's rational analysis of the best identity for one's other life goals. Therefore, it would seem that passing effectively engages the moral concept of autonomy.

This concern about autonomy and passing is contained by the concept of practical identity. Because Korsgaard conceives of the role of autonomy as arising primarily in the freedom of the individual to establish the law-like and obligating contours of one's own practical identity whether socially assigned or chosen, she limits the scope of moral consideration. Practical identities in this regard are pre-moral.

The final important moral element in the normative force of practical identities is obligation. Autonomy, Korsgaard has already argued, is the source of our obligation. Inside our practical identities is where we establish the law-like commitments to our own behavior and treatment of others based on our rational evaluations of how to achieve excellence, or the best versions of ourselves given the identities we employ in order to live our lives. So inside the autonomous portions of practical identities we find our greatest source of obligation to humanity.

Here are some things that Korsgaard has to say about obligation: it makes us human;[17] it is always unconditional;[18] it is associated with the idea of law; and it is compulsive.[19] This means that the force of obligation within our practical identities creates a significant and deep connection to humanity such that we are in a compulsive relationship with others who share our practical identities. We are also obligated to greater humanity in alignment with those values established within our practical identities. Korsgaard writes, "it is the conceptions of ourselves that are most important to us that give rise to unconditional obligations."[20] She thinks of this primarily in terms of personal integrity and our commitments to certain identities. We create a sense of self-value and value in our lives through our identity commitments. So, what happens when we experience a conflict in our values through a conflict of the values held within our independent practical identities?

Identity Conflict

Clearly it is the case that sometimes one of our identities will commit us to one set of values and behaviors, while a different mutually-held identity will commit us to an equally obligatory value that conflicts with the first. Examples for gay people abound. Our religious identities may tell us that we are to reject queer people and queer behavior, while our gay identities obligate us to certain gay sexual behaviors in our pursuit of happiness. This conflict may be exacerbated by the obligation imposed by both identities to disclose the true natures of ourselves to our loved ones in the name of honesty and authenticity. Korsgaard writes, "conflicts that arise between identities, if sufficiently pervasive or severe, may force you to give one of them up."[21] This acknowledgement is important. Conflicts between practical identities will arise, and this is not a significant problem for practical identities; in fact, it captures something true about life: we can feel problems in our integrity, sense of self, and identity based on conflicting sense of obligations driven from mutually exclusive values established by cherished practical identities. One of Korsgaard's inviting examples that is particularly relevant for the gay community is the experience of falling in love. She writes that "falling in love with a Montague may make you think that being a Capulet does not matter after all."[22] One could either think here that the experience of falling in love with someone complicates or changes one's identity (which is certainly true in our culture), or that the practical experience of falling in love teaches certain new practical values and lessons about obligation to humanity that can compromise one's previously held deep convictions and obligations.

Korsgaard clearly thinks that there are times when the shedding of parts of one's identity is warranted. She writes, "some parts of our identity are easily shed, and, where they come into conflict with more fundamental parts of our identity, they should be shed."[23] This can be one way in which we enhance and tone our identities: by catching conflicts that can be resolved through simple shedding of less important or superficial elements of our identity in order to allow the deepest portions of our identities, and most closely held convictions, the capacity to flourish and grow. In general, Korsgaard appeals to a concept of personal integrity to solve the problem of identity conflicts, with this process of shedding, reorganizing, and dismissing identities as a solution to practical identity conflict.[24]

Practical Identity and Narrative

Kim Atkins does an excellent job in combining Korsgaard's conception of practical identity with a concept of narrative. I have previously established the importance of narrative in the process of creating gay identity [early in chapter 1, and early in chapter 4]. Atkins describes narrative as integral to the ethical perspective, as "only the narrative model preserves the first-person perspective, which is essential to an ethical perspective."[25] And this is also the same way in which she connects the importance of narrative to Korsgaard's practical identity, because the normative force of practical identity is to be found in the first-person perspective.[26]

The role of narrative in practical identity is not something that Korsgaard clearly articulates, but it is something she clearly implies by attaching normativity firmly to our considerations and internal—as well as external—articulations of self. This fact of the inherent connection between narrative and practical identity makes it more attractive for our purposes. Gay identity is sometimes only identifiable through the self-articulations and disclosures that gay people make in public. The dependence of gay identity on narrative makes practical identity an even stronger candidate for describing and allowing for the contours gayness to come to the fore.

Gayness as a Practical Identity

The model of practical identity that I'd like to suggest for LGB/Q people is "gayness." This is meant to be one model of moral and political engagement for people who engage in same-sex behaviors, or have same-sex desires. In this section I will argue why queer people would benefit from thinking in terms of a practically employed moral identity. I will then argue for some particular features that should be inherent in that moral identity.

The values of gayness should be developed in part from experience, with the expectation that those norms will change as our social and political climates change. Gayness should be modeled on an idea of what it would look like to be a "good queer," and should inspire excellence. Gayness should produce obligations, both to other queer people (gayness identified as well as others) and to the LGB/Q political landscape. It should be derived from political motivations as well as be continually developing in line with the political climate. Reason and reflection should be continuously used in outlining the new developments in sexual politics. Gayness should always be directed towards the future, but take seriously the data of the past.

One of the most important normative aspects of practical identity is that it provides a reasoned reference point to decide how and when to enact our desires. This provides due cause for creating practical identities that center on questions of sexual desire and the social regulation of those desires. Given that Korsgaard (and Kant) think that a reasoned set of law-like principles are necessary for maintaining our humanity and desires, a model of gayness in the current political climate is unavoidable.

Gayness is particularly a type of what queer scholars have recently been referring to as "homonormativity"[27] which broadly refers to a system of moral and ethical thinking that is developed to address the needs of people who enter into same-sex relationships. When people choose to pass, they are choosing to engage in heteronormativity. By embracing the practical identity of "gayness" an individual is making a commitment to begin participating in homonormativity.

What I have discussed so far are the theoretical considerations that provide a motivation for embracing a concept of gayness. What I'd now like to discuss are the particular elements of gayness that I think are necessary for our current political climate. The first, and perhaps most obvious element of gayness is the obligation to come out as gay (queer, bisexual, lesbian, etc), to provide visibility and to make oneself a social member of the gay community more broadly. This is both a duty to self, and a duty to community.

In our current political climate the desiderata that should be employed for gayness ought to include:

1. commitment to fighting sexual shame (the psycho-social battle against abjection as advocated by Warner in *Trouble with Normal*)
2. commitment to fighting heterosexism
3. commitment to fighting internalized homophobia
4. a dedication to rupturing the social conception of "normal"—in the heterosexual community
5. commitment to fighting the convention of "The Secret" in the gay community
6. provision of role models and resources to subsequent generations of queer people

7. willingness to step in on behalf of queer individuals when homophobia is being used against him/her

The first desideratum takes its inspiration from Michael Warner's *The Trouble with Normal* in which he argues that we ought to take on a psycho-social battle against abjection. Practical applications of this desideratum include openly celebrating sexual diversity, and encouraging sexual health education that is inclusive and non-judgmental. It would include advocating honest conversations about sexual exploitation, rape, sexual harassment, and sexism in polite company, as well as encouraging respectful and celebratory conversation about sexuality and sexual desire.

The second desideratum primarily involves combating assumptions that everyone is heterosexual. It requires advocating for equal rights for gay partnerships and committed relationships including access to health benefits, marriage, divorce, and social support and sanctioning of same-sex relationships.

The third desideratum requires critical analysis of self, and the psychology of oppression and shame that all gay people have been raised into. The commitment to fight internalized homophobia is also a commitment to developing a gay consciousness. Fighting internalized homophobia involves both identifying and replacing problematic and self-defacing behaviors and thought patterns.

The fourth desideratum takes its cues from queer theory and is specifically driven at rupturing the idea of normal that heterosexuals apply to certain types of other heterosexuals (monogamous, reproduction driven, with limited or sanitized kink). This conception of normal and its associated sense of "natural" creates privilege for some and judgments of sub-humanity on others.

Desideratum five takes its inspiration from Richard Mohr's *Gay Ideas* in which he argues that at the center of gay life is the convention of what he calls: "the Secret" (with a capital "S"). The socializing force that keeps gay people from participating in most public life and public conversation is the shaming force of "the Secret." The idea is that gay identity is still a secret, should still be honored as a secret for those who wish to remain in the closet, and should be kept out of view in polite and particularly intergenerational company. Mohr argues that this convention is perpetuated most vehemently by members of the gay community who see it as a governing social force that demands we ought protect one another's secret. Given that most gay people see it as a violation of another gay person's rights to disclose his/her sexuality without express permission, or sometimes even with express permission, means that we continue to respect and maintain the idea that gay sexuality is something that should be treated as a secret. Gay people more than straight people are put into positions to employ discretion about gay sexuality, and this is doing immense damage to our community and our political goals.

The sixth desideratum simply requires that queer people in positions of social authority maintain and advertise their own visibility so as to be visible role models for the next generation. It may also have soft requirements that older queers try to provide general mentoring services for the younger generation.

The final desideratum takes its inspiration from Sarah Schulman's *Familial Homophobia*, in which she advocates for third party interventions anytime that homophobia is witnessed and recognized. Schulman argues that the intervention of a third party on behalf of the homophobia victimized gay person demonstrates to the perpetrator that the gay person is both valuable, and that homophobia is unacceptable. She argues that these third party messages are more effective because more socially forceful than a gay person advocating for his/her own well-being/dignity.

Gayness as a practical identity is both predicated on the idea that gay individuals need an overarching identity and set of normative laws to guide their behavior and desires in light of their queerness and same-sex relationships. Gayness as a practical identity is also about a commitment to the gay community and to an eschatological image like "queertopia" mentioned in the opening section of this chapter. In order to think more philosophically about the nature of community commitment and responsibility, I'd like to return to a discussion of Korsgaard and her understanding of responsibility.

Responsibility—Citizens of Queertopia

The question of responsibility is deeply embedded in the ways in which we define our identity-based norms and decide how to act in accordance with those norms. We must think both in terms of behavior and self-regarding moral assessments, but we must also consider how others will perceive and judge our actions. Korsgaard clearly thinks that our practical identities will provide us with communal understandings of responsible behavior as well as define who will be in the position to hold us responsible. Walter Glannon argues that being responsible "presupposes the capacity to respond to practical and theoretical reasoning concerning what one ought to do or not do."[28] The relationship here to practical identity should be clear. Responsibility relies on exactly the framework practical identities employ to create identity-based norms and commitments. Glannon takes the position that responsibility "supposes a conception of personal identity consisting in psychological connectedness and continuity based on moral structural and functional properties of body and brain."[29] When we assign responsibility to others for their previous behaviors, we employ a practical sense of their identity as continuing over time.

Korsgaard argues that prior to receiving the assignment of responsibility, one must take ownership of his/her responsibility. She writes, "responsibility is in the first instance something taken rather than something assigned."[30] Much like practical identity, responsibility is something we take on. Korgaard also argues that our normativity is to be found in part in the identification of ourselves as a "Citizen in the Kingdom of Ends."[31] This is an appropriation of a Kantian concept, and she contextualizes it in terms of the practical identities we claim for ourselves. For Kant, being a Citizen of the Kingdom of Ends meant something like taking the Categorical Imperative as the defining feature of your moral responsibility towards others, and thereby seeking to live towards an ideal of a community in which each and every individual treats each and every other individual as an end in themselves. For Korsgaard, the defining features of our practical identities will guide the ways in which we pursue a perfect moral community of co-treatment in alignment with the normative prescriptions of our practical identity. Kant and Korsgaard both employ an eschatological image to guide their considerations of moral responsibility that transcends the individual and instead guides the community. Remember at the beginning of chapter 5, I began with an eschatological image of queertopia as a guiding feature for building a practical identity of gayness. Individuals who employ gayness as a practical identity should also consider themselves to be Citizens of Queertopia.

As Citizens of Queertopia, it becomes necessary that we treat the political ends of other citizens as our own. Korsgaard would argue for this in a more theoretically abstract way by saying "to treat another as an end in itself is to make her ends your own."[32] This could also translate to promoting "each other's projects as routinely as [we] do [our] own."[33] It is key to remember in the communal development of gayness that the interest of certain subgroups of the queer community shall be promoted by all subgroups. And it is our commitment to our selves as Citizens of Queertopia that creates this obligation.

Holding others responsible is also something we do for moral reasons, and in light of our identities. Korsgaard writes that we hold others responsible because they are both rational persons and a psycho-social phenomenon.[34] We recognize and respect both of the aspects in a person that makes practical identity possible in order to hold them responsible, and for this reason we must seriously take into consideration how the other individual considers his/her/hir assigned identities as practical identities involving normative claims on his/her/hir behavior. This means that when we hold a woman responsible, we hold her responsible in part as a woman. If she is a feminist, we may assign judgment in particular ways that we would not if she identified more strongly as a traditional housewife, and vice versa. If we are assigning judgment as a woman, our own moral conceptions of womanhood will infuse how we hold the other accountable. The same is true when we assess the responsibility of someone who is queer. We will consider, as part of our judgment, how one handles her gayness as well as consider (if we ourselves are queer) how we conceive of our own normative obligations as queer people. Korsgaard sees this process of holding others responsible as granting a base level of respect to others, and as part of taking a "chance on some form of reciprocity."[35] She writes, "holding someone responsible can be insensitive or merciless; failing to hold someone responsible can be disrespectful or patronizing."[36] Responsibility is a part of our relationships with others, and when we appropriately hold another responsible we make room for a moral friendship and collaboration to develop.

The connection between reciprocity and responsibility is especially keen for Korsgaard who writes that, people who enter into relations of reciprocity must be prepared to share their ends and reasons; to hold them jointly; and to act together. Reciprocity is the sharing of reasons, and you will enter into it only with someone you expect to deal with reasons in a rational way. In this sense, reciprocity requires that you hold the other responsible.[37]

Holding others responsible in order to enter into relations of reciprocity with them makes it possible to create communities of obligation alongside shared goals. It makes it possible to create communities of shared practical identities. Korsgaard continues "when you hold someone responsible . . . you are prepared to accept promises, offer confidences, exchange vows, cooperate on a project, enter a social contract, have a conversation, make love, be friends, or get married."[38] The reciprocity found in the willingness to hold others responsible involves the expectation that we have shared reasons and respected ends with the person we are engaging. This also explains why those individuals who have already entered into a model of creating norms around gay identity have an investment in getting others to do the same. We want our reasons and ends to be shared, especially by those we are the most intimately involved with.

Gayness as a practical identity creates obligations to others through our shared commitment to the political ends of the LGB/Q community. It allows for reciprocity in our friendships, love relationships, political co-organizers, queer co-workers, queer mentors, and queer social leaders. The key commitment that must arise first and foremost to guarantee these relationships of reciprocity is an open commitment to the practical identity of gayness. Passing, in this regard, is the most significant threat to relationships of reciprocity and responsibility for the LGB/Q community.

Gayness and Power

LGB/Q people will continue to be the victims of abuses of power from a homophobic culture for some time. Gay-bashings and other hate crimes will continue to occur and exist as a specter of a threat for many visibly queer people as they traverse certain social spaces. We will continue to have our voices and experiences ignored by those who think they occupy a position of moral superiority. Oppression of LGB/Q people will continue. The history of homosexuality tracing back to sexology in the latter part of the 1800's and the discourse of sickness surrounding gay people that is now over a century old will continue to effect the social hierarchy and ensure our lowered place in relation to others, illustrated by social policies such as "Defense of Marriage Act."[39] To combat these models of power-over oppression and symbolic social hierarchies we will need to continue to employ modes of power that include empowerment and coalition-building.

The power at work in political perversity as well as in gayness as a practical identity needs to be articulated and explored. In brief, the power of political perversity resides in the power to transgress and also the power to make cultural meanings for a group of persons who have been starved of cultural resources for meaning-making. The power to transgress the pre-established culture of heteronormativity with visible perversion, and the power to infuse our media and academic resources with positive and realistic images of queer folk, is both a deconstructive power and a power that forges new meanings. The commodification of gay style into mainstream culture will establish political visibility in the form of empowerment, as well as expose class issues and new oppressions hidden underneath within our own community.[40] Style, especially gay style, requires financial resources that are unfairly available to some and not to others. Hennessey writes,

> The commodification of gay styles and identities in corporate and academic marketplaces is integrally related to the formation of a postmodern gay/queer subjectivity, ambivalently gender coded and in some instances flagrantly repudiating traditional, hetero, and homo bourgeois culture.

Commodified style is appropriated in political perversity. The underbelly of that "flagrant repudiation," as Hennessey argues, does class-based damage. That location of damage is where we should focus some of our gayness norm building. Yes, I think we can and should have both: the employed transgressive power of political perversity based in style and commodification as well as the norm-building power of gayness.

The power in gayness as a practical identity is transformative. In order to explain the transformative power of gayness, I will employ a model of subject repetition that allows for an ethical shift descriptively written by Judith Butler in *The Psychic Life of Power*. She describes a consideration of power, and our subjective relations to power, but also how identity can occupy that site of repetition with agency for positive moral change.

In her model of power, Butler begins with a basic dual defining aspect of power: power is something that controls us, subordinates us, and to which we must submit. However, power is also something that produces and forms us as subjects. So when we think about power in its psychic manifestation, what does it look like? She argues that our subjection is both the process of "becoming subordinated by power as well as the process of becoming a subject."[41] Because gayness as a practical identity is derived from our subject formation, or subjection, understanding the role of both the power of our oppressors who define us as gay through shame, and our coming to self in that identity through the forces of insidious power as well as power that creates us as creatures of moral character and political insight, Butler's idea of subjection gives us a model of power that both explains the internal workings of identity under oppression, as well as draws attention to moments of transformative repetition that can allow us to create better norms of gayness both for ourselves and for the next generations that will be formed in the power and image of the gayness created now.

Our subordination is the condition of possibility for our agency. For Butler a prime example of our subordination is our passionate attachment to our parents or care-takers as children as our only mode of survival. If our parents are homophobic (which many parents of gay children are) how can we have agency that runs in opposition to that homophobia? Butler argues, "while power is *exerted* on a subject, subjection is nevertheless a power *assumed* by the subject."[42] And it is in this assumption of power that we have the room to enact our agency in accordance with our norms, even if some of the structural aspects of our repetition may be unavoidable. It is also this assumed power that becomes the power that we wield. Butler thinks of this as the "reiteration" of power in the subject. It is the temporalization of power that is the "route by which power's appearance shifts and reverses."[43] So, if our care-takers were, for example, theologically homophobic, we have the power to enact and practice our gayness in our theological lives.

We are all vulnerable to categories of social organization through our desire for sociality. Butler argues that to be visible, we must be recognizable, and we can only be recognized through prior social categories. Therefore, to be recognized we must submit to subordination. And it is our desire for sociality that becomes an "exploitable desire" or a site of reception for power. Being labeled as queer by society carries with it the possibility for sociality, particularly in adult life in the forms of romantic connections. That label carries with it moral judgment, primarily at this time in the form of the paradox of the liar or the pervert. It is required that we take in this power of moral judgment, wield this power as our own, and transform our social norms regarding gayness into norms that allow us to fight for the dignity and equality of our lives, loves, and rights, as well as to express our cultural truths, learned moral lessons, and ethical insights.

Civil rights movements have always employed transformative models of power, the type of which is described above and integral to practical identity. The gay version must be both transgressive (stylistically perverse) and transformative in its moral and normative endeavors. Because our lives have been defined by others through our sex acts and sexual desires, we must claim both our sexual behaviors and desires as integral to, but not the total of what and who we are. We must have both the performativity of shame and the building of dignity through the pursuit of our civil rights, and we must see both as forms of the transformation of the oppression we have survived and the relationships, culture, and community we are creating.

Notes

1. Christine Korsgaard, *The Sources of Normativity* (Cambridge: Cambride University Press, 1996), 101.
2. Korsgaard, *The Sources of Normativity*, 101.
3. Raymond Geuss, "Morality and Identity," in *The Sources of Normativity*, 191. He locates this discussion in the *Critique of Pure Reason*.
4. Korsgaard, *The Sources of Normativity*, 120.

5. Geuss, "Morality and Identity," 109.
6. Korsgaard, *The Sources of Normativity*, 120.
7. Geuss, "Morality and Identity," 191.
8. Korsgaard, *The Sources of Normativity*, 121.
9. Korsgaard, *The Sources of Normativity*, 97.
10. Korsgaard, *The Sources of Normativity*, 94.
11. Christopher Gowans, "Practical Identities and Autonomy: Korsgaard's Reformation of Kant's Moral Philosophy," in *Philosophy and Phenomenological Research* 64, no 3 (May 2002), 553.
12. Korsgaard, *The Sources of Normativity*, 101.
13. Korsgaard, *The Sources of Normativity*, 103.
14. Korsgaard, *The Sources of Normativity*, 3.
15. Korsgaard, *The Sources of Normativity*, 91.
16. Gowans, "Practical Identities and Autonomy," 548.
17. Gowans, "Practical Identities and Autonomy," 5.
18. Gowans, "Practical Identities and Autonomy," 103.
19. Gowans, "Practical Identities and Autonomy," 4.
20. Gowans, "Practical Identities and Autonomy," 102.
21. Gowans, "Practical Identities and Autonomy," 120.
22. Gowans, "Practical Identities and Autonomy," 120.
23. Gowans, "Practical Identities and Autonomy," 102.
24. Korsgaard, *The Sources of Normativity*, 103.
25. Kim Atkins, "Narrative Identity, Practical Identity, and Ethical Subjectivity," *Continental Philosophy Review* 37 (2004), 341.
26. Atkins, "Narrative Identity, Practical Identity, and Ethical Subjectivity," 342.
27. The scholar most readily associated with the term is Lisa Duggan.
28. Walter Glannon, "Moral Responsibility and Personal Identity," *American Philosophical Quarterly* 35, 243.
29. Glannon, "Moral Responsibility and Personal Identity," 231. It is worth mentioning this as a philosophical concern about identity regarding the nature of responsibility. Glannon is particularly concerned to establish that nature of personal identity that could allow us to assign responsibility to a person retroactively to events having occurred in the past. To do this, we must have a sense of a person continuing psychologically through time. There may be analogies here to show the problem with passing as a morally problematic choice in terms of responsibility, claiming, holding, and being able to have responsibility assigned. Passing always involves a break in identity from a former disclosed and socially received identity to a new contrived identity. This complicates our ability to assign responsibility prior to the shift in identity.
30. Christine Korsgaard, "Creating the Kingdom of Ends: Reciprocity and Responsibility in Personal Relations," in *Philosophical Perspectives* 6 (1992), 306.
31. Korsgaard, *The Sources of Normativity*, 100.
32. Korsgaard, "Creating the Kingdom of Ends," 309.
33. Korsgaard, "Creating the Kingdom of Ends," 309. Korsgaard sees this as an obligation of friendship in a moral context.
34. Korsgaard, "Creating the Kingdom of Ends," 321.
35. Korsgaard, "Creating the Kingdom of Ends," 312.
36. Korsgaard, "Creating the Kingdom of Ends," 314.
37. Korsgaard, "Creating the Kingdom of Ends," 311.

38. Korsgaard, "Creating the Kingdom of Ends," 306.

39. Rosemary Hennessy, *Profit and Pleasure: Sexual Identities in Late Capitalism* (New York; London: Routledge 2000), 118.

40. Hennessy, *Profit and Pleasure,"* 111. Some of this class oppression also takes the form of gender biased oppression within the gay community that privileges the greater incomes of men (and therefore gay men) over women (and therefore gay women).

41. Judith Butler, *Psychic Life of Power: Theories in Subjection* (Stanford: Stanford University Press, 1997), 2.

42. Butler, *Psychic Life of Power,* 11.

43. Butler, *Psychic Life of Power,* 16.

Conclusion
Social and Legal Implications of Sexual Deceit

Chapters 1 through 4 of this book analyze passing in fairly abstract terms. Chapters 5 and 6 set out a practical solution to passing, and general questions of LGB/Q visibility that can counter both active and passive passing. But, for as long as passing remains an option, there will remain other areas of practical inquiry in which passing must play a conceptual, always moral, and sometimes legal role. This conclusion will sketch out some areas of application for an indepth ethical analysis of passing and its implications, including a preliminary look at questions in sexual politics: outing and privacy, questions relevant to professional ethics and social role morality; and the application of Title VII/Sexual Harassment Law to cases of same-sex harassment.

Implications for Sexual Politics: Passing/Outing, Public vs. Private Debate

Why and When Should a Person be Outed?

Outing is the corollary to passing. We can think of it in terms of a personal disclosure (i.e., outing oneself) or as a third party disclosure (i.e., outing someone else). Outing someone else comes with a different set of moral questions from outing oneself, and in both cases there are concepts as well as social and cultural consequences that need to be explored. Questions regarding outing other people—particularly celebrities—and its ethics were debated, especially in the early 1990's in gay publications such as *Village Voice, OutWeek, The Advocate* as well as a few mainstream news publication: including *The New York Times,* and the *Chicago Tribune.* The public posthumous outing of Malcolm Forbes in June of 1990 became a major source of controversy.[1]

Some writers oppose outing others under almost all circumstances, citing its brutality and violation of privacy. These individuals will usually only make one exception to their moral rule: if a public official is doing damage to the LGB/Q community, then he or she deserves to be outed.[2]

Others argue that outing individuals, especially those who are famous, provides very needed role models for the gay community.[3] It has been argued that the dead have no privacy rights and therefore posthumous outing can always be justified. Others have argued that as long as one is promoting his/her own dignity and self-respect as a queer person, then outing is morally justified and is in fact a consequence of living morally.[4] Others cite consequentialist reasoning to justify outing or not outing: namely, if the individual to be outed has something significant to lose (employment, child custody, etc), then outing can simply not be justified.[5] Others cite outing as the only legitimate strategy to fight pervasive homophobia.[6] In what follows, I will briefly look at these arguments focusing on the contentious ethical values at play.

In general, an ethical assessment of outing (whether oneself or another) is dependent on agreed upon benefits within the LGB/Q community: authenticity, self-affirmation of gayness, (individual) psychological health, happiness, group liberation, and progress on gay causes.[7] Other key ethical questions and values to be taken into consideration include privacy, secrecy, freedom, coercion, truth, lies, knowledge, the first amendment, sex, sexuality, dignity, and happiness.[8] Outing, it is often argued will have long-term utilitarian benefits for individuals and communities.

Outing Oneself

To analyze outing oneself using a utilitarian calculus is unlikely to produce the necessary foundation for visibility. Outing oneself certainly has positive consequences in terms of a greater connection and honest disclosure of one's life, but it often fails to produce social goods, and can in fact lead to disastrous social consequences. A better ethical framework for outing oneself can be grounded in deontology and duties to one-self that enhance dignity and self-respect.[9] Richard Mohr argues that gay people have a moral obligation to provide their love relationships with equal respect (to that of heterosexuals). He argues that this can be founded minimally on the duty to respect persons, and the obvious observation that one is, oneself, a person. The only way to honor one's love relationship is to make that love relationship visible through self-outing or coming-out.[10] The duty-to-self to out oneself is sometimes extended to a duty-to-community. It is argued that the visibility of individuals makes it easier for the community as a whole to receive the social recognition and rights it deserves.[11]

Outing Others

It is assumed by the rhetoric of the gay community that outing oneself is of value and should be done autonomously when one is ready. However, the debate on the outing of others tends to lean towards questions of immorality. Violations of autonomy are raised as the highest concern, and stringent parameters and situations are imposed to determine when the morally problematic elements of outing a third party have been relinquished.

Outing others is best defended on a utilitarian calculus; in fact, this is the only defense it usually receives. The basic argument is that the community will benefit if the true sexual orientation of others is known, therefore one is justified in outing a closeted homosexual. There are certainly other arguments to be made in favor of outing people. One might produce an argument through the use of virtue ethics that a decent queer person would be open and honest about his/her/hir gayness, therefore holding a person accountable to that decency is justifiable. One could also argue that if one has personal, first-hand knowledge about someone else's queer sexuality (either through having been sexually intimate with that person, or knowing intimate details), than the burden of keeping that knowledge is a moral compromise of one's own honesty and autonomy. Under these circumstances, the person with the knowledge of the gayness is forced to participate in the deception of the closeted individual. Under cases of abuse by the closeted individual this claim ought to be enhanced.

Arguments against outing others have centered on concerns about violations of autonomy, privacy and legalistic concerns about libel. The concerns about libel are misplaced if the information is true,[12] but the concerns themselves demonstrate a deeper more problematic element to the social perception of gayness. Vito Russo argues that "if being gay is *not* disgusting, is *not* awful, then why can't we talk about it?"[13]

The argument against outing from autonomy suggests that autonomy ought to be "understood as the ability to discover and pursue those purposes which are congenial to one's self." In order to respect the autonomy of others, we must at minimum respect their right to engage these abilities.[14] A solution to this problem of autonomy might entail encouraging and prodding others to come out of the closet, using whatever tools of influence one has to employ.

The argument against outing based on privacy depends on a confused conflation of the terms of privacy and secrecy. This will be discussed at much greater length below. But first, I will discuss two systemic pieces to problems of outing: closetude, conventions of secret keeping and LGBT/Q community considerations more broadly.

Closetude and the Secret

At times the arguments for outing are inversely framed through the harms of "closetude" (a term for passively/actively allowing others believe one is a heterosexual). The most important, morally relevant, aspect of the closet is that it is maintained by coercion. All gay people must go through a stage of being closeted, and this stage is both a moral and spiritual coercion.[15] When one accepts the parameters of the closet, one accepts the view of society that gayness is something to be hidden, one accepts that his/her/hir relationships are to be dishonored and kept secret, one passively if indirectly accepts oppression, and one avoids direct harms. The option of the closet is maintained by force. But it is important to note that the closet does not constitute a "right." Therefore queer people do not have a right to their own closetude. Richard Mohr argues, "The dynamics of the closet do not comport with what a right is. At a minimum, a right means a permission to act in accordance with one's own desires, to live by one's own lights rather than by the dictates of others, whether the others are majorities or a tyrant or anyone else who might coerce one."[16] More accurately, gay people have a right not to be coerced into closetude. Actions of outing approximate this combating of the closet.

Closely related to the concept of closetude is what Richard Mohr refers to as the convention of "the Secret" (employed in chapter 6). It is broadly understood within the gay community that you do not out other gay people in the heterosexual world, particularly if tangible repercussions will be felt as a result of that outing. The code of secrecy is so thorough and internally reinforced by members of the gay community that few individuals step outside that convention to question the damage to civil rights and moral fortitude that the secrecy is perpetuating. This code of secrecy, Mohr argues, is one that each gay person is born into, and to which no one grants individual consent.[17] He argues that the secrecy of the closet is greater than a set of rules employed. Rather, it is a convention, the conscious breaking of which causes civil unrest, anger, and fear from those in charge. Outing is an act of civil disobedience in a culture that defines invisibility and silence as the only proper place for what it sees as a group of moral degenerates. Mohr continues on to argue that the convention of the secret is *the* social convention that most centrally defines the gay community.[18] If we are looking to redefine the gay community for the purposes of social justice gains in

LGBT/Q rights, there is a strong argument to be made that regular and casual—non-punitive—outing is the way to move forward.

Outing and a Right to Privacy

The strongest argument against outing is an individual's right to privacy. Particularly beginning with the 1986 U.S. Supreme Court case *Hardwick vs. Bowers* concerns over the right to privacy within the gay community has taken a front row seat. In the Hardwick case, a gay man was prosecuted with the Georgia anti-sodomy law for having private consensual anal sex in his home with another man. He argued for his right to privacy, which the courts denied. The gay community viewed this as a huge defeat, and since that time has been focused on rights rhetoric based on privacy.

The problem with basing LGBT/Q rights on demands for privacy is the possible slippery slope into secrecy which is the mainstay of the rhetoric which reinforces our oppression and invisibility. Privacy is the right to have "control over the access that others have to one." This must be distinguished from secrecy, which is "the intentional concealment of something."[19] Sissela Bok argues "privacy need not hide and secrecy hides far more than what is private."[20] Clearly the two concepts are related on a continuum, but secrecy is a more severe form of privacy. Even our most ordinary rhetoric suggests that our private lives, especially for heterosexuals, are not also secret lives. Wedding rings, family photos, and casual conversation about family all evidence that private lives are often exposed in structure—if not detail—in very public ways. It is clear that the private lives of gay and lesbian individuals have suffered from a lack of respect, invasion, and oppression from the court system and society at large. But maintaining the convention of the secret deepens and sustains this damage. LGBT/Q individuals have a right to privacy (even when the courts deny them this right), but LGBT/Q individuals should not have a right to secrecy.

"Gayness" in Positions of Social Authority: Role Morality, Professional Ethics, and "Gayness"

Arguments for an Obligation to Model

In addition to general claims about the obligation to community that all LGBT/Q persons share to 'come out' of the closet, there are particular arguments that emphasize the obligation that certain LGBT/Q individuals have to community in light of the social roles they occupy. Professional ethics ought to also be affected by claims of obligations to be role models. Are these claims legitimate? Under what circumstances does a person's sexual identity necessarily impact their professional performance or ability to effectively be placed in fiduciary relationships with LGBT/Q patients, clients, parishioners, or students? What about the responsibility of famous people (actors and public personalities) and politicians to be role models for gay community?

Once upon a time—beginning with the both the invention of the closet and the public visibility of gay and lesbian persons starting after the second half of the 20th century—gay people were told that a certain amount of notoriety required invisibility. Larry Gross quotes a famous now-known gay writer " 'One of the unwritten laws of gay life,' [writer Armistead] Maupin sighs, 'is when you reach a certain level of fame, you shut up about your homosexuality. You're not told this by straight people, you're told it by other famous homosexuals who are ushering you into the pantheon of the right."[21] It was not until very recently that the LGB/Q community began to demand something more of its community members.

Current arguments in favor of public visibility for all famous and professional LGB/Q persons center on a number of positive and negative positions. For professions that inspire and guide young adults, such as teachers, individuals argue that visibility provides much needed role models[22] which, in addition, diminishes teen suicides.[23] The status of role model is essentially included in the professional description; it is considered to be an ethical part of the person's role and function in society.

For those who resent individuals who decide to stay in the closet—despite their role obligations and ability to be out of the closet—elements that are cited include the frustrations that their closetude helps to "perpetuate the invisibility that fuels anti-gay stereotypes . . . [and] reinforces the belief that homosexuality is shameful."[24] Public and famous closeted gay and lesbian individuals inevitably benefit from the social progress made within the LGB/Q community, without contributing themselves to its contours through the most important resources they have: their visibility and public personae.[25] Others have cited the poor effects on the gay community itself for loving and embracing its closeted celebrities arguing that it is "our own internalized homophobia that makes us want to love [them]."[26] Clinging to the few available LGB/Q persons publicly known within the LGB/Q community—yet still closeted for the general public—does not add to our sense of political empowerment. Some have even argued that the closetude of gay people in the public eye is itself "treason" against the gay community.[27]

Positions of Public Trust

Positions of public trust present particular challenges to questions about the ethics of the closet in public and professional life. Minimum standards of public accountability have claimed that if someone is doing direct harm to the LGB/Q community vis-à-vis their closeted identity or despite their closeted identity, then he or she deserves to be outed. A more sensitive and LGB/Q-positive look at the requirements of professional ethics suggests greater standards for people in positions of public trust if we take seriously the importance of role morality.

It is worth noting that historically, role morality is a fairly new invention, younger even than homosexuality as a social identity. Despite its proposed presence in Plato's *Republic*, our modern understanding of role morality did not begin to develop until the work of late 19th and early 20th century sociologists Durkheim and Mead.[28]

In certain positions of public trust—therapist, judge, and clergy—there is something about the role that requires integrity and honesty.[29] The requirement may extend to any profession that requires/demands trust as part of professional function:[30] medical practitioner, professor, lawyer, even perhaps under some rubrics public officials and politicians, despite the social cynicism regarding the untrustworthy politician. If individuals in these roles lie about their identity and their personal life, the trust instilled in the profession, based on the expectation of integrity, has been violated.[31] Mark Chekola also uses this line of reasoning to argue that the outing of such public officials becomes justified in order to protect the invested trust of the public. This is true, he argues, even if the individual would be opposed to this outcome based on the demand of honesty and integrity of the social role s/he occupies.[32] This of course follows if we establish honesty and integrity about one's sexual identity and personal life as relevant to the trust granted to the professional role s/he occupies.

The role of honesty and integrity in certain professions is particularly important because those who trust the individual are doing so in light of their professional role, not because they have the chance to spend the time cultivating a human relationship that would create the bonds of trust needed. The professional role is meant to profoundly expedite this process. The role of expert demands an ethic, because it is the expertise that is being trusted. Those who enter into the professional relationship without expertise are trusting a personae, and in general do not know the individual as a person, but rather know him/her as an occupant of a given social role.[33] In order to protect the social responsibility and services provided by all those in that professional role, certain ethical requirements must be firmly in place.

These requirements of trust are amplified when the professional is in a fiduciary relationship with a particular individual. A fiduciary relation is "a situation where various professionals 'in equity and good conscience' are 'bound to act in good faith and with due regard to interests of one reposing the confidence.'"[34]

When in a fiduciary relationship, the professional is thought by both parties to be "bound to act as if their interests were those of their clients and hence to sacrifice their own interests for the sake of their client's interest."[35] Fiduciary relationships clearly arise in counseling, legal, and medical settings. It could be argued that elements of pedagogical relationships are fiduciary, as well as certain aspects of a politician's relationship to his/her constituents. Larry May acknowledges that complete loyalty to a client's interest may not be realistic or possible, but the careful consideration of those interests must remain paramount for the fiduciary relationship to remain ethical.[36] What is particularly important for the professional to recognize is that any client/patient is expecting the professional to take their role obligations seriously, and that expectation binds the professional to do so.[37]

It seems clear that one could easily argue that if questions of sexuality or sexual identity are at work within the fiduciary bond, then the professional has increased responsibility to disclose his/her own sexual identity or possible sexual identity prejudices/conflicts to the non-professional. It remains an open question as to whether or not information about one's sexual identity or prejudice is part of professional ethics or role obligations more broadly, since it is broadly in the interest of every LGB/Q non-professional to be able to find professionals that are openly LGB/Q-identified. I will discuss this again at the end of this section, but first I want to briefly discuss public positions that don't involve fiduciary trust.

Public Positions without Trust

When we think about the arguments for LGB/Q visibility for people in the public eye who are not in positions of trust—i.e., actors, actresses, or other public media figures—the arguments based on trust and made in regards to honesty and integrity won't work. Often in these cases the arguments in favor of their ability to choose the closet are founded in arguments of the right to privacy.[38] The discussion of the conflation of privacy and secrecy is particularly relevant here. Public figures assent to a certain amount of publicity; they assent to having portions of their lives lived very much in public. The question that must remain is whether or not they have a right to their closetude. This begs a fundamental question about the role of media in the process of gay liberation: what are the expectations are of people who are in a position to promote or destroy the maintenance of those closets, namely those who report on their lives and keep them in the consciousness of the general public?

When it comes to questions of how the media should handle the known sexuality of public individuals, general journalistic ethics suggests that reporting on the private lives of public figures should be equalized across sexual identities. The press respects the private lives of non-famous individuals; but those in the public eye must accept both the benefits and liabilities of their publicity. Gay liberation demands equalization, and the media could and ought to be an important tool in this equalization of treatment for all famous people in regards to their private lives.[39]

Role Obligations: Problems for Gayness Generally

Chapter 6 advocates that we begin to think of gayness as a kind of practical identity. It is an identity that comes with certain moral and political commitments, primary of which is a commitment to visibility. Would gayness as a practical identity also carry with it certain role responsibilities?

A role is defined as a "constellation of institutionally specified rights and duties organized around an institutionally specified social function."[40] Role obligations, then become moral requirements that attach to that institutional role, "whose content is fixed by the function of the role, and whose normative force flows from the role."[41] There are some roles that are fairly easily defined as such: professional roles. But there are also other social roles, more commonly and loosely defined, that are considered roles for the purpose of institutionalized morality: husband, wife, daughter, son, sister, brother, (serious) girlfriend, (serious) boyfriend. These social relations become roles because certain behaviors are expected of the individuals in light of their relationship with others within a larger institution: the immediate family. Because these roles are institutionally defined, they are genuine institutional roles.[42] The relationships of sexual intimacy have their contents generated from the context of heterosexuality, which is itself considered an institution by a number of moral thinkers. Marriage, for example, is referred to as an institution. This should immediately raise questions for LGB/Q people. The relationships of boyfriend, girlfriend, and partner are not institutionally defined through the larger organizing institution of the family, or heterosexuality. And the appropriated institution of marriage for gay people is not an uncomplicated or particularly helpful institution. Michael Hardimon argues that when we debate the appropriate titles to provide ourselves in our relationships such as boyfriend vs. partner vs. roommate we are debating the nature of "our station" and therefore "it's duties."[43] This is a particularly insightful observation for the gay community. The closet often encourages people to deny the romantic nature of their connection to their lovers. And it is clear from the moral expectation of the social roles one claims (or does not claim), that the individual is owning or denying certain sets of moral responsibilities. We use our defined social roles in our relationships in order to get moral guidance in our treatment of others.[44] Our defined roles allow us to invite in the moral perspectives of other people on our most dear and cherished relationships, or our most pressing professional obligations.

It should be clear that our role obligations are a significantly important part of our moral lives. Confusingly, however, Hardimon does not think that being a member of an ethnic group constitutes a role.[45] It should be clear, however, from the exploration of Korsgaard's practical identities in chapter 6 that if one thinks through one's relationships to others significantly through the lens of an ethnic identity, then an ethnic identity can take on a kind of role obligation. Modern sexual identity falls somewhere between the ethnic identity and the roles produced by the more intimate institution of family and personal relationships. Hardimon does advocate that individuals can rework certain prescribed social roles because the social constraints placed upon them do not make room for an individual's politics. For example, the social institution of mother, wife, or sister may need to be reworked by a feminist wishing to fill those roles.[46] This provides an excellent way to think about the interventions of gayness into traditional social and professional roles.

It is my position that gayness creates an obligation to the LGB/Q community for us in all our professional and social roles. This obligation requires that we out ourselves, maintaining visibility, and furnishing the world with role models however imperfect or inspirational. I think that in tandem to this work of being visible in our social roles, we must also use our gayness and political ideals to critique the classic institutions already established by social morality. Institutions that are hostile to the insights of gayness should be critically examined as creating moral hazards for gay people.[47] This places my perspective on professional ethics and role morality as subsumptionist, meaning that I see professional ethics and role morality as subsumed by social morality which in turn is subsumed by critical morality. Other potential perspectives include a non-subsumptionist view that would hold that professional ethics has a smaller domain than social morality and that the two are separate from eachother.[48]

What about social roles and professional obligations that directly demand closetude? This will be a guiding question in the next section, which discusses the topic of gay military service and the previously legalized and enforced congressional act that demanded passing of all LGBT/Q military personal: "Don't Ask, Don't Tell" and what the moral implications are of such a social policy.

Legal Implications: Don't Ask Don't Tell; Title VII and Sexual Harassment

If gayness can make moral demands on us in terms of our social ethics, and our role obligations can also make moral demands on us in terms of our institutional commitments, we will find in our modern culture role obligations that directly conflict with gayness; and we must be able to put the two in conversation and sort out the appropriate ethical response. Should our social ethics override our institutional obligations, or vice versa? Wueste argues that there is not an *a pri-*

ori way in which we can determine which aspect of our lives should take precedence.[49] Therefore, I would like to take a very recent paradigm case of institutionally enforced passing that directly conflicts with the moral obligations of gayness as outlined in chapter 6: "Don't Ask, Don't Tell," [DADT] the military policy forbidding openly gay men and women to serve in the U.S. military.[50]

DADT History, Statistics, and Definitions

Conduct and Propensity

"Don't Ask, Don't Tell" began with a promise from President Clinton that he would lift the ban on gay servicemen and women in the U.S. military.[51] It is clear that Clinton had the good intention to protect homosexuals as a class of persons from direct discrimination by making it illegal for the military to ask questions regarding sexual orientation on its entrance forms. What came of this promise was a cemented homophobic law that obscured conduct and status, made insidious outcomes of suspicions of private conduct, and ended the military careers of over 12,500 individuals. Many Americans had hoped this new policy would be an improvement on the previous ban. Some believed it was an improvement because it was supposed to sanction military personal, not for "who they are" but for "what they do." Janet Halley argued that the revised policy of "Don't Ask, Don't Tell" was "*much, much worse* than its predecessor."[52]

Sodomy, whether cross-sex or same-sex, was considered a violation of the military code of conduct.[53] This provided the footing for making same-sex sexual conduct a punishable and discharging offense for gay servicemen and women. But the application of sodomy was a crime was disproportionately applied to same-sex participants over cross-sex participants.[54] "Conduct" became a euphemism for "status," where the conduct of one class of persons was considered career ending, and the same conduct for another class of persons was considered an offense, but not necessarily a career ending offense.[55] However, sodomy is not the only actionable conduct crime for gay service men and lesbian service women. The military extended its definition of what constituted "homosexual conduct" to include behaviors well beyond consensual sex acts.

The military also considered "telling" to be homosexual conduct. If a serviceman or woman discloses to *anyone* that he or she is gay, the mere act of "coming out" is considered homosexual conduct. By *anyone,* the military includes family, friends, people in one's civilian community, and even a therapist.[56] According to the military it is gay to come out; however, it is not gay to remain closeted.[57]

But more than just telling—using a verbal locution—the military also considered homosexual conduct to include "bodily contact which a reasonable person would understand to demonstrate a *propensity or* intent to engage in" homosexual conduct.[58] This became the most insidious aspect of "Don't Tell." A propensity can be anything a commander thinks it is: and if a commander preconceives that every woman who wants to serve in the military is probably a lesbian, then anything any service woman does can be interpreted as a propensity.[59]

Although the title "Don't Ask, Don't Tell" seems to suggest that servicemen and women had the right to keep their sexual orientations private if they were willing not to disclose their sexual orientations. The right of "don't ask" suggests there is a safe guard against intrusion. But, in practice servicemen and women who have been asked about their sexual orientations have no legal recourse.[60]

DADT Anti-Gay Ethic

From the Perspective of the Government
The U.S. military argued that it has an invested interest in keeping openly gay men and lesbians out of the service because the presence of homosexuals

> adversely affects the ability of the Military Services to maintain discipline, good order and morale; to foster mutual trust and confidence among service members, to ensure the integrity of rank and command; to facilitate assignment and worldwide deployment of service members who frequently must live and work under close conditions affording minimal privacy; to recruit and retain members of the Military services; to maintain the public acceptability of military service; and to prevent breaches of security.[61]

It was not the *presence* of homosexuals in the military that was the problem: "Don't Ask, Don't Tell" makes is possible for homosexuals to be present in theory. Instead, it was the presence of honest and openly gay men and women, or even just the *perception* of these individuals in the military that was the problem.[62] Richard Mohr points out that none of these concerns have anything to do with the ability of gay men and lesbians to perform the duties prescribed to them by their post.[63] What the U.S. military was trying to formulate in the passage quoted above was an anti-gay ethic. The ethical starting point was heteronormativity, which is a social, not a sexual ethic. Articulation of this ethic began with the premise that to break with the social code of heteronormativity is to rupture the trust, integrity, discipline, and public acceptability that this social norm has put in place.[64] However, "Don't Ask, Don't Tell" may have had the opposite effect when it came to maintaining the "safety" of their heterosexual servicemen and women. The military is concerned about same-sex sexual predation of heterosexuals by homosexuals that takes advantage of the psychological and physical proximity, integrity and bonding that is created while living and working "under close conditions affording minimal privacy." By keeping the identity of homosexuals hidden, but still allowing them to be present if they can keep hidden enough, this bonding is built upon a deception. Janet Halley argues, then, that the possibility for seduction was increased not decreased by "Don't Ask, Don't Tell."[65]

The U.S. government could have produced or enhanced its sexual ethic in order to deal with problems of unwelcome sexual conduct in a same-sex context. However, DADT moved in the opposite direction of that, too. The Department of Justice had an exception to their discharge policy referred to as the "queen-for-a-day" exception. Under this exception, individuals who were caught having same-sex sexual conduct could save their position in the military if they could evidence that it was a one-time event and that it did not speak to a deeper set of urges: namely if the servicemen or women involved can provide evidence of their heterosexual identity, then they can be freed from charges. In addition, the military will not discharge a "heterosexually loyal bisexual." If an individual can evidence that despite urges to be with both sexes, s/he will remain loyal to heteronormativity and only find sexual release with the opposite sex, the military will keep the individual.[66] Both of these strategies for exemption evidence that the military was trying to maintain an anti-gay ethic rather attempting to regulate sexual conduct.

From the Perspective of LGB/Q People

The military produced a social ethic that was anti-gay, masking it as an ethic about sexual conduct. What might be some of the moral burdens placed on gay folk who, during DADT, decided to remain in the military anyway, devoted to the profession they have chosen to enter, and were able to keep their identity from their colleagues? Claudia Card outlines the basic problems of "Don't Ask, Don't Tell" for gay people as: 1) rewarding lying and penalizing honesty, 2) demeaning "all lesbians and gay men by upholding a stance that would be justified only if lesbians and gay men were in truth responsible for the fear, disgust, or revulsion of others . . . it encourages the false assumption that lesbians and gay men *are* responsible for those reactions," and 3) deterring "quests for self-knowledge" and rewarding "closed-mindedness."[67] Card evidences that "Don't Ask, Don't Tell" was damaging to the individual moral sense of gay and lesbian individuals willing to remain in the military. It was also damaging to the social psychology of gay and lesbian people. And finally, and perhaps most importantly, it cut gay and lesbian people off from their own sense of selves.

This last effect, Card argues, can have the consequence of "doubling." Doubling is a term she borrows from psychologist Robert Lifton who uses it to explain how Nazi doctors were able to perform the heinous crimes against humanity that their jobs demanded while otherwise having sustainable and loving home lives. These doctors needed to make a division within themselves for different contexts so that they literally had two incompatible sets of values and emotional responses.[68] Card uses this concept to describe the split between the lives of military commanders who must maintain personal gay and lesbian lives, yet go to work and discriminate thoroughly against all displays of gayness, even their own. Card worries this means that any gay person who was willing to enter the military and maintain its values, while using systematic deception to remain positioned in the institution, is a potential moral monster.

Moral Solutions

The clearest moral solution to "Don't Ask, Don't Tell," and any other professional ethic that forbids gayness outright, is to eradicate the forbidding professional ethic. To quote Claudia Card, "a policy that encourages and rewards dishonesty about the things that are most important in our lives . . . our intimate relationships . . . is disgraceful."[69] The removal of the policy of "Don't Ask, Don't Tell" only increases the integrity, accountability, and professional performance of all gay and lesbian military personnel. Given the real moral and professional risks to those who are gay but wish to enter a forbidding profession, it ought to be advocated—I would advocate—that LGB/Q persons do not enter into forbidding professions, even at the expense of a life-calling. Christine Korsgaard acknowledges that these kinds practical identity conflicts can be some of the most potent resources for our human drama. This is not to claim that abandoning one's profession in the service of their personal lives and sexual orientation is going to be an easy process. But the moral argument to be made is that integrity demands tough decisions like this. The grave moral consequences of choosing systemic deception should be avoided at all costs.

Sexual Harassment

Quick History

Sexual harassment and sexual harassment law is another major legal sphere in which heteronormativity rules the day at the expense of the professional, psychological, and sometimes physical safety of LGB/Q individuals in the workplace. It also fails to recognize the potential harms that LG/Q (the "B" here is purposely left out) persons can do to each other in the workplace. Framed through feminist heterosexual models, the application of Title VII to cases of sexual harm in relationships of power differences means that same-sex harassment is difficult to recognize. Curiously, as it is currently interpreted, sexual harassment law makes it easier for bisexual people to be sexual predators in the work place as long as they harass men and women equally.

The history of sexual harassment as a legally prohibited form of sex discrimination is relatively new. It is clear from accounts of women who worked outside the home in the 19th and early 20th centuries that the practice of sexual harassment is an historic part of the American work experience. Ranging from sexual assault to unwanted physical and verbal advances, women have reported significant harms caused by their male employers.[70] But until the 1970's, women had no legal protection from such assaults at work. Indeed, even the term "sexual harassment" was not coined until 1974.[71]

Sexual harassment law is based on Title VII, a civil-rights act passed in 1964 that prohibits discrimination based on a number of different identities, including sex. For a number of years, however, the courts refused to recognize that sexual harassment was in any way a form of discrimination "on the basis of sex." The courts initially argued that only if the harassment was based on an immutable quality about a person's sex, could it constitute discrimination based on sex: in the case of women these "sex-plus" qualities included things such as marital status, pregnancy, and having children. If the characteristics are mutable, than it doesn't count as sex-based discrimination. Mutable characteristics include: attractive women with long blonde hair, or women who wear pants, or men who display effeminate qualities. The initial logic of the courts argued that if a woman was given unwanted sexual attention at work because she had a lovely figure and wore tight fitting clothes, then she wasn't being discriminated against "on the basis of sex" but instead on mutable features, in this case her shapely figure and revealing clothes. The courts have since changed their position on mutable and immutable characteristics with the help of decades of feminist legal intervention.[72] Indeed that "sex-plus" requirement, while no longer being used against women who have been sexually harassed, is still being used to discriminate against gender-deviant LGBT/Q people.[73]

In the case of the sexual harassment of women, it is now generally understood by the courts that unwanted sexual advances in the workplace are not expressions of desire so much as expressions of power, privilege, dominance, coercion, and corrosive gender relationships, directed in the service of the men in charge. This sexual misconduct is seen as perpetuating gender norms established in favor of the patriarchy.[74]

Gay History

Sexual harassment law has only successfully been applied to one same-sex case: *Oncale vs. Sundowner Offshore Services* (1998). The Oncale case in an interesting and possibly damaging court case in the history of LGB/Q workplace rights. On the face of it, it is seemingly a victory for gay people: Joseph Oncale worked for a shipping company and received numerous sexually harassing comments from a male supervisor, and was physically restrained by a group of men twice: once so that his supervisor could place his penis on his body, and a second time in a shower where a piece of soap was used "to prepare" him for anal penetration by his supervisor. The courts determined that the behavior inflicted upon him constituted sexual harassment, and that Oncale was legally entitled to sue his former employer. Success for gay men, right?! Unfortunately it is not that simple.

To begin, neither the plaintiff nor any of the men involved in his assault were homosexual, nor did any of the decisions reached by the justices mention anything about homosexuality. Nothing in this case was about protecting gay people from injury on the job, or even protecting someone heterosexual from injury by a gay person on the job. The court's decision, in fact, depended on an acknowledgement that damage was done to Joseph Oncale on the basis of his sex, insofar as they stripped him of his masculinity and effeminized him. Essentially, Oncale's discrimination reflected "hostility to women in the workplace," and this is why he could sue for damages based on his sex.[75] The court reasoned its way through the case based on the problem of unequal treatment.[76] The court was trying to decide whether or not a woman in Oncale's case would have been treated differently. The court decided that it was the "social context" and "common sense" that the harassment Oncale received went well beyond male-on-male pranks and had descended into effeminizing discrimination. I will say more about the problematic reasoning in this rightly decided court case in the section below.

Application to LG/Q People

Jospeh Oncale was not gay. But if he had been, would his case still have passed through the Supreme Court in the way that it did? Would the courts have declared the violence as sexism, and would this have been satisfying to a gay victim of sexual harassment by straight men? What if his harassers had been gay? Would it matter that they found him sexually attractive? I would hope that the courts would have still decided in favor of Oncale in this case, regardless of the sexual orientations involved. But, I do not think that a gay Oncale would have felt seen as a victim of homophobia. Whether Oncale was gay or not, the actions his supervisor and helpmates perpetuated on him were clearly entrenched in homophobia, in using same-sex sexuality to humiliate and terrorize someone. If the harassers were themselves gay, the courts may have used homophobia against the defendants, not in deeming the actions and treatment of another person illegal and immoral, but instead using same-sex sexuality, primarily, as the form of terror and abuse. Neither of these interpretations capture the complexity of how homophobia interfaces with this case. Oncale was a first time victim of homophobia (rather than life-long); his harassers were exploiters of homophobia (without having themselves suffered a lifetime of its oppressive forces). The mere fact that the court has a hard time recognizing same-sex harassment as sexual harassment without using sexism is itself a by-product of homophobia.

Some legal thinkers have argued that sexual orientation shouldn't be of consideration in this particular case. They argue the only thing of concern should be the way sexuality can be used as a form of violence on the job. Christopher Kendall, for example, argues that the only concern is the way sexual harassment on the job can be a presentation of sexuality as power-based, and if we can understand this, then we will see that the "preservation of the gender hierarchy (cruelty, violence, aggression, homophobia, sexism, racism, and ultimately compulsory heterosexuality)" are all intertwined.[77] The problem is that we have in place legal restraints on racism, violence, and even sexism, but we don't have legal protections in place for homophobia or compulsory heterosexuality. Kendall goes so far as to blame the constructs of masculinity as that which must prove its "adequacy and superiority" as the root cause of homophobia and specifically the attacks that were perpetuated on Joseph Oncale.[78] If masculinity is the problem for Oncale, how could we interpret a similar case in which a feminine woman sexually violates a butch lesbian?

Excluding LG/Q People

When same-sex sexual harassment can only be analyzed under the terms of sexism, the particulars of gay experience, and the real harms to LG/Q persons perpetuated by heteronormativity, are simply excluded. It may be convenient that same-sex harassment can collapse into sexism, but it doesn't address the legal needs for protection that LG/Q people experience in the workplace in regards to their sexuality. As the courts have currently arranged their interpretations, it is illegal under Title VII to discriminate based on someone's gender, but it is not illegal to discriminate based on the gender of someone's lover. In fact LG/Q persons are often harassed for their sexuality, without anything overtly sexual being stated.

Sexual harassment law makes it illegal for men to talk about their female colleagues as "bitches" or "cunts," but sexual harassment law can't protect gay people from even a group of collegial feminists who wish to sit around referring to them as "fags" and "dykes." Violence to gay people and violence done by gay people is not simply reified male-female power relationships.

This is a problem: a moral and legal problem.

Against LG/Q People

In addition to not protecting LG/Q people in the workplace, sexual harassment law can actually be used against gay people. Remember that one way in which Oncale could have proceeded with a case against his employers would have been to prove that they were sexually interested in him: that they were gay. Joseph Oncale suffered real harms in terms of his employer's actions, but legal theorist Janet Halley has expressed anxiety that without those real harms, a case of homophobic panic could have been rallied against his employers had they been gay. Remember that one of the conclusions in the case of Oncale, offered by Justice Scalia, was that "common sense" will help determine if harassment has occurred. Halley straight-forwardly writes: "homophobia and homosexual panic are common sense."[79] In a fictional scenario, she imagines that a still heterosexual Oncale experiences non-threatening and non-harassing behavior by his gay supervisor as threatening and harassing simply because the supervisor is an openly gay man. Perhaps the gay supervisor talks to his lover on the phone in front of his employees, or kisses him hello and goodbye when he arrives on the worksite. Or maybe his supervisor likes to share ordinary details about his non-sexual life with his partner in obnoxious attention seeking ways (we all know heterosexuals who talk too much about their partners and children). Might the common sense of many Americans—who would deem this behavior inappropriate—make it actionable? As Richard Mohr argues "since most people find the existence of gays offensive, it might turn out that any recognizably gay behavior or discussion of gay sex might "reasonably" be found to be sexual harassment."[80] We have seen that this is exactly the kind of reasoning employed in "Don't Ask Don't Tell" to discharge gay and lesbian soldiers.

Queering Sexual Harassment—More Problems

Many of the problems of application of Title VII have to do with ambiguities in the use of word "sex." The writers of the Civil Rights Act of 1964 could not have had sexual harassment in mind when writing out the list of identities that should not be used against people in employment. So, when analyzing this particular application of "sex," the courts have turned to the definition of "sex" in 1964. There are, broadly speaking, 3 definitions of sex: 1) sex as biological dimorphism: or the division of organisms into male and female, 2) sex as gender: or the sphere of behavior dominated by the relationships between men and women, 3) sex as sexuality: or the whole sphere of sexual and pleasure-seeking conduct.[81] If definition 1) is employed, then there can be no such thing as a bisexual harassment (because the harasser is always an equal opportunity harasser). If definition 2) is employed there can be no same-sex harassment. And if definition 3) is employed, then desire plays the central role, and no one can be harassed by someone who does not see his/her own sex as the target for sexual activity. Everything goes to hell with the application of each of these three definitions if we throw in cases of people who are passing in the role of the harasser, especially definition 2) if the individual is gender passing, and especially definition 3) if the individual is sexual identity passing.
This is a legal interpretation and civil rights problem.

Often times when we need to dissect and localize definitions of complex social and historical terms such as "sex," scholars would be inclined to turn towards queer theory. However, a significant set of problems arise when we use queer theory in conjunction with sexual harassment law. I will briefly discuss a few here.

Because queer theory regards the homosexual-heterosexual distinction as suspect it cannot recognize discrimination that is directed at sexual orientation.[82] And while queer theory recognizes that sexuality is shot through with power, it does not recognize that power as structurally organized by gender or sexual identity.[83] In fact queer theory is worried about sexual harassment law regulating sexual desire whatsoever.[84]

In the case of a homophobic panic, queer theory would be inclined to interpret the scenario as arising from a conflict of desire. The panic is a result from not wanting a social identity associated with same-sex sexuality while at the same time wanting to participate in same-sex sexuality. A panic then becomes the manifestation of this internal conflict. This would lead queer theorists to question the claims of harm that were cited by victims such as Oncale. This immediately puts queer theory in tension with feminist legal theory that seeks to advocate on behalf of the truth of the sexual harms experienced by sexual harassment victims. This interpretation of homophobic panic by queer theorists leaves many people vulnerable, perhaps most notably closeted and even openly gay people who may experience real sexual harm as victims of same-sex sexual harassment,[85] and protects predatory same-sex sexual harassers whether openly LG/Q identified or passing for heterosexual. Marc Spindelman argues that undermining the truth-telling capacity of gay men and lesbians in this way is heteronormative.[86] Queer theory's concern over protecting sexual desire and sexuality from punishment leaves LG/Q and even heterosexual people exposed and vulnerable to predation from the un-punishable. When it comes to LG/Q persons, this involves no movement forward by the courts or our legal system that already leave us exposed and vulnerable to social harms done because of—or even through our sexualities.

Gayness as a Possible Solution—Legal Protections for Gayness

The clearest solution to the problems presented by sexual harassment law is to create a civil rights act that protects against discrimination based on sexual orientation: an act that can distill the insidious elements of homophobia from sexism, and provide for legal cases in which the transgression of sex or sexuality was in terms of LG/Q or even heterosexual identity. While sexual harassment law does, as Oncale evidences, prepare the way for a heterosexual to file a same-sex harassment case against someone who violates the masculinity of a subordinate; a civil rights act that protected sexual orientation would provide for same-sex harassment when the harasser was a woman—or most importantly for this book—if the harasser was passing for heterosexual and abusing that privilege with an openly gay person, a closeted gay person, or even a heterosexual.

One of the legal liabilities of passing, in combination with the convention of the secret within the gay community, is the ability to use heterosexual privilege against those who are openly gay and working within or towards the ethical norms of gayness. Without legal protections for gayness, ones that particularly defend against harassment and other evil doings by passers, heterosexuals, and even other LGBT/Q identified individuals, the social trajectory towards justice will be continuously compromised as those who are fighting the good fight are damaged without recourse. Sexual harassment law and "Don't Ask, Don't Tell" are just two of the legal considerations that evidence this need. Legal protections for visibility will undermine closetude; legal protections against passing will undo the convention of the secret. Legal protection will make it more possible for LGBT/Q social ethics to develop; legal protections will be the undoing of the moral compromise of passing.

Notes

1. Larry Gross, *Contested Closets: The Politics and Ethics of Outing* (Minneapolis: University of Minnesota Press, 1993), 262.

2. Richard Mohr, "The Outing Controversy: Privacy and Dignity in Gay Ethics," in *Gay Ideas* (Boston: Beacon Press, 1992), 22.

3. The debate here then becomes whether or not someone who is forcibly outed constitutes a desirable role model for the community. Is nearly total invisibility better than the visibility of self-loathing would-be closet cases? See: Randy Shilts, *Is "Outing" Gays Ethical?* New York Times Op-Ed page, April 12, 1990 and Steve Berry, "Liz Smith Mon Amour" *Outweek* May 16, 1990.

4. Mohr, "The Outing Controversy," 35, 43.

5. Jeremiah McCarthy, "The Closet and the Ethics of Outing," in *Gay Ethics: Controversies in Outing, Civil Rights, and Sexual Science,* edited by Timothy Murphy (Binghamton: Haworth Press, 1994), 39.

6. Gross, *Contested Closets,* 261.

7. Raja Halwani et al., "What is Gay and Lesbian Philosophy?," *Metaphilosophy* 39 (October 2008), 438.

8. Mohr, "The Outing Controversy," 12.

9. Halwani et al., "What is Gay and Lesbian Philosophy?," 440; Mohr, "The Outing Controversy," 31.

10. Richard Mohr, *Gays/Justice: A Study of Ethics, Society, and Law* (New York: Columbia University Press, 1988), 333.

11. Halwani et al., "What is Gay and Lesbian Philosophy?," 439.

12. "Libel is based on the premise that the statement in question is both untrue and intentionally malicious." Michael Bronski quoted in Gross, *Contested Closets,* 266.

13. Gross, *Contested Closets,* 67.

14. McCarthy, "The Closet and the Ethics of Outing," 31.

15. Mohr, "The Outing Controversy," 26.
16. Mohr, "The Outing Controversy," 25.
17. Mohr, "The Outing Controversy," 27.
18. Mohr, "The Outing Controversy," 30.
19. Mohr, "The Outing Controversy," 12.
20. Quoted in Mohr, "The Outing Controversy," 14.
21. Gross, *Contested Closets*, 45.
22. Mark Chekola, "Outing, Truth-Telling, and the Shame of the Closet," in *Gay Ethics: Controversies in Outing, Civil Rights, and Sexual Science*, edited by Timothy Murphy (Binghamton: Haworth Press, 1994), 87.
23. Gross, *Contested Closets*, 126. Statistics on the rates of LGB/Q teenage suicides compared with those of heterosexual teenagers vary between 3 to 1 and 5 to 1. This is particularly alarming given the significantly smaller portion of LGB/Q teenagers compared to heterosexuals. (Somewhere between 3% and 20% overall population. Again estimates vary.)
24. Gross, *Contested Closets*, 23.
25. Gross, *Contested Closets*, 129.
26. Heide Dorrow, a lesbian activist, quoted in Gross, *Contested Closets*, 80.
27. Vito Russo quoted in Gross, *Contested Closets*, 181.
28. Daniel E. Wueste, "Role Moralities and the Problem of Conflicting Obligations," in *Professional Ethics and Social Responsibility* edited by Daniel E. Wueste (Lanham, Maryland: Rowman and Littlefield Publishers, Inc. 1994), 105.
29. Chekola, "Outing, Truth-Telling, and the Shame of the Closet," 87.
30. Daniel Wueste argues that "because they profess, professionals ask that they be trusted" Wueste, "Introduction," 7.
31. Chekola, "Outing, Truth-Telling, and the Shame of the Closet," 87.
32. Chekola, "Outing, Truth-Telling, and the Shame of the Closet," 88.
33. Wueste "Introduction," 20.
34. Larry May, "Conflict of Interest," in *Professional Ethics and Social Responsibility,* 79.
35. May, "Conflict of Interest," 79.
36. May, "Conflict of Interest," 79.
37. Wueste, "Role Moralities and the Problem of Conflicting Obligations," 114.
38. Chekola, "Outing, Truth-Telling, and the Shame of the Closet," 88.
39. Gross, *Contested Closets,* 279-280.
40. Michael Hardimon, "Role Obligation," *Journal of Philosophy* 91 (1994), 334.
41. Hardimon, "Role Obligation," 334-5.
42. Hardimon, "Role Obligation," 336.
43. Hardimon, "Role Obligation," 340.
44. Hardimon, "Role Obligation," 341.
45. Hardimon, "Role Obligation," 335.
46. Hardimon, "Role Obligation," 349.
47. This is an insight of Joan Callahan as cited in Wueste, "Introduction," 27.
48. I am grateful to Wueste's introduction to *Professional Ethics and Social Responsibility* in describing the contours of the subsumptionist/nonsubsumptionist distinction.
49. Wueste, "Role Moralities and the Problem of Conflicting Obligations," 110.
50. When I first wrote this conclusion, "Don't Ask, Don't Tell" was still an active military policy, however, serious changes were being discussed and advocated by the

Obama Administration. On September 20,[th] 2011 "Don't Ask, Don't Tell" was repealed. This section now refers to a historical policy that lasted from 1993-2011. The changing landscape is hopeful for the broader installation of gayness as a social ethic to our culture. "Don't Ask, Don't Tell" is particularly interesting for this book because it was institutionalized passing. The policy before 1993 was an outright ban on all LGBT/Q persons in the military. I considered removing the section, however, it remains clear that the corrosive effects on the morality of our service men and women will out last this repeal by many years. And of course, its lasting cultural impact on the military and broader American society cannot be overlooked.

51. Austria, Belgium, Denmark, France, Finland, Germany, Italy, Japan, the Netherlands, and Spain all allow openly gay man and women to serve in their militaries. Claudia Card, "The Military Ban and the ROTC: A Study in Closeting," in *Gay Ethics: Controversies in Outing,* 122. Australia, Canada, Israel, and Britain have all lifted bans on homosexual servicemen and women. Editorial of *The New York Times*: Sunday October 4th, 2009. "The Damage of Don't Ask, Don't Tell"

52. Janet Halley, *Don't: A Reader's Guide to the Military's Anti-Gay Policy,* (Durham: Duke University Press, 1999), 1.

53. This military law was repealed in early December 2011, nearly three full months after the repeal of "Don't Ask, Don't Tell."

54. For a thorough explanation of the parallels and influence of Bowers vs. Hardwick, see Halley, *Don't,* 5-10.

55. Halley writes that in the case of male-female fellatio, a commander my institute separation proceedings, but does not need to do so, while in the case of male-male fellatio, he or she has no choice. The servicemen must be discharged. Halley, *Don't,* 38.

56. Halley, *Don't,* 52.

57. Gay experience will evidence again and again that remaining closeted is a very gay thing to do.

58. Halley, *Don't,* 57.

59. Halley, *Don't,* 5. Indeed, lesbians are discharged at "many times the rate of gay men." Card, "The Military Ban and the ROTC," 125.

60. Halley, *Don't,* 50.

61. Official military policy cited in Card, "The Military Ban and the ROTC," 133.

62. I am grateful to Claudia Card for the perception/presence distinction.

63. Richard Mohr, "Black Law and Gay Law: Do Civil Rights Have a Future?," in *Gay Ideas,* 62.

64. I am reminded here of an interesting outcome of a socialized sexual ethic in Ancient Rome that our modern minds (feminist and otherwise) would revolt at. In Ancient Rome, seducing the wife of another man was considered a worse crime than raping her. In the latter case, only property was damaged, but in the former case the basic fabric of society has been violated.

65. Halley, *Don't,* 31-2.

66. Halley, *Don't,* 100.

67. Card, "The Military Ban and the ROTC," 128-9.

68. Card, "The Military Ban and the ROTC," 130.

69. Card, "The Military Ban and the ROTC," 121.

70. Reva B. Siegel, "Introduction: A Short History of Sexual Harassment," in *Directions in Sexual Harassment Law,* edited by Catharine A. MacKinnon and Reva B. Siegel (New Haven: Yale University Press, 2004), 3.

71. Siegel, "Introduction: A Short History of Sexual Harassment," 8, as part of a consciousness-raising session held during a course on women and work by Lin Farley at Cornell University.

72. Particularly notable here is Catherine Mackinnon and her 1979 publication of *Sexual Harassment of Working Women* (New Haven: Yale University Press).

73. Siegel, "Introduction: A Short History of Sexual Harassment," 14.

74. Katherine Franke, "What's Wrong with Sexual Harassment," in *Directions in Sexual Harassment Law*, 173.

75. Siegel, "Introduction: A Short History of Sexual Harassment," 25.

76. Franke, "What's Wrong with Sexual Harassment," 172.

77. Christopher Kendall, "Gay Male Liberation Post Oncale: Since When is Sexualized Violence Our Path to Liberation?," in *Directions in Sexual Harassment Law*, 226.

78. Kendall, "Gay Male Liberation Post Oncale," 226.

79. Janet Halley, "Sexuality Harassment," in *Directions in Sexual Harassment Law*, 182-3.

80. Mohr, *Gays/Justice*, 326-7.

81. Eskridge, William N. Jr., "Theories of Harassment 'Because of Sex,'" in *Directions in Sexual Harassment Law*, 156.

82. Halley, "Sexuality Harassment," 194.

83. Halley, "Sexuality Harassment," 194.

84. Marc Spindelman, "Discriminating Pleasures," in *Directions in Sexual Harassment Law*, 203.

85. Halley, "Sexuality Harassment," 196. Feminists have also advocated on behalf of plaintiffs in sexual harassment cases to have their sexual history kept out of the court proceedings. This, too, would make it very difficult for gay and lesbian individuals who have regularly acted on their same-sex sexual desire to defend themselves against the homophobic panic defense advocated by queer theory.

86. Spindelman, "Discriminating Pleasures," 214.

Bibliography

Adler, Jonathan. "Lying, Deceiving, or Falsely Implicating," *The Journal of Philosophy* 94, no. 9 (September 1997): 435-452.

Alexander, Larry and Emily Sherwin. "Deception in Law and Morality," *Law and Philosophy* 22 (2003): 393-450.

Alison, James. *Undergoing God: Dispatches From the Scene of a Break-In.* New York; London: Darton, Longman, and Todd, 2006.

Allen, Amy. "Foucault on Power: A Theory for Feminists," in *Feminist Interpretations of Foucault,* edited by Susan J. Hekman, University Park: Penn State Press, 1996.

———. "Rethinking Power," *Hypatia* 13 no.1, Winter 1998: 21-40.

Altieri, Charles. "Personal Style as Articulate Intentionality," in *The Question of Style in Philosophy and the Arts*, edited by Caroline Van Eck, James McAllister and Rene e van de Vall. Cambridge: Cambridge University Press, 1995.

———. "Style as the Man: From Aesthetics to Speculative Philosophy," in *Analytic Aesthetics,* edited by Richard Shusterman. New York: Basil Blackwell, 1989.

Appiah, Anthony Kwame. *The Ethics of Identity.* Princeton: Princeton University Press, 2005.

Atkins, Kim. "Narrative Identity, Practical Identity, and Ethical Subjectivity," *Continental Philosophy Review* 37 (2004): 341-366.

Balkun, Mary McAleer. *The American Counterfeit: Authenticity and Identity in American Literature and Culture.* Tuscaloosa: University of Alabama Press, 2006.

Ball, Carlos. *The Morality of Gay Rights: An Exploration in Political Philosophy.* New York: Routledge, 2003.

Bartky, Sandra Lee. *Femininity and Domination: Studies in the Phenomenology*

Oppression. New York: Routledge, 1990.

Beardsley, Monroe. "Verbal Style and Illocutionary Action," in *The Concept of Style,* edited by Berel Lang. Philadelphia: University of Pennsylvania Press, 1979.

Beauvoir, Simone de. *The Second Sex,* translated by H.M. Parshley. New York: Vintage, 1989.

Bell, Vikki. *Culture and Peformance: The Challenge of Ethics, Politics, and Feminist Theory.* New York: Berg, 2007.

Bergoffen, Debra. "Simone de Beauvoir," edited by Edward N. Zalta. *The Stanford Encyclopedia of Philosophy* (Summer 2009 Edition) http://plato.stanford.edu/archives/sum2009/entries/beauvoir/

Bernauer, James and Michael Mahon. "The Ethics of Michel Foucault," in *The Cambridge Companion to Foucault,* edited by Gary Gutting. Cambridge: Cambridge University Press, 1994.

Bersani, Leo. *Homos.* Cambridge: Harvard University Press, 1995.

Bok, Sisela. *Lying: Moral Choice in Public and Private Life.* New York: Pantheon Books, 1978.

Bordo, Susan. "The Body and the Reproduction of Femininity," in *Gender, Body, Knowledge,* edited by Alison Jaggar and Susan Bordo. London; New Brunswick, N.J.: Rutgers University Press, 1989.

Brown, Alison Leigh. *Subjects of Deceit: A Phenomenology of Lying.* Albany: State University of New York Press, 1998.

Brown, Laura. "Beyond Thou Shalt Not: Thinking About Ethics in the Lesbian Therapy Community," in *Loving Boldly: Issues Facing Lesbians,* edited by Esther D. Rothblum and Ellen Cole. New York: Harrington Park Press, 1989.

Broyard, Bliss. *One Drop: My Father's Hidden Life – A Story of Race and Family Secrets.* New York: Little, Brown, and Co., 2007.

Brummett, Barry. *A Rhetoric of Style.* Carbondale: Southern Illinois University Press, 2008.

Buccino, Daniel. "Homosexuality and Psychosis in the Clinic," in *Homosexuality and Psychoanalysis,* edited by Tim Dean and Christopher Lane. Chicago: University of Chicago Press, 2000.

Butler, Judith. *Gender Trouble.* Routledge: New York, 1990.

———. *Precarious Life: The Powers of Mourning and Violence.* London and New York: Verso, 2004.

———. *Psychic Life of Power: Theories in Subjection.* Stanford: Stanford University Press, 1997.

Butler, Paul. *Out of Style: Reanimating Stylistic Study in Composition and Rhetoric.* Logan, Utah: Utah State University Press, 2008.

Cahill, Ann J., "Continental Feminism," *The Stanford Encyclopedia of Philosophy* (Fall 2008 Edition), edited by Edward N. Zalta. http://plato.stanford.edu/archives/fall2008/entries/femapproach-continental/

Callahan, Joan C. "Professions, Institutions, and Moral Risk," in *Professional*

Ethics and Social Responsibility, edited by Daniel E. Wueste. Lanham, Maryland: Rowman & Littlefield Publishers Inc., 1994.

Cameron, Deborah. "Peforming Gender Identity: Young Men's Talk and the Construction of Heterosexual Masculinity," in *The Discourse Reader* (2nd Edition), edited by Adam Jaworksi and Nikolas Coupland. London: Routledge, 1999.

Card, Claudia. "Groping Through Moral Gray Zones," *On Feminist Ethics and Politics.* Lawrence: University of Kansas Press, 1999.

———. "The Military Ban and the ROTC: A Study in Closeting," in *Gay Ethics: Controversies in Outing, Civil Rights, and Sexual Science,* edited by Timothy Murphy. Binghamton: Haworth Press, 1994.

Carver, Terell, and Samual A. Chambers. *Judith Butler's Precarious Politics.* London: Routledge, 2008.

Caughie, Pamela. *Passing and Pedagogy: The Dynamics of Responsibility.* Urbana: University of Illinois Press, 1999.

Champagne, John. *The Ethics of Marginality: A New Approach to Gay Studies.* Minneapolis: University of Minnesota Press, 1995.

Chatman, Seymour. "The Styles of Narrative Codes," in *The Concept of Style,* edited by Berel Lang. Philadelphia: University of Pennsylvania Press, 1979.

Chauncey, George. *Gay New York: Gender, Urban Culture, and the Makings of the Gay Male World 1890-1940.* New York: Basic Books, 1994.

Chekola, Mark. "Outing, Truth-Telling, and the Shame of the Closet," in *Gay Ethics: Controversies in Outing, Civil Rights, and Sexual Science,* edited by Timothy Murphy. Binghamton: Haworth Press, 1994.

Clifford, P. and A.F. Heath. "The Political Consequences of Social Mobility," in *Journal of the Royal Statistical Society* 156, no. 1 (1993): 51-61.

Cohen, Gerald. "Beliefs and Roles," *Proceedings of the Aristotelian Society* (1966-7), Compton Press.

Connell, R.W. "A Very Straight Gay: Masculinity, Homosexual Experience, and the Dynamics of Gender," *American Sociological Review* 57, no. 6 (December 1992): 735-751.

Corvino, John. "Why Shouldn't Tommy and Jim Have Sex?," in *Social Ethics* (7th Edition), edited by Thomas Mappes. Columbus: McGraw Hill, 2006.

Crimp, Douglas. "Mario Montez, For Shame," in *Regarding Sedgwick,* edited by Barber and Clark. New York: Routledge, 2002.

Crouch, Robert. "Betwixt and Between: The Past and Future of Intersexuality," in *Intersex in the Age of Ethics,* Edited by A.Dreger. Hagerstown, M.D.: University Publishing Group, 1999.

Cryle, Peter and Christopher E. Forth. *Sexuality at the Fin de Sie'cle: the Makings of a Central Problem.* Newark: University of Delaware Press, 2008.

Cudd, Ann. *Analyzing Oppression.* Oxford: Oxford University Press, 2006.

Cuomo, Chris. "Thoughts on Lesbian Differences," *Hypatia* 13 no.1, Winter 1998: 198-205.

Dean, Carolyn. " The 'Open Secret,' Affect, and the History of Sexuality," in

Sexuality at the Fin de Siecle, edited by Cryle and Forth. Newark, NJ: University of Delaware Press, 2008.

Deigh, John. "Shame and Self-Esteem: A Critique," in *Ethics* 93, no. 2 (January 1983): 225-245.

Deveaux, Monique. "Feminism and Empowerment: A Critical Reading of Foucault." *Feminist Studies* 20, no.2 (Summer 1994): 223-247.

Diamant, Louis. "Sexual Orientation: Some Historical Perspective," in *The Psychology of Sexual Orientation, Behavior, and Identity,* Edited by Louis Diamant and Richard D. McAnulty. Wesport: Greenwood Press, 1995.

Dondiger, Wendy. "The Mythology of Self-Imitation in Passing: Race, Gender and Politics," *Martin Marty Center Religion and Culture Web Forum.* December, 2004.

Dowds, Alan. *The Velvet Rage.* Cambridge MA: Perseus Books Group, 2005.

Dreger, Alice Domurat. "A History of Intersex: From the Age of Gonads to the Age of Consent," in *Intersex in the Age of Ethics*, edited by A. Dreger, Hagerstown, M.D.: University Publishing Group, 1999.

Eskridge, William N. Jr. "Theories of Harassment 'Because of Sex' in *Directions in Sexual Harassment Law,* Edited by Catharine A. MacKinnon and Reva B. Siegel. New Haven: Yale University Press, 2004.

Fanon, Frantz. *Black Skin, White Masks.* New York: Grove Press, 1967.

Fausto-Sterling, Anne. "Dueling Dualisms" in *Gender, Sex and Sexuality,* edited by Abby Ferber et al. New York: Oxford University Press, 2009.

Feinberg, Leslie. *Stone Butch Blues.* Ann Arbor: Firebrand Books, 1993.

Flynn, Bernard, "Maurice Merleau-Ponty," *The Stanford Encyclopedia of Philosophy* (Fall 2008 Edition), edited by Edward N. Zalta. http://plato.stanford.edu/archives/fall2008/entries/merleau-ponty/

Foster, Gwendolyn Audrey. *Class Passing: Social Moblity in Film and Popular Culture.* Carbondale: Southern Illinois University Press, 2005.

Foucault, Michel. *Discipline and Punish: the Birth of the Prison*, translated by Alan Sheridan. New York: Pantheon Books, 1977.

———.*The History of Sexuality,* translated by Robert Hurley. New York: Vintage Books, 1985.

———. *Politics, Philosophy, Culture*, Edited by Lawrence Kritzman. Routledge: New York, 1988.

———. "The Subject and Power," in *Power,* edited by James D. Faubion. New York: The New Press, 1994.

Franke, Katherine M. "What's Wrong with Sexual Harassment," in *Directions in Sexual Harassment Law,* Edited by Catharine A. MacKinnon and Reva B. Siegel. New Haven: Yale University Press, 2004.

Frankfurt, Harry. *On Bullshit.* Princeton: Princeton University Press, 2005.

Fraser, Nancy. *Unruly Practices: Power, Discourse, and Gender in Contemporary Social Theory.* Minneapolis: University of Minnesota Press, 1989.

Frye, Marilyn. *The Politics of Reality: Essays in Feminist Theory.* Trumansburg, New York: Crossing Press, 1983

Gallagher, Shaun and Dan Zahavi, "Phenomenological Approaches to Self-Consciousness," *The Stanford Encyclopedia of Philosophy* (Spring 2009 Edition), edited by Edward N Zalta. http://plato.stanford.edu/archives/spr2009/entries/self-consciousness-phenomenological//

Garber, Marjorie. *Vested Interests*. New York: Harper Collins, 1992.

Gates, Henry Louis. Jr. *Thirteen Ways of Looking at a Black Man*. New York: Random House, 1998.

Geuss, Raymond. "Morality and Identity," in *The Sources of Normativity*. Cambridge: Cambridge University Press, 1996.

Gilman, Sander. *Making the Body Beautiful: A Cultural History of Aesthetic Surgery*. Princeton: Princeton University Press, 1999.

Ginsberg, Elaine K. ed. *Passing and The Fictions of Identity*, Durham, NC: Duke University Press, 1996.

Glannon, Walter, 1998, "Moral Responsibility and Personal Identity," *American Philosophical Quarterly* 35: 231-249.

Glaus, Kathleen O'Halleran."Alcoholism, Chemical Dependency, and the Lesbian Client," in *Loving Boldly: Issues Facing Lesbians*, edited by Esther D. Rothblum and Ellen Cole. New York: Harrington Park Press, 1989.

Goffman, Erving. *Stigma: Notes on the Management of Spoiled Identity*. New York: Simon and Schuster, 1963.

Goodman, Nelson. *Ways of Worldmaking*. Indianapolis: Hackett Publishing Company, 1978.

Gowans, Christopher. "Practical Identities and Autonomy: Korsgaard's Reformation of Kant's Moral Philosophy," in *Philosophy and Phenomenological Research* 64, no. 3 (May 2002): 546-570.

Green, Stuart. "Lying, Misleading, and Falsely Denying: How Moral Concepts Inform the Law of Perjury, Fraud, and False Statements," *Hastings Law Journal* 53, 2001-2002: 157-212.

Gross, Larry. *Contested Closets: The Politics And Ethics of Outing*. Minneapolis: University of Minnesota Press, 1993.

Groveman, Sherri. "The Hanukkah Bush: Ethical Implications in the Clinical Management of Intersex," in *Intersex in the Age of Ethics*, edited by A. Dreger, Hagerstown, M.D.: University Publishing Group, 1999.

Halberstam, Judith. "Between Butches," in *Butch/Femme: Inside Lesbian Gender,* edited by Sally R. Munt. London: Cassell, 1998.

———. *Female Masculinity*. Durham: Duke University Press, 1998.

Halley, Janet. *Don't: A Reader's Guide to the Military's Anti-Gay Policy*. Durham: Duke University Press, 1999.

———. "Sexuality Harassment," in *Directions in Sexual Harassment Law*, edited by Catharine A. MacKinnon and Reva B. Siegel. New Haven: Yale University Press, 2004.

Halperin, David. *What Do Gay Men Want?: An Essay on Sex, Risk, and Subjectivity*. Ann Arbor: The University of Michigan Press, 2007.

Halwani, Raja et al. "What is Gay and Lesbian Philosophy?," *Metaphilosophy*

39 (October 2008): 434-471.
Hardimon, Michael. "Role Obligations," *Journal of Philosophy* 91 (1994).
Hennessy, Rosemary. *Profit and Pleasure: Sexual Identities in Late Capitalism.* New York; London: Routledge, 2000.
Holstein, James and Jaber Gubrium. *The Self We Live By: Narrative Identity in a Postmodern World.* New York: Oxford University Press, 2000.
Hostert, Anna Camaiti. *Passing: A Strategy to Dissolve Identities and Remap Differences,* translated by Christine Marciasini. Madison N.J.: Fairleigh Dickinson University Press, 2007.
Ikuenobe, Polycarp. "The Meta-Ethical Issues of the Nature of Lying: Implications for Moral Education," *Studies in Philosophy and Education* 21, (2002): 37-63.
Jagose, Annamarie. "Queer Theory," *Australian Humanities Review,* December 1996.
Johansson, Warren. *Outing: Shattering the Conspiracy of Silence.* Binghamton: Haworth Press, 1994.
Katz, Jonathon. *The Invention of Heterosexuality.* New York: Dutton, 1995.
Kemel, Salim. "Style and Community," in *The Question of Style in Philosophy and the Arts,* edited by Caroline Van Eck; James McAllister and Rene e van de Vall Cambridge: Cambridge University Press, 1995.
Kendall, Christopher N. "Gay Male Liberation Post Oncale: Since When is Sexualized Violence Our Path to Liberation?," in *Directions in Sexual Harassment Law,* edited by Catharine A. MacKinnon and Reva B. Siegel. New Haven: Yale University Press, 2004.
Kirby, Vikki. *Telling Flesh: The Substance of the Corporeal.* New York: Routledge, 1997.
Kirchick, James. "Fallen Soldier" in *The Advocate,* October 2009: 16.
Kitzinger, Celia. "Problematizing Pleasure: Radical Feminist Deconstructions of Sexuality and Power," in *Power/Gender,* edited by Lorraine Radtke. Newbury Park: Sage, 1994.
Korsgaard, Christine. "Creating the Kingdom of Ends: Reciprocity and Responsibility in Personal Relations," in *Philosophical Perspectives* 6 (1992): 305-332.
Korsgaard, Christine. *The Sources of Normativity.* Cambridge: Cambridge University Press, 1996.
Kroeger, Brooke. *Passing: When People Can't Be Who They Are.* New York: Public Affairs, 2003.
Lang, Berel. *Writing and the Moral Self.* New York: Routledge, 1991.
Lipman-Blumen, Jean. "The Existential Bases of Power Relationships: the Gender Role Case," in *Power/Gender*, edited by Lorraine Radtke, Newbury Park: Sage, 1994.
Loizidou, Elena. *Judith Butler: Ethics, Law, Politics.* New York: Routledge, 2007.
Lopreato, Joseph. "Upward Social Mobility and Political Orientation," *American Sociological Review* 32, no.4 (August 1967): 586-592.

Love, Heather K. "Spoiled Identity: Stephen Gordon's Loneliness and the Difficulties of Queer History." *GLQ* 7(4), 2001: 487-519.

Mackinnon, Catherine. "Desire and Power: A Feminist Perspective," in *Marxism And the Interpretation of Culture*," edited by Cary Nelson. Urbana: University of Illinois Press, 1988.

———."Feminism, Marxism, Method and the State: An Agenda for Theory," *Signs 7, no. 3* (1982): 515-544.

———."Feminism, Marxism, Method and the State: Toward Feminist Jurisprudence," *Signs* 8, no. 4 (1983): 635-658.

———.*Toward a Feminist Theory of the State*. Cambridge: Harvard University Press, 1989.

Mallon, Ron. "Passing, Traveling, and Reality: Social Constructionism and the Metaphysics of Race," *Nous* 38 (2004): 644-673.

Margolies, L., M. Becker, and K. Jackson-Brewer. "Internalized Homophobia: Identifying and Treating the Oppressor Within," in *Boston Lesbian Psychologies Collective, Lesbian Psychologies: Explorations and Challenges*. Urbana: University of Illinois Press, 1987.

Martell, Christopher et al. *Cognitive-Behavioral Therapies with Lesbian, Gay, and Bisexual Clients.* New York: Guilford Press, 2004.

May, Larry. "Conflict of Interest," in *Professional Ethics and Social Responsibility*, edited by Daniel E. Wueste. Lanham: Rowman & Littlefield Publishers Inc., 1994.

McCarthy, Jeremiah. "The Closet and the Ethics of Outing," in *Gay Ethics: Controversies in Outing, Civil Rights, and Sexual Science*, edited by Timothy Murphy. Binghamton: Haworth Press, 1994.

McCarthy, Joan. *Dennett and Ricoeur on the Narrative Self.* Amherst: Prometheus Books, 2007.

McCune, Jeffrey Quinn Jr. *Doin' the Down Low, Remixin' the Closet: Black Masculinity and the Politics of Sexual Passing.* Dissertation, Northwestern University, 2007.

McGreevey, James E. *The Confession.* New York: Harper, 2006.

Merleau-Ponty, Maurice. "Cezanne's Doubt," in *Sense and Nonsense*, translated by Huber and Patricia Dreyfus. Evanston: Northwestern University Press, 1964.

———. "Indirect Language and the Voices of Silence", in *Signs*, translated by R. McCleary. Evanston: Northwestern University Press, 1964.

———. *Phenomenology of Perception*, Routledge: London, 1945.

Meyer, Leonard. "Toward a Theory of Style," in *The Concept of Style.* Philadelphia: University of Pennsylvania Press, 1979.

Miller, William Ian. "Passing and Wishing You Were What You Are Not," in *Faking It*. Cambridge: Cambridge University Press, 2003.

Mills, Claudia. "'Passing': The Ethics of Pretending to be What You Are Not," *Social Theory and Practice* 25(1), Spring 99: 29-51.

Mohr, Richard. "Black Law and Gay Law: Do Civil Rights Have a Future?," in

Gay Ideas. Boston: Beacon Press, 1992.

———. *Gays/Justice: A Study of Ethics, Society, and Law*. New York: Columbia University Press, 1988.

———. "Gay Studies as Moral Vision," in *Gay Ideas*. Boston: Beacon Press, 1992.

———. "The Outing Controversy: Privacy and Dignity in Gay Ethics," in *Gay Ideas*. Boston: Beacon Press, 1992.

Moore, Honor. *The Bishop's Daughter*. New York: W.W. Norton & Co., 2008.

Morrish, Liz and Helen Sauntson. *New Perspectives on Language and Sexual Identity*. New York: Palgrave Macmillan, 2007.

Murphy, Timothy ed. *Gay Ethics: Controversies in Outing, Civil Rights, and Sexual Science*. Binghamton: Haworth Press, 1994.

Myrdal, Gunnar. *An American Dilemma: The Negro Problem and Democracy*. New York: Harper and Row, 1944.

Nichols, Margaret. "Therapy with Bisexual Women: Working on the Edge of Emerging Cultural and Personal Identities," in *Women in Context: Toward a Feminist Reconstruction of Psychotherapy*, edited by M.P Mirkin. New York: Guilford Press, 1994.

Oksala, Johanna. "Anarchic Bodies: Foucault and the Feminist Question of Experience," in *Hypatia* 19 no. 4 (2004): 97-119.

O'Leary, Timothy. *Foucault and the Art of Ethics*. London: Continuum, 2002.

Parker, David. *The Self in Moral Space*. Ithaca: Cornell University Press, 2007.

Peek, Lori. "Becoming Muslim: The Development of a Religious Identity," *Sociology of Religion* 66, no. 3 (Autumn 2005): 215-242.

Pellegrino, E. D., R. M. Veatch and J. P. Langan, ed. 1991a. *Ethics, Trust and the Professions: Philosophical and Cultural Aspects*. Washington, DC: Georgetown University Press, 1991.

Piper, Adrian, "Passing for White, Passing for Black," in *Passing And The Fictions of Identity*, edited by Elaine K. Ginsberg. Durham, NC: Duke University Press, 1996.

Plato. *The Symposium*, Translated by Alexander Nehamas and Paul Woodruff, in *Plato: Complete Works*, edited by John M. Cooper. Indianapolis: Hackett, 1997.

Preves, Sharon. "For the Sake of the Children: Destigmatizing Intersexuality," in *Intersex In the Age of Ethics*, edited by A. Dreger. Hagerstown, M.D.: University Publishing Group, 1999.

Rich, Adrienne. "Compulsory Heterosexuality and Lesbian Existence. *Signs: Journal of Women in Culture and Society* 5, no. 4 (1980): 631-660.

Roof, Judith. "The Community of Dolphins vs the Safe Sea of Women: Lesbian Sexuality and Psychosis," in *Homosexuality and Psychoanalysis*, edited by Tim Dean and Christopher Lane. Chicago: University of Chicago Press, 2000.

Rudy, Kathy. "Toward a Progressive Sexual Ethic," in *Sex and the Church: Gender, Sexuality, and the Transformation of Christian Ethics*. Boston: Beacon Press, 1997.

Ryan, Joanna. "Can Psychoanalysis Understand Homophobia," in *Homosexuality and Psychoanalysis,* edited by Tim Dean and Christopher Lane. Chicago: University of Chicago Press, 2000.

Samar, Vincent J. "A Moral Justification for Gay and Lesbian Civil Rights Legislation," in *Gay Ethics: Controversies in Outing, Civil Rights, and Sexual Science.* Binghamton: Haworth Press, 1994.

Sanchez, Maria Carla and Linda Schlossberg. *Passing: Identity and Interpretation in Sexuality, Race, and Religion.* New York: New York University Press, 2001.

Sanders, Jimy M. "Ethnic Boundaries and Identity in Plural Societies," *Annual Review of Sociology* 28 (2002): 327-357.

Sartre, Jean-Paul. *Being and Nothingness.* New York: Washington Square Press, 1956.

———. *Black Orpheus.* Translated by S.W. Allen. Paris: Gallimard, 1949.

Scanlon, T.M. *What We Owe to Each Other,* Cambridge: The Belknap Press of Harvard University Press, 1998.

Schlossberg, Linda. "Introduction: Rites of Passing," in *Passing: Identity and Interpretation in Sexuality, Race, and Religion,* edited by Maria Carla Sanchez and Linda Schlossberg. New York: New York University Press, 2001.

Schulman, Sarah. *Ties that Bind: Familial Homophobia and Its Consequences.* New York: The New Press, 2009.

Sedgwick, Eve Kosofsky. *The Epistemology of the Closet.* Berkely: University of California Press, 1990.

———. "Queer Performativity: Henry James's *The Art of the Novel.*" *GLQ* 1: 1-16.

Serano, Julia. *Whipping Girl: A Transsexual Woman on Sexism and the Scapegoating of Femininity.* Emeryville, CA: Seal Press, 2007.

Siegel, Reva B. "Introduction: A Short History of Sexual Harassment," in *Directions in Sexual Harassment Law,* edited by Catharine A. MacKinnon and Reva B. Siegel. New Haven: Yale University Press, 2004.

Singer, Linda. "Merleau-Ponty on the Concept of Style," *Man and World,* 1981.

Smith, Olav Bryant. *Myths of the Self: Narrative Identity and Postmodern Metaphysics.* Lanham: Lexington Books, 2004.

Snorton, C. Riley., "A New Hope: The Psychic Life of Passing." *Hypatia* 24, no.3 (Summer 2009): 72-92.

Sontag, Susan. "Notes on Camp," in *Against Interpretation.* New York: Doubleday, 1966.

———. "On Style" in *Against Interpretation.* New York: Doubleday, 1966.

Spindelman, Marc. "Discriminating Pleasures" in *Directions in Sexual Harassment Law,* edited by Catharine A. MacKinnon and Reva B. Siegel. New Haven: Yale University Press, 2004.

Stryker, Susan. *Transgender History.* Berkeley: Seal Studies, 2008.

Sycamore, Mattilda Bernstein. *Nobody Passes: Rejecting the Rules of Gender and Conformity.* Emeryville, CA: Seal Press, 2006.

Systema, Sharon. *Ethics and Intersex.* Dordrecht: Springer, 2006.
Tarnopolsky, Christina. "Prudes, Perverts, and Tyrants: Plato and the Contemporary Politics of Shame," *Political Theory* 32, no. 4 (August 2004): 468-494.
Taylor, Charles. *The Ethics of Authenticity.* Cambridge: Harvard University Press, 1992.
———. *Sources of the Self: The Making of Modern Identity.* Cambridge: Harvard University Press, 1989.
Teichert, Dieter. "Narrative, Identity, and the Self," *Journal of Consciousness Studies,* 2004, no. 11: 175-191.
Todorov, Tzvetan. *Facing the Extreme.* New York: Henry Holt and Company, 1996.
Turner, William B. *A Genealogy of Queer Theory.* Philadelphia: Temple University Press, 2000.
Van Eck, Caroline; James McAllister and Rene e van de Vall. "Introduction," to *The Question of Style in Philosophy and the Arts.* Cambridge: Cambridge University Press, 1995.
Vincent, Norah. *Self-Made Man.* New York: Penguin, 2006.
Wald, Gayle. *Crossing the Line: Racial Passing in Twentieth Century U.S. Literature and Culture.* Durham: Duke University Press, 2000.
Walker, Lisa. *Looking Like What You Are: Sexual Style, Race, and Lesbian Identity.* New York: New York University Press, 2001.
Warner, Michael. *The Trouble with Normal: Sex, Politics, and the Ethics of Queer Life,* Cambridge: Harvard University Press, 1999.
Warner, Michael. "Unsafe: Why Gay Men are Having Risky Sex," reprinted in David Halperin, *What Do Gay Men Want?: An Essay on Sex, Risk, and Subjectivity.* Ann Arbor: The University of Michigan Press, 2007.
Wilkerson, William. *Ambiguity and Sexuality: A Theory of Sexual Identity.* New York: Palgrave Macmillan, 2007.
Williams, Bernard. *Truth and Truthfulness.* Princeton University Press, 2002.
Wueste, Daniel E. "Introduction," in *Professional Ethics and Social Responsibility,* edited by Daniel E. Wueste. Lanham, Maryland: Rowman & Littlefield Publishers, Inc., 1994.
———. "Role Moralities and the Problem of Conflicting Obligations," in *Professional Ethics and Social Responsibility,* edited by Daniel E. Wueste. Lanham, Maryland: Rowman & Littlefield Publishers, Inc., 1994.
Yoshino, Kenji. *Covering: The Hidden Assault on Our Civil Rights.* New York: Random House, 2006.
Young, Iris Marion. "The Five Faces of Oppression," in *Justice and the Politics of Difference.* Princeton: Princeton University Press, 1990.

Index

abjection, 99, 100, 105-6, 108, 146, 169-70
accountability, 25, 185, 192
actors/actresses, 186
The Advocate, 180
aesthetics, 124, 130-31; of living, 155, 156; of shame, 149, 156
Alison, James, 155, 157-59
Altieri, Charles, 119, 129, 131
Althusser, Louis, 133
ambiguity, 54, 56n8, 66, 80, 106, 108, 127-28, 163
anti-gay, 76; ethic, 190-91; legislation, 80, 105; stereotype, 184
anti-homophobic, 18
anxiety, 5, 10, 12, 14-15, 21, 24, 44, 48, 88, 98, 101, 196
Appiah, Kwame Anthony, 6, 38-39, 41-42
Aristotle, 63, 84, 120
ascesis, 159
assimilationist, 24, 33, 144
Augustine, 62-64
Austin, J. L., 145
authentic, 14, 18, 36, 44, 49, 65, 86, 113, 116, 149; ally 16, 50, 76; expression, 1, 3; identity, 36, 39, 48, 50, 62, 87; relationships, 16, 77, 159; self 79, 89

authenticity, 3, 33, 36, 45, 47, 51, 73, 77, 87, 102, 154, 167, 180
autonomy, 11, 44, 70, 144, 160, 166-67, 181

Barthes, Roland, 99
Bartky, Sandra, 78
Baudrillard, Jean, 86
Beauvoir, Simone de, 96, 116-17, 127; *See also The Second Sex*
Bell, Vikki, 55, 83, 126
Berlin, Isaiah, 45
Bersani, Leo, 142, 146-47
betrayal, 2, 5, 19, 37, 70, 99
birth gender, 12-14
black media, 21
Bok, Sissela, 62, 64-66, 70, 183
bullshit, 67-69, 74
Butler, Judith, 46, 51-55, 83-85, 97-98, 103-4, 113, 125-26, 145, 174-75; *See also* performativity

camp, 36, 132, 135, 154
Card, Claudia, 25, 79-80, 82, 191-92
caring, 81-82, 92n61
Cass, Vivienne, 101-2
Categorical Imperative, 165, 172
Catholic Church, 152, 157-58
Caughie, Pamela, 36-37
Chekola, Mark, 185

Chicago Tribune, 180
circumlocutions, 63
cissexual, 13, 15, 16; assumption, 12-13; privilege, 12, 14, 15
civil disobedience, 182
civil rights, 143, 182, 197; act of 1964, 191; movement, 175
class, 4, 9, 13, 61, 79, 103, 124, 174
clergy, 138n74, 157, 185
Clinton, Bill, 189
the closet, 3-4, 17-21, 38-39, 75-76, 80, 82, 133, 144, 151-53, 157, 170, 181-86, 189, 197
closetude, 76, 182, 184, 186, 188, 198
coalition-building, 156
"coerced hypocrisy," 152
coercion, 71, 180, 182
coextensivity, 55, 85
coming-out, 6, 17, 76, 108, 152, 157-58, 189; narrative, 19
commodities, 132
compass, 88-9
complicity, 80
comportment, 131
concentration camps, 79-82
consensual sex, 183, 189
consequentialism, 63-65, 67, 76, 180
continental feminism, 117
corporeality, 46, 116-17, 126-27
counter-factuals, 40
Crimp, Douglas, 147, 149
cross-dressing, 9-10, 128-29

D'Augelli, Anthony, 102
deceit, 2, 13, 19, 62, 69-71
decency, 181
deception, 4, 7, 14, 24-25, 37, 61-64, 66-68, 70-74, 77, 89n4, 157, 181, 191-92
decision-making, 61
Defense of Marriage Act (DOMA), 173
deontology, 65, 180; ical, 63, 75
Department of Justice, 191
depersonalization, 81-82
dignity, 39, 63-65, 73, 76-77, 81-82, 92, 144, 146, 149, 154-56, 171, 175, 180
disclosure, 10-11, 35, 50, 62-63, 73-75, 144, 153, 168, 179-80

discourse, 16, 18, 33, 37, 46, 49, 52-53, 55, 73, 84-86, 89, 103-4, 106-8, 123, 132-33, 147, 154-56, 164, 173
discrimination, 12-13, 20, 24, 29n42, 42, 48, 99, 104, 189, 192-95, 197
disguise, 10, 38, 48, 66
dishonesty, 37, 151-52
Don't Ask, Don't Tell (DADT), 189-91
Dowds, Alan, 102
down low, 20-23
drag, 9-10, 51, 126-27, 146, 149
duty, 72, 75-76; to community, 181; to self, 169, 181

effemimania, 10
effeminate, 6-7, 58, 96, 132, 193
Ellis, Havelock, 42
embodiment, 17, 42, 44, 78-79, 117, 126
empowerment, 173-74, 184
enjoyment of power, 81-82
enlightenment, 44, 89
epistemology, 18, 34, 47, 73, 106-7, 114
Epistemology of the Closet, 18; *See also* Sedgwick, Eve Kosofsky
erotophobia, 148
essentialism, 18, 51, 164
ethical, 1-3, 11, 16, 18-20, 25-26, 33, 37, 41, 51, 54, 61, 72, 77, 79, 83-85, 87, 94-95, 103-7, 116, 131, 141-43, 149, 155, 160, 162n69, 168, 174-75, 179-80, 184-86, 188, 190, 198; dilemma, 8, 86, 160; obligation, 37
ethics of outing, 27, 179-182
ethics under oppression, 25, 77-89
etiology of sexual orientation, 93, 105
evil, 80, 91n58, 198

falsehood, 68
familial homophobia, 147, 171
family, 5, 6, 9, 20-21, 40, 65, 72-76, 101-2, 134, 141-44, 147, 151, 183, 187-89
Fanon, Franz, 77-78
feminism, 97, 104-5
fidelity, 2
fiduciary, 184-86; relationships, 184-86; trust, 186

flourishing, 36, 79, 156
Forbes, Malcolm, 180
Foucault, Michel, 85, 103, 106, 108, 155, 159-60, 162
fragmentation of behavior, 81-82
Frankfurt, Henry, 67-69
Freud, Sigmund, 94-95, 97-98
FTM, 11, 24

Garber, Marjorie, 47-48
gay liberation, 39, 186-87
gay style, 109, 132-35, 174
gayness, 2, 22, 27, 28n1, 43, 73, 75-76, 108, 152, 155, 160, 163, 168-69, 171-75, 180-83, 187-89, 192, 197-98
gender, 6, 8, 9,10, 11, 12, 13, 14, 16, 28n2, 41, 51-53, 61, 78, 91n48, 93, 97-98, 101, 105, 123, 128, 141-42, 148, 174, 193, 195-96; and sex discrimination, 104; and sexuality, 3, 103, 109; and sexual identity 25, 51, 103, 197; and sexual non-conformity, 145; binary, 3, 9, 16; conformity, 146; deviant, 9, 24, 35, 47, 48, 127, 142, 193; dystopia, 133 entitlement, 13; expression, 1, 9, 125, 142; identity, 6, 7, 8, 9, 11, 12, 13, 14, 27n1, 36, 50-52, 97-98, 103, 123, 126, 134, 141-42, 150; identity and expression, 29, 134; norms, 145, 193; oppression 79; passing, 2, 6-7, 9-10, 12, 14, 24, 28n23, 47, 58, 196; performance, 127; politics 4, 11, 117; regulation, 9; self-presentation, 6; style, 124, 134; theory, 54
Gender Trouble, 50; *See also* Butler, Judith.
gendered, 12, 15, 117; pronoun 57n18; sexuality, 6
gendering 12, 13, 15
genderqueer, 9, 10, 47
genealogy, 104, 106
Genet, Jean, 99-100
Gide, Andre, 99
Gilman, Sandra L., 44-45
Goffman, Erving, 151-52, *Stigma*, 151
the good, 84, 129-31, 151-52
Gross, Larry, 184

habituation, 121, 123, 132
Halberstam, Judith/Jack, 35, 126
half-truths, 63, 90n11
Halley, Janet, 189, 191, 196
Halperin, David, 98-100, 110n26
happiness, 36, 44, 64, 69, 75, 156, 167, 180
Hardwick vs. Bowers, 183
Heidegger, Martin, 164
hermaphroditism, 10, 29n35, 95
heroic virtues, 82
heteronormativity, 3, 18-19, 21, 25, 50, 73-74, 133, 143, 154, 169, 190, 192, 195
heterosexuality, 1, 3, 5, 7, 13, 17-20, 22-23, 37, 75-76, 94-95, 97, 101, 104, 107, 126, 129, 133-35, 139n92, 141, 143-44, 147-48, 152, 154-56, 159, 169-70, 180, 187, 191-92, 194-98; privilege, 91, 128, 198
Heyd, David, 82
HIV/AIDS, 21, 75, 100
homonormativity, 26, 169
homophobic, 95, 138n68, 149, 173, 175, 189; attacks 42; behavior, 20; panic, 196-97
honesty, 71, 73, 152, 154, 157-59, 167, 181, 185-86, 191
hooks, bell, 43
Husserl, Edmund, 116

infidelity, 2, 22
informed consent, 11
institution, 4, 49, 52, 76, 83-84, 95, 97, 103-4, 118, 152, 187-89, 200
integrity, 46, 71, 167-68, 185-86, 190, 192
intellectualism, 81-82, 92n6
interiority, 55, 83, 85
internalized homophobia, 20, 27, 148-49, 169-70, 184
interpellation, 53, 58n49, 105, 126, 133, 145-46
intersex, 6, 10-11, 31n96
intersubjectivity, 62, 69-75
invasion, 183
invert, 53, 94, 98, 128, 134, 149

Jagose, Annemarie, 106
Jew, 34, 45, 54, 79

journalistic ethics, 186

Kantian, 54, 56n8, 64, 164, 172; ethics 2
Kapos, 80
Kato, David, 81
Kiernan, James, 94-95
kin network, 6
Kingdom of Ends, Citizen of 171-72
Kinsey, 101, 103; model 101
Korsgaard, Christine, 2, 27, 153, 163-69, 171-173, 188, 192; *See also* practical identities
Krafft-Ebing, Richard von, 30n79, 42, 94, 128
Kristeva, Julia, 99

Lacan, Jacques, 96
Laurentis, Teresa de, 103, 105
legal, 2, 12, 27, 28n9, 33, 52, 64, 90n25, 124-25, 138n61, 174, 181, 186, 188, 190, 192-98
lesbian, 6, 7, 12, 15, 31, 36, 96-98, 104, 108, 128-29, 133-34, 142-44, 146, 148-49, 155, 157-58, 169, 183-84, 189-192, 196-97; butch, 6, 10, 28n23, 36, 127-28, 133, 142, 146, 150, 161n37, 195
Levi, Primo, 79-80, 91n49
LGBT/Q social ethics, 2, 26, 27, 198
the liar vs. the pervert, 2, 26, 142, 150-54, 156, 159, 175
liars, 64-66
libel, 181
liberalism, 104, 107-8
lies, 16, 44, 62-73, 89n4, 110n26, 144, 180
Love, Heather, 149-150
lying, 2, 22, 25, 51, 61-74, 76, 89, 152, 157, 191
Lyotard, Jean-François, 85

marriage, 5, 21, 36, 75, 101, 144, 170, 187
masculinity, 6-7, 12, 14, 36, 40, 51, 104, 126-29, 150, 194-95, 197
Maupin, Armistead, 184
Merleau-Ponty, Maurice, 26, 85, 113-118, 135
Mills, Claudia, 34

misleading, 67, 71
Mohr, Richard, 76, 152, 154-56, 170, 180, 182, 190, 196
monstrous, 81-82
moral, 16, 19, 23, 25-27, 36, 53-55, 62, 67-85, 87-91, 95, 100, 107-9, 130, 134-35, 143, 150, 152, 164, 169, 172-175, 179-183, 187-192; agency, 15; agents, 20, 26, 80, 164; ambiguity, 62, 80; assessment, 68, 171; authority, 85, 157; blame, 69, 80; career, 88; commitments, 50; compass, 89, 141; complexity, 2, 55, 72, 81; compromise, 80, 181, 198; concerns, 25, 68; condemnation, 37, 68; consideration, 26, 63, 75, 152, 167; continuum, 53, 63; convictions, 158; core, 26, 69, 88; credibility, 157; decision, 166; demands, 188; development, 69, 144; dilemma, 142, 151; discourse 19; disdain, 33; education, 131; element, 167; erasure, 26; failure, 78; framework, 79, 152, 163; formation 162n69; fortitude, 182; grey zones, 25, 79-82, 92n61; ideal, 26; identity, 169; implications, 36-37, 188; judgment, 80, 108, 153, 175; justification, 164; knowledge, 157; lives, 2, 61, 79, 81-82, 91n48, 188; majority, 26, 141, 143; monster, 192; norms, 54, 85, 154; obligations, 89, 164, 166, 180, 189; observation, 166; opinion, 156-57; outcomes, 67, 88; panic, 22; paradox, 26, 80, 151, 154-55, 159; perspective, 49, 62, 187; philosophers, 1, 62, 66, 68; practice, 160; protection, 19; reasons, 172; respect, 157; responsibility, 55, 79-80, 85, 88, 156-57, 172, 187; questions, 22, 26, 65, 74, 107, 157, 159-60, 180; shame, 53; space, 91n49, 129; standards, 158; story, 37, 81; theology, 157; theory, 153; value, 154; violence 69; *See also* professional ethics; role morality

moralism, 142-44

MTF, 11, 24
mulatto, 3, 54
Murphy, Timothy, 154-55

narrative, 2, 7-9, 17, 19-20, 23-24, 26, 35, 37-40, 42, 47, 49, 57n15, 78, 86-88, 115, 118-123, 129-135, 151-52, 168
norms, 10, 12, 39, 51-54, 75, 83, 88, 126, 134, 145, 153-4, 169, 171, 173, 175, 193, 198; of repression 75; of responsibility 75

obligation, 26, 33, 38, 49, 72-74, 76, 156, 164, 166-69, 172-73, 183-188
Oncale vs. Sundowner Offshore Services, 193-97
one-drop rule, 4, 22
"open secret," 94
openly gay, 23, 81, 157, 189-90, 196-98
oppositional sexism, 12
oppression, 17, 25, 34-35, 37, 40, 42-43, 48, 55, 62, 65-66, 74-83, 89, 90n20, 91n48, 99, 115-16, 170, 173-75, 182-83
ordinary vices, 81
orientation, 126, 141; orienting, 88
outing, 75, 179-83, 185; self, 27, 180-81; others, 180-81; posthumous, 180
OutWeek, 180

passionate attachment, 84, 175
performativity, 25-26, 34, 51-55, 61, 83-85, 113, 125-29, 145-46, 153, 175
performed identity, 35
phenomenology, 2, 9, 73
plastic surgery, 44-45, 56n3, 58
Plato, 156; proto-feminism, 117; *Republic,* 185
political perversity, 26, 141-42, 153-54, 174
politicians, 80, 184-86
popular culture, 125, 154
postmodern, 25, 34, 46, 86-89, 122-23, 174
power, 1, 13, 16, 20, 25, 27, 49, 52-55, 58n26, 61-63, 74, 77-79, 81-84, 86, 89n1, 91n58, 97, 100, 103-6, 117-18, 122-25, 148, 173-75, 192-93, 195, 197
practical identity 2, 27, 153, 163-69, 171-75, 187-88, 192
prejudice, 14-15, 65, 90, 99, 186
pretense, 25, 61-62, 71
pride parades, 145, 153
privacy, 27, 67, 73, 179-83, 186, 190
privilege, 1, 12-15, 18, 21, 47, 56n6, 61, 77, 91n48, 95, 114, 128, 154, 170, 193, 198
procreation, 94, 95
professional ethics, 27, 164, 179, 183, 185-86, 188
propensity, 184; *See also* Don't Ask, Don't Tell (DADT)
Proust, Marcel, 99
"psychical hermaphroditism," 95
psychic alienation, 78
The Psychic Life of Power, 84, 174; *See also* Butler, Judith
Psychoanalysis, 93, 98-100, 105
public, 1, 5, 9, 11, 14-15, 18-19, 27, 35-36, 40, 47-48, 74, 94-95, 102, 123-24, 143, 153-57, 168, 170, 179-80, 183-87, 190; accountability, 185; - morality 152; trust, 107, 185
publicity, 100, 186-87

queer, 1, 7, 17-18, 22, 24-27, 27n1, 28n1, 28n3, 31n96, 35, 50, 58n51, 73, 78, 83, 99-100, 104, 106-8, 126, 128-9, 134, 141-50, 152, 156-57, 160, 163-64 167, 169-75, 180-82; ethics, 132, 151, 153; identity, 7, 18, 21, 53, 106, 121, 133, 143, 149-50 153, 156; shame, 145, 149-50, 155; style, 133; youth, 4
queer theory, 2, 25, 94, 103, 105-7, 111n57, 146-7, 153-54, 170, 197; and sexual harassment, 196-97; *See also* Sexual Harassment/Title VII
queertopia, 141-2, 171-72; citizen of 172
Quintilian, 121

racial, 1, 2, 9, 21-22, 24, 37, 42, 79, 98; identity, 6, 22, 43, 76, 123; passing, 3-6, 21, 28, 37, 59, 78

reciprocity, 64, 77-78, 96, 164, 172-73
recognition, 7, 13, 16, 74, 77, 99, 117, 128, 144, 146, 148, 154, 181; misrecognition, 14, 16, 43
religion, 31, 35, 37, 43, 47, 76, 134, 151, 164
respect, 16, 39, 45, 63, 65, 70, 76, 81, 95, 98, 131, 133, 143, 152-53, 156-57, 170, 172-73, 180-81, 186
responsibility, 25, 27, 33, 55, 71, 74-75, 79-80, 85, 87, 89, 91n49, 149, 156-57, 164, 166, 171-73, 176n29, 184-86
right to privacy, 183, 186
righteous indignation, 70
ritual, 52, 76
role, 4, 6, 26, 38, 40, 42-43, 45, 49-50, 53, 55, 58, 78, 82, 89, 97, 107-08, 118, 124, 127, 130-34, 142, 147, 155-57, 159-60, 166, 168, 170, 179, 185, 187, 196; models, 27, 75, 150, 170, 174, 180; morality, 27, 154, 174, 183-85, 188; obligations, 186-88
Russo, Vito, 181

Sartre, John Paul, 115-16
saturated self, 86, 88
Scalia, Justice Antonin, 196
The Second Sex, 96, 117, 127; *See also* Beauvoir, Simone de
second wave feminism, 97
secrecy, 4, 21-23, 152, 180, 182-83, 186
"the secret," 27, 115, 169-70, 182-83, 198
Segwick, Eve Kosofsky, 18, 103, 139, 142, 145-47, 153, 160
self, 8, 9, 11, 16-20, 24, 32, 34-35, 37-38, 42, 44-45, 47-50, 53, 55, 63, 65-66, 70-89, 92, 96, 99, 102-7, 114-15, 121-24, 128-30, 134-35, 141-45, 150, 153-56, 158-60, 166-71, 174, 180-81, 191; blame, 70-71; fashioning, 159; loathing, 17, 49, 58, 144, 149; presentation, 1, 6, 35, 49, 66, 122-23, 128; respect, 76, 156, 180; stylization, 159
Senghor, Leopold, 115
Serano, Julia, 10, 12-16

sex-plus (mutable characteristics), 193; *See also* Sexual Harassment/Title VII
sexology, 11, 25, 93-95, 101, 134, 173; sexologist, 10, 42, 95, 128
Sexual Harassment/Title VII, 27, 170, 179, 188, 192-98
shame, 2, 7, 10-11, 26-27, 49, 53, 74, 77-78, 95, 99, 102, 133-34, 141-56, 169-70, 174-75, 184; as gender failure 150
shunning, 147
sincerity, 64, 69, 157-58
sinful, 64
slaves, 3
Snorton, C. Riley, 16-17
social, 1-7, 9-27, 32-36, 39-43, 45, 48-53, 56, 62-64, 67-70, 72-79, 81-84, 86-89, 93-95, 97-104, 107-109, 115-118, 120-125, 127-29, 132-135, 142-43, 146-49, 151-55, 163-66, 169-73, 175, 179-85, 187-91, 194, 197-98; constructionism, 18, 27, 36, 44, 51, 83-88, 154; ethics, 188; identity, 2, 6, 17, 38, 40-42, 134, 166, 185, 197; justice, 36, 42, 89, 138, 142, 182; responsibility, 149, 185; role morality, 179
Socrates, 154, 156
sodomy, 30, 94, 183, 189
Solomon, Robert, 155, 162n48
Some Like it Hot, 48, 56n2
Sontag, Susan, 114, 132
Sources of the Self, 129; *See also* Taylor, Charles
speech acts, 18, 52-53, 84, 145
stereotypes, 6, 41-45, 50, 96, 102, 184
stigma, 11, 15, 21, 99-100, 124, 144-46, 149-152
stoicism, 100
Stonewall, 39, 99, 149; pre-, 150; post-, 93, 98
Stramel, James, 76
Stryker, Susan, 11
style, 2, 7, 19, 23, 26, 85, 93, 98, 109, 113-38, 149, 153, 156, 159-60, 174
stylized corporeality, 116, 126-27, 133
subjection, 162, 174-75
subsumptionist, 188
Sullivan, Andrew, 144
supererogatory duties, 79, 82-83

Tarnopolsky, Christina, 154, 156
Taylor, Charles; 38, 88, 129-30, 151;
    See also Sources of the Self
third-gendered, 9-10
third wave feminism, 97
Todorov, Trvestan, 79-83
Torr, Dianne, 127
transgender, 1, 5-7, 9-16, 27n1, 28n2, 29n42, 31n96, 41, 47, 104
trans-misogyny, 12
transphobia, 12, 14
transvestite, 9-10, 47
trust, 7, 49, 52, 62-64, 67, 69-74, 106-7, 122, 147, 157, 185-86, 190
truth, 4, 23, 49, 51, 63-65, 68-73, 90, 112, 131, 151, 156, 158-59, 175, 180, 191, 197; telling, 63-64, 67, 72, 74, 134, 152, 155-57, 159, 197
Turner, William, 106-8

Ulrichs, Karl Heinrich, 41, 92

ungendering, 13
utilitarian, 64, 180-81

Village Voice, 180
virtue, 15, 25, 63-64, 68-69, 73, 77, 79-83, 92, 120-21, 152, 158-59; ethics, 75, 159, 181; theory, 2
visibility, 3-4, 18, 20-22, 42-44, 75, 133, 142, 145-46, 149-54, 169-70, 174, 179-81, 184, 186-88, 198

Walker, Lisa, 42, 128, 138n68
Warhol, Andy, 149
Warner, Michael, 75, 99-101, 142-44, 169-70
The Well of Loneliness, 149
white lies, 67
Wilde, Oscar, 99
Williams, Bernard, 64, 69, 72

xenophobia, 148

About the Author

Kelby Harrison has a PhD in philosophical ethics, gender, and sexuality from Northwestern University. From 2010 to 2012, she was the social ethics post-doctoral fellow at Union Theological Seminary. She is coeditor of *Passing/Out: Sexual Identity Veiled and Revealed*, an intergenerational, interdisciplinary, and intersubjective anthology on issues of sexual identity closeting and revelation.

DOWNTOWN CAMPUS LRC

J.S. Reynolds Community College
3 7219 00176202 3

HQ 76.25 .H369 2013
Harrison, Kelby.
Sexual deceit

DISCARDED